THE
JEWS

THE
JEWS

CHAIM BERMANT

Times
BOOKS

Library of Congress Cataloging in Publication Data

Bermant, Chaim I
  The Jews.

  Bibliography: p.
  Includes index.
  1. Jews—Politics and government—1948-   —Address-
es, essays, lectures. 2. Jews—Social life and customs—
Addresses, essays, lectures. 3. Jews—Civilization—
Addresses, essays, lectures. I. Title.
DS143.B5   1977   301.45'19'24   77-79020
ISBN 0-8129-0705-1

Contents

Acknowledgments

I have wandered into many strange fields in the course of writing this book and have needed the reassurance of many friends that I have not gone too far astray. I am particularly grateful to the following for their help: Dr Anthony Goldberg, Dr Lionel Kochan, Professor Walter Laqueur, Mr Chaim Raphael and Mr Charles Spencer. I am also indebted to John Curtis of Weidenfeld and to Roger Jellinek of Times Books for invaluable advice, to my editors Linda Osband and Adeline Sneider, and to Sharon Ross, who typed my manuscript with her usual efficiency and speed.

Chaim Bermant
April 1977
Iyar 5737

PUBLISHER'S ACKNOWLEDGMENTS

The author and publishers would like to thank the following for kind permission to reprint quotations from: *Arnold Schoenberg: Letters*, edited by Erwin Stein, Faber and Faber Ltd; *The Jews*, Hilaire Belloc, A. D. Peters and Co. Ltd; *World of Our Fathers*, Irving Howe, Routledge (London), and Harcourt Brace Jovanovich Inc. (New York).

THE
JEWS

CHAPTER ONE

The Jews

It's good to be a Jew, which is a somewhat un-Jewish thing to say, for Jews are rather more accustomed to hugging their wounds than counting their blessings and are nervous of suggesting that things may be going well in case they should start going badly. Not every Jew is superstitious, but almost all are familiar with the Yiddish expression, *kein-ein hora* – let not the evil eye behold it.

And there are many evil eyes about. There are people who don't like Jews. There are also people who don't like Italians, Irish, the Scots, Welsh, Greeks, Turks, Russians, Poles, Hottentots, Arabs, Herzogovinians, but those who dislike Jews do so with a particular passion, and they have been doing so for rather longer. Among some it is something of a national inheritance and there are people who have never seen a Jew, and are never likely to see one, but whose hackles rise at the very sound of the word. Jew-haters are like other haters, only more so, and if they have been quiescent of late it is because they have a lot to be quiescent about. Various publicists have in recent years suggested that the Nazis haven't killed six million Jews, but only three million, or six hundred thousand, or sixty thousand, or that those who did die were but casualties of war. It is all part of an effort to ease the burden of guilt. Wouldn't the suggestion that Jews were again riding high, do it for them?

Anti-semites, however, may have been kept quiescent by a feeling of horror not only at what happened to the Jews, but at what happened to mankind. Not only did six million Jews die in the holocaust, but twenty million Russians, and millions of others, not all of them casualties of war. If one lesson has been learned from the Hitler years it is that if any one group of humans is thought to be expendable, then all of humanity is at risk. Thus if greater attention is paid to the needs of the Blacks in America, or the coloured immigrant in Britain, and if the whole world is determined to end white domination in southern Africa, it is partly because of what has happened to the Jews in Europe. All of which does not mean that the Jew-hater must remain for ever silent, but neither does it mean that he will suddenly find his voice through the discovery that Jews are not only alive, but prospering.

Throughout the Middle Ages, wherever Jews enjoyed a lesser or greater degree of autonomy they passed numerous laws against luxury and ostentation, limiting the number of guests at weddings, the number of courses at meals, the quality of garments to be worn in public, partly because ostentation was regarded as sinful in itself, but largely because it was feared that it could excite the envy and hatred of gentiles. Jewish commentators have sometimes been moved by the same fears and much of their work falls into what one might call the *Oy Vei is mir* (O woe is me!) school of writing or, to use the more elegant expression of Professor Salo Baron, 'the lachrymose conception of Jewish history and martyrology'. It is not that anyone faked events to make them seem worse than they were, but that in happy times people were, as a rule, sufficiently glad of their good fortune to keep quiet about it. Jews were rarely in control of their own destinies and where they impinged upon history it was because they were troublesome or in trouble.

But if things were not quite as bad as they have been made out to be, they were bad enough. The central events of post-Biblical Jewish history are misfortunes, with the holocaust as the greatest misfortune of all. To have one's very existence made a capital offence is not a fact which can fade quickly from the memory, yet the decade of Auschwitz also saw the emergence of Israel. One cannot set triumph against calamity and say the score with fate has been settled, especially as the struggle to keep Israel in being is by no means over, yet it does permit one a spasm of elation. To take pleasure in what is, is not to overlook what was, and the Jew tends to let his memory lean too heavily on his spirit.

There is the story of the Jew on a train who kept moaning: 'Oy, have I got a pain . . . Oy, have I got a pain . . . Oy, have I got a pain . . . Oy . . .' Finally one of the passengers, who could stand it no longer, jumped to his feet, searched the length and breadth of the train and came back with a doctor, who gave the Jew a pill, and all was quiet for a minute or two till the voice began again: 'Oy, did I have a pain . . . Oy, did . . .'

It is perhaps time for an end to oying. A sense of guilt does not make for a healthy relationship between ex-persecutor and ex-victim.

Yet if Jews are too preoccupied with the past, are things going so well in the present that one may shout Hallelujah? What of Russian Jewry? It is, to be sure, no joy to be a Russian, and rather less of one to be a Russian Jew, yet if to be a Jew in Russia means an extra degree of oppression, it also affords an extra degree of hope. To be Jewish is to be aware of other Jews and to be concerned about them; but awareness is the beginning, and this awareness is a source of hope: one is not forgotten. Any Russian Christian anxious to celebrate his rituals may find himself subject to harassment or persecution, but with no certainty that Christians in the outside world will exert themselves on his behalf. They may remember him in their prayers, but they will not take to the streets.

The readiness of Jews to intercede for one another is as old as their history. Wherever a few of them reached a haven, among their first acts was to establish a fund for those still in peril, and wherever any acquired influence they were quick to intercede for the oppressed, but in the past such intercessions tended to be private – sometimes very private – and discreet. What is new is the readiness, perhaps even the over-readiness, of Jews to take to the streets.

Jews too have a conscience about the holocaust, for to survive at all where so many have perished is to experience a feeling of guilt, and if they should appear to over-react to even minor incidents, it is perhaps because they feel that they may have been too timid and ineffectual in the past, and this is particularly the case with American Jewry. They have the numbers, the wealth, the influence and, to use a Yiddish expression which may be said to encompass all three, they have the *mazel*, which means good fortune, and good fortune means being in the right place at the right time. They are also the dominant influence, material *and* cultural – more so, as we shall see, than Israel – in the Jewish world.

There are leading American Jews who like to give the impression that there is no such thing as an American Jewish lobby. There is, and there would be something amiss with American Jewry if there was not. If farmers can combine to get improved prices for their hogs, Jews may be forgiven for uniting to get improved conditions for their co-religionists, and if they have done so with marvellous effect, it is partly because circumstances have been in their favour. It is not merely that the holocaust has established a vast fund of sympathy for the Jew, but it is infinitely easier to lobby for Russian Jewry now than it was to lobby for German Jewry in the 'thirties, even though the enormities perpetrated by Hitler were incomparably greater, because a large part of American opinion is inherently pro-German and anti-Russian, and certainly anti-Communist.

It is even easier to lobby on behalf of Israel, for Israel represents the simple qualities of grit and heroism still admired by the American public. Here is the New Frontier, and here are the new frontiersmen with (especially since Entebbe) a touch of Superman thrown in. Moreover, it is the one area where all the virtues beloved of July 4th oratory have been seen to work. Israel is not without its imperfections (in some ways it is America writ small), but it still remains a living vindication of democracy, and it has not only raised the esteem of the Jew in his own eyes, but in the eyes of his gentile neighbours.

Jews in other countries have not the same tide of popular feeling on their side. Western Europe (which contains about a million Jews) does not share America's fundamentalist commitment to democracy, and its sympathy for Israel is tempered by misgivings about its own colonial past. Israel is not Rhodesia or Algeria, but not all Europeans understand why two or three million Jews should want to hold on to a barren strip of Asia when they could be doing so well elsewhere, and the European Jewish communities are too small and fragmented to form a potent force. When one talks of World Jewry today, one talks essentially of America and Israel – perhaps even in that order.

Until a generation ago – or even less – no one was more inclined to share America's exalted view of itself than the Jew. He really did believe that it was God's own country, opened up just as the position of European Jewry was becoming untenable, whose very creed might have been laid down by the Prophets, a new world without the phobias and dogmas of the old, where past histories were written off and each individual could advance on his own merits. In Europe, the Jew, anxious to integrate within the host society, was subject to rebuffs. He liked to think of himself as a German, Frenchman or Englishman of the Mosaic persuasion, but to the Englishman, Frenchman or German he was but a Jew who was trying to rise above himself. The Jew could, however, be an American without presumption or abasement and he gloried in the role. America had no more eager proselytes than the Jews who had found prosperity and acceptance, so that when the 'huddled masses' came ashore towards the end of the nineteenth century, they were met not only with soup kitchens set up by the earlier arrivals, but with a whole apparatus of schools and welfare institutions to bring them into the mainstream of American life. Some struggled against the process on religious, cultural or political grounds, but if they did not succumb, their children almost invariably did, and by the outbreak of World War II American Jewry was no longer an immigrant community.

The rise of the American Jew in American life was not effortless. That America was not *die goldene medineh* (the golden land) of lore was only to be expected – neither was Canaan. Nor was it quite as open or as devoid of dogmas as it was said to be, and if being Jewish was no longer an insurmountable obstacle, it was assuredly no advantage. Even in Jewish circles, the quickest way, and sometimes the only way, of getting to the top of a company was to marry the boss's daughter. But Jews still believed in the concept of America as something uniquely wholesome and that if it did not quite represent the Millennium it could serve as one until the real thing came along. And so they beavered on and moved from the slums into the suburbs, from the work-bench into the professions, from the small businesses into large. No Jew, even of the Episcopalian persuasion, has as yet become President of the United States, or of General Motors or of the Chase Manhattan Bank, but Jews cannot, for all that, be regarded as uniquely disadvantaged. They have come to the forefront of American life, have savoured its pleasures and enjoyed its privileges, yet their feeling has been one of anti-climax. Was *this* what they had been struggling for?

It was as if the meek, having inherited the Kingdom of Heaven, decided that they were after all better off on earth. America still offered opportunities absent elsewhere. It was still the most open and spacious country in the world. It was still the most likely place to get rich and stay rich, but it had lost the most American quality of all, its confidence. It was no longer sure what it stood for or where it was going. Jews had striven for a place in a self-assured commonwealth, and had arrived upon a diffident one, with the result that they have since been asking themselves whether they may not have paid too high a price to get there. Not a few have begun to re-trace their steps, which may explain the rediscovery of Isaac Bashevis Singer, the elevation of Elie Wiesel to a cult figure, the established place of Chaim Potok's novels on the best-seller lists, and the phenomenal success of Irving Howe's *World of Our Fathers*. Nor are Jews singular in this respect. The success of the television programme *Roots* has been even more phenomenal. One can observe a similar process of rediscovery among American Poles, Greeks, Italians, Germans and, indeed, Arabs.

When the whole fails, the parts begin to look to themselves. The Jew has given up trying to be someone else and is rediscovering the pleasures of being himself, which does not mean that every Jew fading out of Jewishness has reversed his direction. On the contrary, not a few may have felt induced to hasten the process, but a growing number have added an extra dimension to their lives in re-discovering their origins.

The following pages will attempt to examine what it means and has meant to be a Jew, the traits and obsessions, the ambiguities and dangers which go with Jewishness and, not least, the rewards. The Jew, for all the disciplines of his faith – some might say because of them – has not always been a model citizen and he can sometimes be a public nuisance: but it can, on the whole, be shown that the world is a better place for the fact that he is still around.

· CHAPTER TWO ·

Good God

Not all Jews believe in God, but most like to think that God believes in them. He is so central to their history that to suggest that He never existed in the first place would be to question the purpose of their own existence.

Jews have been around for a very long time, longer perhaps than is good for them or, as some might suggest, for anyone else. Their being is a tacit assertion of His being, and whether He in fact exists or not is almost beside the point, for belief imposes its own realities and God, in a manner of speaking, has been placed in His heavens by the sheer insistence of the faithful that He is there. In a sense, therefore, the Jews are, as Zangwill once said, the choosing people rather than the chosen.

In May 1948, when Arab armies were massing on what were to be the frontiers of the Jewish state, and Arab irregulars were already in action in Galilee and Jerusalem and a pall of smoke hung over the Judean hills, Jewish leaders were closeted in anxious, and often acrimonious debate. The Declaration of Independence was before them, and the Rabbis demanded an affirmation of belief in God. Others protested that God had done too little to deserve such credit, and the term Rock of Israel was suggested instead. And Rock of Israel it remained, for as Ben-Gurion said, everyone, right, left and centre, believed in the Rock of Israel in his own way.

The same may be said of the central event in Jewish history, *Matan Torah*, the giving of the Law of Moses on Sinai, a code which, its own language makes clear, was not thrust on the Israelites, but offered conditionally:

. . . if you will obey my voice and keep my covenant, then ye shall be a peculiar treasure unto me above all people, for all the earth is mine.

And ye shall be unto me a kingdom of priests and a holy nation . . .

There are traditions which suggest that the Jews did not even get the first option and that the Torah was first offered to all the other nations of

7

the world. The response of the others, however, was luke-warm, which, given the sort of demands made by the Torah, was understandable. The Jews alone, or so the legend goes, were prepared to accept the entire code without reservation:

And Moses came before the elders of the people, and laid before their faces all these words which the Lord commanded him.

And all the people answered together and said, All that the Lord hath spoken will we do . . .

– which on the face of it seemed a rash thing to do, for in accepting the Torah they accepted God, and the choice of a God is, after all, a fairly lasting commitment. But then, until Sinai, the Israelites' experience of heaven had been largely benign.

God had, after all, redeemed them from Egyptian bondage, shielded them from their enemies, fed them when they were hungry, given them water when they were thirsty and led them through the wilderness with a pillar of cloud by day and a pillar of fire by night. Yet as their wanderings continued the relationship deteriorated, and the first crisis came even while Moses was on Sinai:

And when the people saw that Moses delayed to come down off the mount, the people gathered themselves unto Aaron and said unto him, Up, make us gods, which shall go before us; for as for this Moses, the man who brought us out of the land of Egypt, we know not what has become of him.

Aaron sought to calm their anxieties by creating the golden calf and thereby breached the second commandment almost in the moment of utterance. He had created a graven image:

And the Lord said unto Moses, I have seen this people and behold it is a stiff-necked people.

Now therefore, let me alone that my wrath may wax hot against them, and that I may consume them . . .

And Moses pleaded with God, saying:

Wherefore should the Egyptians speak, and say, for mischief did He bring them out to slay them in the mountains, and to consume them from the face of the earth? Turn away Thy fierce wrath and repent of this evil against Thy people . . .

Now there is almost an element of rebuke in these words, as if Moses was asking God to see reason, and what is more God saw reason, 'and repented of the evil which He had thought to do unto His people'.

If this was the first time the Israelites incurred the wrath of Heaven, it was assuredly not the last. They had been sufficiently warned:

If ye walk in My statutes and keep My commandments, and do them, then I will give you rain in due season, and the land shall yield her increase, and the trees of the field shall yield their fruit . . . And I shall give peace in the land, and ye shall lie down and none shall make you afraid . . .

But if you don't:

I will even appoint over you terror, consumption and the burning ague that shall consume the eyes, and cause sorrow to the heart; and ye shall sow your seeds in vain for your enemies will have eaten it . . . And I will make your heaven as iron and your earth as brass . . .

And I will bring a sword among you that shall avenge the quarrel of my covenant; and when ye are gathered together in your cities I will send the pestilence among you . . . And ye shall eat the flesh of your sons, and the flesh of your daughters shall ye eat. And I will destroy your high places, and cut down your images, and cast your carcases upon the carcases of your idols . . . And I will scatter you among the heathen, and will draw out a sword after you: and your land shall be desolate and your cities laid waste . . .

But it was all to little avail, for if there is one recurring theme in Scripture, it is 'and the people did evil in the sight of God', and what had occurred in the days of Moses recurred in the days of Joshua and Ehud, and Deborah and Gideon, and Samuel and Saul and David, and right down through the centuries to the destruction of the first Temple by the Babylonians in 586 BC. Nor, in general terms, did later Jewish history follow a different pattern. Jewish misfortune, explained the Rabbis, as they explain it still, was the measure of Jewish iniquity.

But yet if a people sins and is punished and sins again and is punished again, and the process continues for four thousand years without either an improvement in their ways or an end to their misfortunes, then it might be reasonably inferred that the deterrent does not deter and that there was perhaps some imperfection in the divine plan. It certainly confirms the reputation of Jews as a stiff-necked people, but what is more remarkable is their continuing re-affirmation of faith. They are troubled by the ways of God, but they forgive Him for they know not what He is doing. They only hope that He does.

There is a sense in which the Jewish idea of God transcends the image conveyed in Scripture as someone almighty, jealous and vindictive. There is indeed something contradictory in the idea of a God who is at once omnipotent and jealous, for if there is abundant proof of His forgiveness, the thing He finds least forgiveable is Israel's tendency to go 'whoring after strange Gods'. Here, one might think, was the reaction, not of a supreme deity, but of a wife with fading charms who needs constant reassurance of her husband's fidelity.

One of the most sacred prayers in the Jewish liturgy defines the thirteen attributes of God:

The Lord, the Lord God, merciful and gracious, long suffering and abundant in goodness and truth. Keeping mercy for thousands, forgiving iniquity and transgression and sin.

Maimonides, the eleventh-century polymath who was the Aristotle of Jewish thought and whose work as codifier and commentator has made him the supreme authority on Jewish life (though in his own life-time much of his work was considered to be heretical and was consigned to the flames by the Rabbis), argued that God, being godly, could have no human attributes and that epithets applied to Him, whether benign or otherwise, merely represented the human view of His actions, which suggests that God was made in man's image, and that the whole scheme of crime, punishment and forgiveness was not so much part of a divine plan as man's own idea of how God should respond to human frailties.

The complex relationship between God and Israel is perhaps best summed up in one of the most mysterious and intriguing volumes in the entire canon of the Bible, the Book of Job:

There was once a man in the land of Uz, whose name was Job, and that man was perfect and upright, and one that feared God and eschewed evil.

And Job prospered and had sons and daughters and great herds of sheep, cattle and oxen, 'and a very great household so that this man was the greatest man in all the east'.

Then Satan came before God and asked:

Doth Job fear God for nought? Hast Thou not made an hedge about him, and about his house, and all that he hath on every side? Thou hast blessed the work of his hands, and his substance is increased in the land. But put forth Thy hand now and touch all he hath, and he will curse Thee to Thy face.

And within a day all that Job had was turned to ashes. His children died, his servants perished, his goods were stolen, yet his faith remained:

Naked came I out of my mother's womb, and naked shall I return; the Lord gave and the Lord hath taken away, blessed be the name of the Lord.

Then on top of his other afflictions came bodily torment and he was smitten 'with sore boils from the sole of his foot unto the crown of his head'.

Then said his wife unto him, Dost thou still retain thy integrity? Curse God and die. But he said unto her, What? Shall we receive good at the hands of God, and not receive evil?

But when his neighbours – the original 'Job's comforters' – suggest that his sufferings may be due to his sins his patience finally snaps. All that has been welling up within him breaks out in a prolonged cry of mortification, and he turns to Heaven demanding: 'Show me where I have erred!'

Then God appears to him out of a whirlwind to chastise him for his want of faith, and he finds his answer in His very appearance: 'I have heard Thee by the hearing of the ear; but now mine eye seeth Thee. Wherefore I abhor myself and repent in dust and ashes.' And all ends happily. His wife bears more sons and daughters, he acquires more cattle and sheep, and 'the Lord blessed the latter end of Job more than his beginning'.

But the happy ending is almost irrelevant. What was important was the recovery of faith, for if God did exist then Job's torments were not without purpose. The Israelites have out-Jobbed Job in that they have seen God's presence in their very suffering, but more, they have seen in their exceptional misfortunes proof of exceptional merit, and religious revivals have tended to follow national calamities.

Jewish exile may be said to begin with the destruction of the second Temple by the Romans in AD 70. Their years in their own land were not free of travail, but at least they were masters of their own fate. For the next 1900 years they were to be wanderers, always self-conscious, and usually unwelcome guests. Their torments were not as constant nor their sufferings as profound as writers in the lachrymose tradition of Jewish historiography would have one believe, but law and order are comparatively novel to European society, and where a country passed through a dark age the experience of its Jewish population tended to be that much darker. But though there was harassment, oppression and confiscatory taxation, actual physical attacks tended to be sporadic, and arose less from the abuse of authority than from its breakdown. Jews were always among the first victims of anarchy and among the first casualties of war.

A map of Jewish migration would offer an outline of Jewish experience. Jews moved like a river, prodding out the areas of least resistance. Tolerance brought an influx, persecution an exodus, and so Jews moved eastwards into the Parthian empire in the first and second centuries, westwards into North Africa and thence into Moorish Spain in the eleventh and twelfth centuries and finally from the thirteenth century there came a great movement across the face of Europe, which was to continue for the next four centuries, to the hospitable lands of Poland and Lithuania.

If the best that Jews could hope for elsewhere was tolerance, or indifference, newcomers to Poland were positively welcomed. They became administrators, merchants, lessees of the great estates of the Polish nobility, tax-farmers and tax collectors and, as Poland expanded eastwards into the Ukraine, they moved with the armies as agents of the ruling power. Thus when, in 1648, the Ukrainians under Chmielnicki rose against Polish dominion the Jews were to bear the main brunt of their fury. Within eighteen months over three hundred Jewish townships were destroyed and over one hundred thousand Jews – about a fifth of Polish Jewry – perished. It was the greatest calamity Jews were to experience until the rise of Hitler. The suffering was so wide-spread and the agonies so acute that mystics began to ask themselves whether these were not perhaps the *chevlei Moshiach*, the birthpangs of the Messiah.

The Messiah as a figure who will return Jews to their homeland and establish the Kingdom of Heaven largely derives from Jewish exile. Had the idea crystallized earlier, it is likely that Christianity would have spread more widely among Jews, but it was in medieval Europe that Messianism came into its own. At the source of the idea was Jewish suffering, which might have clashed with the idea of a beneficent God had it not, in itself, been taken as an oblique hint of beneficence, a sign that salvation was at hand. Thus in 1096, when the first Crusade moved like a scythe through the Jewish communities of Europe, there was talk of signs and miracles, as survivors hugged their wounds and prepared themselves for redemption. Further spasms of Messianic fervour occurred during the Black Death in the fourteenth century, and after the expulsion of the Jews from Spain in 1492, but the most serious revival came in the aftermath of the Chmielnicki massacres.

Jewish minds and imaginations were straining for signs and portents and when the son of a Smyrna merchant, called Shabbetai Zevi, came out of nowhere and proclaimed himself 'the first begotten son of God' and 'messenger and redeemer of Israel', thousands abandoned their homes and possessions to follow him across Europe to Jerusalem. They got no further than Constantinople, where Shabbetai Zevi was arrested and, given the choice between Islam and death, chose Islam. His wife, a survivor of the

Chmielnicki massacres, did the same. Yet it was out of this time of darkness that there came a movement which was to revitalize Judaism, give it new energy and hope and sustain it through centuries of rapid change up to our own time – Hassidism.

Hassidism created an inner world free of the harassment, humiliations and disappointments of the outer one. It brought man in more immediate touch with his maker. It challenged the dry scholasticism of the Rabbis and placed piety, humility and zeal on a par with, if not above, intellectual eminence. It created a Jewish nirvana which each man could attain through the fervour of his own devotion. It made reality seem irrelevant. Basic to the creed is the belief not merely that God is one, alone and unique, but that He is *all* that is, everywhere, everything, and it proved at once awesome and reassuring. It eliminated the space between heaven and earth.

Yet at the same time God was seen in almost homely terms and addressed in the affectionate diminutive as *Gottinke*, little God, often – as in the style of Sholem Aleichem's Tevye – with a sort of familiar deference – not unmixed with exasperation. God was open to private entreaty and if one was unfamiliar with the language of prayer any language sufficed; and if entreaties remained unanswered, then no doubt there was cause. *Mi frekt nit by Got kashes*, 'one does not ask God questions', was the refrain, and one didn't, not even Job's cry of anguish: 'Show me where I have erred!'

The eastward movement of Jewry was checked by the Chmielnicki massacres. It reversed in an ever-growing wave which reached its climax in the final decades of the nineteenth century and the first years of the twentieth century, when within a period of thirty years, nearly three million Jews moved from Russia and Poland and settled in the Americas and Western Europe. About three-quarters of the fourteen million Jews in the world today originate from Eastern Europe.

They were quick to shake the snow off their boots and to adapt themselves to their new environments. Some faded out of Judaism, without making any conscious effort to disappear, some sidled out, others fled; but many remained to affirm their faith and to transmit their convictions to their children, and even where the children have not always been convinced, they have kept their reservations silent, or at least muted, for God has formed so much a part of their father's domain, that to renounce the one was tantamount almost to renouncing the other. The Jew's belief in God is tied up with his belief in family. It doesn't quite amount to ancestor worship but there are vague areas where God the Father fades into father the God, especially where father is no more. There are, as there always have been, conflicts between the generations, but a troubled father, anxious to correct an erring son, need only drop dead to have his way.

Thus, for example, the majority of Jews still belong to a synagogue (though only a minority attend them), and even those who don't will take care to receive the last rites through a Jewish burial society and will be buried in consecrated ground. Many Jews (in Britain the overwhelming mass) are still at least nominally Orthodox, and not a few are Ultra-Orthodox and maintain a way of life hardly, if at all, removed from that of the Russian Pale of Settlement in the nineteenth century.

There is one day in the year when most Jews who think of themselves as such will be found at prayer, or at least in a House of Prayer, and that is on *Yom Kippur*, the Day of Atonement. And perhaps the climax of the *Yom Kippur* service is the *Unetane Tokef* which ends with the following paragraph:

On the first day of the year it is inscribed, and on the Day of Atonement the decree is sealed, how many shall pass away and how many shall be born; who shall live and who shall die, who at the measure of his days and who before it; who shall perish by fire and who by water; who by the sword and who by wild beasts; who by hunger and who by thirst; who by earthquake and who by plague; who by strangling and who by stoning; who shall have rest and who shall be restless; who shall be tranquil and who troubled, who at ease and who afflicted; who shall become poor and who shall wax rich; who shall be humbled and who exalted –
> But Prayer, Atonement and Charity
> avert the evil decree.

The prayer is in Hebrew, which is about as familiar to most Jewish worshippers as Latin is to Christians, but the message gets through. It cannot be said that Jews therefore resort to synagogue as a form of insurance. There is a residual feeling that the occasional effort to propitiate one's deity can do no harm and might do good, but in the main, synagogue attendance on a day like *Yom Kippur* has in modern times tended to be less of an affirmation of belief in God than a belief in believing, and *Yom Kippur* itself, an occasion for moral stocktaking, is in a sense the Annual General Meeting of the Jewish people, at which the chairman, who has directed their fortunes for so long, is confirmed in office *nem. con.*[1] It is also an annual roll-call which brings a basic feeling of reassurance, the thought that, after all we've been through, we're still here. Most Jews will recall

14

---

[1] *nemine contradicente : no one contradicting*

that they are slightly less observant than their fathers and their fathers were slightly less observant than *their* fathers, so that in the normal course of events there should have been a gradual phasing out of Judaism. But it hasn't happened and it no longer even seems likely that it will happen. One is left with a feeling that Jews are here because Somebody wants them to be here, and that if God is here to stay, then so are the Jews, or perhaps vice versa. Jews, moreover, have been Jewish for a very long time and there is a natural unwillingness to concede that one's forefathers made a mistake and continued to make it for over three thousand years. It may not be easy to believe in a God with such contradictory qualities as the God of Israel, but it is even more difficult to believe that one hundred generations of Jews could have been wrong.

A gentile who wants to convert to Judaism comes before a *Beth Din* (ecclesiastical court) and is there formally cautioned that as a righteous gentile he need conform only to the seven commandments of Noah to be assured of a place in Heaven, but as a Jew he would have to conform to no less than six hundred and thirteen. Given such expectations it is not difficult to fall short, and on the Day of Atonement the Jew, with hand to his heart, goes through an endless confessional:

We have trespassed, we have been treacherous, we have robbed, slandered, acted perversely. We have been wicked, presumptuous, violent, deceitful. We have counselled evil and spoken falsely. We have rebelled, provoked, committed iniquity. We have transgressed. We have oppressed. We have been stiff-necked. We have acted wickedly. We have corrupted. We have committed abominations. We have erred and have caused others to err . . .

And that is but the preamble. A confession so sweeping may suggest an underlying belief in one's innocence, but the Jew is, in fact, hyper-critical of himself and of his fellow-Jews (while at the same time remaining hyper-sensitive to outside criticism), and, as a rule, the more blameless his life, the more he will be troubled by his imperfections. Accordingly, the difference between the Orthodox Jew, the non-Orthodox Jew and the gentile is that one is a miserable sinner, the other a cheerful sinner, and the third doesn't even know that he has gone wrong. And therein we touch on the concept of the Chosen.

The idea of the Chosen did not confer any special privileges, only special obligations: what was acceptable in others was unforgiveable in the Jew. He was not endowed with special aptitudes or virtues, only special responsibilities. He was prone to the same temptations as other men, but was expected to rise above them. If the favourites of other deities could do no wrong, the Jew, given the demands made on him, could do no right. If it was hard to be a Jew, it was impossible to be a good Jew, and most people have given up trying. But the effect of it all has been to instil in the Jew a troublesome compound of pride and diffidence, the sense that he was among the elect, the suspicion that he was unworthy of election.

It is not a comforting birthright and, as a Sholem Aleichem character once observed (with an irony that sounds better in Yiddish): 'Such a favour, O God, I'll never forget.' The Jewish kingdom is of this world. All the rewards and punishments in Scripture are to be experienced in the here and now, and not in the hereafter, and all its dramatis personae – with the possible exception of Enoch and Elijah – died and stayed dead. There is no Valhalla in Judaism and no Garden of the Houris, and while there was paradise and hell, both were to be experienced mainly on earth. It was only in post-Biblical years that Rabbis concluded that there must be more to life and death than met the eye, and the Talmud paints a picture of paradise as a place where 'there is no eating or drinking, no begetting children, no commerce, envy, hatred or competition, but only this: that the righteous sit with crowns on their heads and delight in the presence of God'. It was the sort of next world which reconciles one readily to this one, but the Jewish attitude to the hereafter tended to vary with their immediate experience and it is of course natural to presume during calamity and misfortune that if there is a God at all, He must have some sort of redress stored up somewhere, and that the good will be rewarded and the wicked punished. No one familiar with Jewish history can believe that virtue is its own reward, or that it is humanly attainable. The Talmud carries the assurance that 'all Israel has a place in the world to come', but it does not suggest that this life is an insignificant preliminary to the life everlasting, nor is it clear that one's actions in this world, whether benign or malign, will necessarily affect one's experience in the next. Neither heaven with all its joys, nor hell with all its torments (which, as described in the Talmud, are akin to those of Tantalus), have a central place in the Jewish faith. Judaism is of this world and in so far as it believes in the Kingdom of Heaven at all it is as something which will become manifest on earth. The devout Jew also believes, or is, at least, expected to believe, in the resurrection of the dead, but the only form of immortality which counts as far as most Jews are concerned is in being reborn through one's children and grandchildren.

'The heavens', say the Psalms, 'the heavens are the Lord's, but the earth has He given to the children of men.' Many lessons have been drawn from these lines, and one, certainly, is to be content with this life and not to probe too far into the beyond. If the Jew is by nature a mystic, he is less concerned with the hereafter than with enlarging his awareness of, and enhancing his gladness in, the here and now.

CHAPTER THREE

In Every Generation . . .

Anti-semitism is a fairly new word for a fairly old sentiment and was invented about a hundred years ago by a German writer, Wilhelm Marr, to describe the particular antipathy which he felt towards Jews. Jews themselves have been aware of such feelings for rather longer and when they assemble to celebrate the Passover they recall – as they have recalled for two thousand years – 'In every generation men rise against us to destroy us . . .'. Things have not been quite that bad, though they often seemed like it, if only because Jews have been scattered, throughout much of their history, over a large part of the globe, and if some, perhaps even most, prospered, there was always a group of them in difficulties somewhere. As Jews have always been sensitive to each other's troubles, it is the troubles which have settled in the memory rather than the joys.

Most Jews have a slight knowledge of Jewish history. This is true even of those in *Yeshiva* (college of higher learning), for the *Yeshiva* is devoted largely to the study of the Talmud, and the Talmud, though encyclopaedic in scope, was completed by the sixth century and events beyond that date are largely *terra incognita*, except where they are echoed in liturgy and lore.

There is one event in the Jewish calendar, the 9th of Av, which is treated as a sort of carnival of grief. The day itself commemorates the destruction of both the first and second Temples (in 586 BC and AD 70 respectively), but it has become a remembrance day for every calamity in Jewish history. People abstain from food and drink, and assemble in the synagogue to read lamentations and tell sad stories of the death of kings and the martyrdom of Rabbis: how one had his head cut open, and another his flesh flayed, how a third was burnt alive wrapped in a holy scroll, and a fourth cast to the dogs without burial; how the Jews of Mayence perished and how their brethren in York were massacred, and so on down the ages to the greatest calamity of all – the holocaust: 'To

Auschwitz, Buchenwald, Bergen-Belsen, Dachau, Meidanek and Treblinka were they taken. . . . They flayed the flesh of our kin, and used their skin for adornment. . . . In want and hunger they gnawed the ground . . .'

The effect of it all is to make the Jew feel that he is a legatee of grief, that Jewish history is one long dark night of suffering and that the rest of mankind was in conspiracy against him.

Jewish history may be said to begin with the Exodus from Egypt and the settlement of the Twelve Tribes in Canaan in the thirteenth century BC. For about two hundred years the tribes remained a fairly united commonwealth ruled by judges and priests. But even then they sought to be 'as other nations' and yearned for the dominion of a king. Saul ascended the throne in the eleventh century BC and the country remained one united kingdom until the death of Solomon about a hundred years later. In 928 BC the kingdom split between Rehoboam in the south and Jeroboam in the north. The northern kingdom was larger in population and size, the southern was more important in terms of Jewish history, for it included Jerusalem and the Temple, but, in common with other petty states in the area, both were at the mercy of their larger neighbours and neither had a truly independent existence.

In 722 BC, the Assyrians came down like a wolf on the fold, destroyed the northern kingdom and took its inhabitants into captivity. Their fate is still a matter of conjecture, hence 'the Ten Lost Tribes'. The two in the south persisted for a further century and a half until Jerusalem was in turn destroyed by the Babylonians and the people taken into captivity.

Judea was resuscitated later in the century but it was never to recover its independence till our own times, and it remained a province first of the Persian, then of the Greek and finally of the Roman Empire. While all Jews continued to pray for the peace of Jerusalem and to pay tribute to the Temple, more Jews were outside the Jewish state than within it. The diaspora had established itself as a lasting fact of Jewish life five centuries before Christ.

The Egyptian city of Alexandria was, for many years, a major centre of Jewish life. The Jews, who were mostly prosperous artisans, had their own quarter near the palace of the Ptolemies and enjoyed a considerable measure of autonomy, but their position was ambivalent. They formed a middle class between the Egyptians, who were regarded as a subject people, and the Greeks, who enjoyed the full privileges of citizens, and when Jews aspired to rise to the level of the Greeks they caused resentment among both Greeks and Egyptians. Strife was not infrequent and a particularly vicious clash in 33 BC, which resulted in the destruction of property, desecration of synagogues and much loss of life, is sometimes referred to as the first pogrom. Yet it would be wrong to see events in Ptolemaic Egypt in terms of what happened to Jews in Tsarist Russia. It had more in common with the type of communal strife to be seen today in Cyprus or Lebanon. Jews were far from defenceless, they gave as good as they got, and they were not infrequently the aggressors.

There were about eight million Jews in the Roman Empire out of a total population of about eighty million, and, though scattered, they were closely linked, so that action against any could mean trouble from all. Moreover, Palestinian Jewry occupied a particularly strategic position astride the major east-west route. Thus, although the Romans accorded a ready tolerance to most cults, they treated Judaism with particular circumspection, so that, for example, Jews were absolved from Emperor worship – obligatory elsewhere as an expression of loyalty to the Empire – in case it should be regarded as a form of idol worship. Similarly, Roman legions in Jerusalem removed human images from their standards, and sometimes even animal images, in case these too should cause offence. Yet Jews were often in conflict among themselves and restive against the very idea of foreign dominion. Trouble in Judea was frequent, and in AD 132, during the reign of Hadrian, there came an uprising which led to great slaughter, took over three years to suppress and disrupted communications in a vital part of the Empire. When peace was restored, Hadrian turned to what he regarded as the source of the trouble and proscribed the practice of Judaism under penalty of death. There were numerous instances of open defiance – and the story of Jewish martyrdom begins with this period of persecution. Many legends arise from it, and some of them, such as the Martyrdom of the Ten Sages (the *Asarah Harugei Malchut*) now form the central part of the *Yom Kippur* liturgy:

> . . . And the dread King
> Bade the ten sages to be slain in woe
> And torture. Lo! I saw them through the years;
> They stepped out of the ages, and they walked
> Before the deathless spirit that is mad
> With hunger for the destruction of God's own.
> Two of the great of Israel were brought forth
> To slaughter first; – The High Priest Ishmael,
> And Rabban Simeon Ben Gamliel
> A Prince in Israel. And this one implored,

'O slay me ere you slay him, lest I see
The death of him who ministers to God . . .'

It has been difficult to trace the foundations of these legends and many
of the known facts contradict them. Not all of the sages mentioned were
contemporaries and could therefore not have been killed at the same time.
Judah Ben Bava, one of the Ten, was, according to another tradition, killed
by Roman troops in a separate incident. Rabbi Akiva features in all the
accounts, but the names of the other nine sages vary from version to
version. That the Jews suffered extreme tribulation in the last years of
Hadrian is without doubt, but whether they took the form described in the
legends is another matter. All nations create legends around their triumphs;
the Jews are perhaps unique in that they build legends round their calamities, but from that day unto this, Rome, or Edom as it is called in
Rabbinic texts, has descended as the archetype of all Jewish enemies: brutal,
remorseless and blood-crazed. Yet Jewish experience under the Romans
was in fact the experience suffered by every small nation restive under the
dominion of a large, and if there is anything unique in the history of those
years, it is not the brutality of the Romans, but the courage and assertive-
ness of the Jews.

It is only after the rise of Christianity that we come upon anti-semitism
in what might be called its classical form, when Jews were attacked not
because they were presumptuous, rebellious, assertive or perverse, but
because they were *Jews*, and because as Jews they often inspired irrational
fears. The collapse of the Roman Empire and the ensuing chaos brought
Jews northwards into areas which had little experience of the diversity
common in the east, and which were ever suspicious of the stranger. And,
of course, there was no-one more strange than the Jew, with his alien
appearance and language, his distinctive and secretive ways and, above all,
his distinct faith. Thus in the wave of religious fanaticism engendered by
the Crusades, the Jews were the most immediate victims, for as the Abbé
of Cluny observed: 'What is the good of going to the end of the world, at
great loss in men and money, to fight the Saracens, when we tolerate
among us other infidels a thousand times more guilty towards Christ than
the Mohammedans.'

The authorities, in almost every case, rushed to the help of the Jews,
but they were helpless before the mob, and the Crusaders' route across
Europe was marked with a trail of Jewish blood. There were many
witnesses to the torments suffered by the Jews, and to their heroism:

The foe killed them even as the others, putting them to the sword. They sustained themselves by the example of their brothers, let themselves be massacred and Hallowed the Name . . . They fulfilled the words of the Prophet: 'The mothers are laid upon their children, the fathers upon their sons.' This one killed his brother, that one his parents, his wife and his children; the betrothed killed each other even as the mothers killed their children. All accepted with full hearts the divine verdict. Recommending their souls to the Eternal they cried: 'Hear O Israel, the Lord Our God, the Lord is One.' The enemies stripped them naked and dragged them off, granting quarter to none, save those few who accepted baptism . . .

The tradition of *kidush hashem*, dying for the Holy Name, sanctified by the tradition of the *Asarah Harugei Malchut*, assumed new life, and community after community perished rather than accept baptism. Five thousand Jews were slaughtered in the Rhine Valley alone.

The medieval Jew had but slight contact with Christians or Christianity, and everything he knew of them both he abhorred. Martyrdom, the choice of death rather than a readiness to share their way of life, was therefore the ultimate mark of contempt, the ultimate gesture of defiance, and, as a medieval document quoted by the bibliographer Abraham Habermann suggests, this world may have been less important to him than the next:

For the time being the enemy will slay us . . . yet we shall live and flourish, our souls will be in Paradise . . . Above all, do not question the justice of the Holy One, Blessed be He, and Blessed be His Name . . . Happy shall we be if we do His will, and happy everyone who is slain and slaughtered and dies for the Sanctification of His Name. Such a one is destined for the World to Come, and shall dwell in the same regions as those righteous men, Rabbi Akiva and his companions, the pillars of the world who were slain for the sake of His Name. Furthermore, for such a one the world of darkness is transformed into the world of light, the world of grief into the world of joy, and the transient world into the world everlasting.

For no one were the Dark Ages as dark and as long as for the Jew.

If one monarch was protector, another might be predator, and worse even than a predatory ruler was a weak one, for Jews were the first victims of disorder. 'Ultimately', as Professor Leon Poliakov, an eminent student of anti-semitism, has written, 'the Jew could live only by means of money – not in the sense in which this is understood in our modern capitalist society, but in a much more significant sense: the right to life, which Christian society granted the merest yokel, had to be *bought* by the Jew at regular intervals. Under these circumstances money acquired for the Jew a quasi-sacred significance.'

But there was more to it than that. Until the Crusades, European Jews were men of substance, owning estates, vineyards, and considerable business houses, and they never reconciled themselves to the lowly status and penury imposed upon them by persecution. Every disaster was thus a challenge to even greater effort, and they acquired an ingenuity and resilience which, where given the breathing space of a generation, placed them ahead of their neighbours.

Moreover the very ceremonies and responsibilities of Judaism called for a certain minimal sufficiency. Jewish dietary laws made it more expensive to feed one's household. Jewish festivals limited the number of working days, but above all, the obligation to teach and to study presumed a degree of leisure not available to the general mass of the host population, and those who could not afford it expected the support of those who could. If study, as the Talmud urged, was the highest good, then the provision of facilities for study was the second highest, and it was this, added to the need to pay for the mere right to live, which gave money its 'quasi-sacred significance', and Rabbis showed a leniency in re-interpreting the fairly restrictive commercial laws of Judaism which they did not show elsewhere. All of this seemed to give divine blessing to what was already a sufficiently pronounced natural tendency, and the Jew strove for money with a determination which brought him into conflict often with the mores of his host society, and sometimes with its laws. It is not true, as Jewish writers often aver, that Jews were *forced* into money-lending, but the very fact of being a Jew was in itself an expense and there were few occupations other than money-lending which would have assured him the necessary income. The Church's attitude to money-lending as un-Christian moreover limited the competition and increased the returns. Some Jews did become rich, but the proportion of rich Jews (and the extent of their riches) may have been exaggerated, if only because the poor tended to be overlooked. If the Jew intruded upon the public's attention it was either as a law-breaker or because he was rich, and if he was rich it was usually because he was a money-lender.

If his money gave him security it also, of course, increased his vulnerability and the opprobrium with which he, and his fellow Jews, were regarded. The rich are always resented by the poor and the foreign rich are doubly resented and so there was sufficient reason for anti-Jewish antipathy in the Middle Ages. But Jews could have lived with rational antipathies. Their lives became untenable only when the irrational intervened, as it did with increasing frequency.

Their sufferings during the Crusades, given the fanaticism of the age, could be ascribed to a type of rational irrationality. Their sufferings during and in the aftermath of the Black Death arose out of crazed fear.

The bubonic plague had been a frequent visitor, but in 1348 it descended with a particular fury and within the next two years killed off more than a third of the population of Europe. The scale and remorselessness of the calamity, its very inexplicability, gave rise to extremes of behaviour and wild speculation. The Jews, it was whispered, were in league with Satan and were poisoning wells. The Black Death, it was suggested, was their doing. They were out to destroy Christendom. The declaration of Pope Clement VI that 'since this pestilence is all but universal everywhere, and by a mysterious decree of God has afflicted, and continues to afflict, both Jews and many other nations [the charge] that the Jews have provided the cause or the occasion for such a crime is without plausibility', proved unavailing. In many towns those Jews who had been spared by the Black Death were cut down by their neighbours and entire communities were wiped out in the Low Countries, France, Germany and Austria.

Spanish Jews had also suffered their tribulations, especially under the Almohades, a fanatical Moslem sect which invaded Spain in the twelfth century; but on the whole, Moslem rule tended to be enlightened and tolerant. Jews were able to prosper and rise to the highest offices of state and there was a flowering of Jewish culture such as had not been known in any of the previous centuries of exile. But as Christianity spread southwards across the face of the peninsula, their day darkened, their culture atrophied, their horizons narrowed. Persecution elsewhere in Europe had been arbitrary and sporadic; in Spain it became systematic and formed part of an attempt to force them into the Church. Elsewhere in Europe most Jews killed themselves rather than embrace the cross. In Spain, often led by their own Rabbis, entire congregations opted for baptism. Elsewhere, as we have seen, the world offered so much harassment to the Jew, and so few compensations, that they showed little compunction in leaving it. In Spain, however, Jews had known what it was to live and to be accepted, even respected members of an open and cultured society, and they felt that life was well worth a Mass. In some cases the conversions may have been sincere, but usually they were not and there emerged a whole caste of Conversos who, while overt Christians, remained covert Jews, and from 1481 the Holy Inquisition began to search into their souls.

It has been argued that the Inquisition was hardly a manifestation of anti-semitism for inquisitors only killed their own, but as most of their victims had been forced into the Church at the point of the sword, this is almost beside the point. Over two thousand Conversos were burnt at the stake as heretics, but it became clear that Conversos would continue to lapse while the Jews were still free to practise their faith in the open. Moreover, the Crown yearned to witness the complete Christianization of Spain, and after the fall of Granada, the last Moorish stronghold on Spanish soil, only the Jews stood in the way of that ambition. In 1492 the Jewish community, numbering some two hundred thousand souls, was expelled.

It was one of the blackest moments in Jewish history, but even while lights were being dimmed at one end of the continent, they were assuming a new effulgence at the other.

Different countries have at different times assumed the status of *die goldene medineh*, the golden land, in Jewish eyes, and if it had been Spain in the tenth and eleventh centuries, it was Poland in the fifteenth and sixteenth.

Poland, which had been devastated by Mongol invaders in the thirteenth century, sought new immigrants to settle her empty acres. They arrived, at first in a trickle and then in a stream, and among them were many Jews who, given opportunities they had not known in other countries, showed themselves to be eager cultivators and able administrators, and were particularly adept in organizing the trade of the country. In time they came to form a middle class between the small peasants and the ruling gentry. As Poland expanded to embrace vast new areas reaching as far as the Black Sea, the interests of the Jews also expanded. Poland, went a saying of the time, was 'heaven for the nobleman, purgatory for the citizen, hell for the peasant and paradise for the Jew'. There is also a Jewish saying that the trouble with paradise is that it doesn't last.

In 1648 the Ukrainian Cossacks under Bogdan Chmielnicki rose against their Polish masters and advanced northwards and westwards like an all-consuming wall of fire, with a barbarity and fury which had not been witnessed since the Mongol invasion. If their main hatred was directed against the Poles, their most immediate target was the Jews. Thousands were flayed alive, others were buried alive. Arms and legs were hacked off and men and women were left floundering in their own blood. Pregnant women were cut open and live cats thrust into their wombs. Thousands of infants were impaled, torn apart, thrown down wells or buried alive. Rape was so widespread that the councils of the Jewish communities came together to consider how to cope with an impending generation of Jewish Cossacks. The event is known in Jewish history as the *Gezeroth tach vetath*, 'the decrees of 1648–49', as if they were another punishment from on high. Over one hundred thousand Jews perished in the uprising. But one cannot see the events of those years as entirely the result of crazed fanaticism or mindless superstition.

The Pentateuch contains innumerable injunctions on how the Jew should treat the stranger in his midst ('Love ye therefore the stranger for ye were strangers in the land of Egypt'), but not how he should behave in the midst of strangers. Perhaps it was unnecessary, for exile, the awareness of being in a minority, imposes its own restraints and if the Jew was not always a model citizen, he was rarely a troublesome one and he generally acted with circumspection. In Poland, the Jews became so numerous, prosperous and entrenched, that they began to lose something of their caution.

Their whole economy was based mainly on the arenda system under which they became tax farmers and collectors for the crown, or lessees of the forests, estates, mills and salt mines of the nobility. Some operated on a large scale, many on a small scale, leasing a few acres of land, or operating a small distillery or tavern, but their utility to their superiors rested in their powers of extraction. The peasantry, the work force, the cattle, the land, were all regarded in much the same light and were pressed for their maximum yield, and if the nobility were thus the ultimate exploiters, the Jews were the visible ones and aroused the most immediate hostility. Rabbis warned that Jews were sowing a terrible harvest of hatred, but while the revenues rolled in the warnings were ignored. Moreover, the Rabbis themselves were beneficiaries of the system. Poland had become a major centre of Jewish learning and was renowned for the number and size of its academies and the quality of its scholarship. A leisured class had begun to emerge (a voluntary one; in later years there was to be an involuntary leisured class) which was also supported by the arenda.

There were, moreover, inherent tensions between the three parties to the system. The landowners were Catholic Poles, the middlemen were Jews, the peasants – and they were hardly more than serfs – were Greek Orthodox Ukrainians. The Pole was almost the reincarnation of Esau, 'a cunning hunter, a man of the field', cheerful, bucolic, feckless, licentious and improvident. The Jew was Jacob, 'a dweller in tents', pensive, prudent, indrawn, and if Pole and Jew regarded each other with derision they both treated the Ukrainians with contempt. When the Cossacks finally burst out of their steppes in 1648 they put an end to the career of Poland as a major power (and prepared the way for her eventual dissolution), and decimated Polish Jewry. The fact that Jews were non-Christians added fury to the onslaught, but they were attacked mainly as henchmen of the Poles.

Order was eventually restored, but the hatreds and fears generated by the uprising never died away, and where Polish Jewry had been confident, hopeful and assertive, it became nervous, apprehensive, on guard. World Jewry today consists largely of the heirs of those Polish Jews, and some of the old apprehensions persist.

Until 1648 there was a continuing *Drang nach Osten* on the part of European Jewry. Now the process was reversed and a westward trek began which is still not complete. Areas of central and western Europe which had been virtually *Judenrein* for centuries found new Jewish communities forming in their midsts and from about the end of the eighteenth century a tacit schism developed between Jews to the west of the Oder and those to the east.

The latter, finding the outer world increasingly untenable, retreated into an inner world and found new meanings and solace in mysticism, while Western Jewry, sensing a more hopeful and enlightened universe, began to emerge in their ones and twos to claim a place in the sun. It does not mean that they were universally welcomed. The Jews, wrote Voltaire, the leading apostle of enlightenment, were 'an ignorant and barbarous people, who for a long time have combined the most barbarous greed with the most detestable superstition and the most invincible hatred of all the people who tolerate and enrich them'. Jews were to receive similar rebuffs from other apostles of progress, but while progress continued their conditions improved. Their disabilities fell away one by one and by 1850, those of them living in central and western Europe were free men.

Gentiles, however, were still that much freer and in his impatience for full acceptance many a Jew, whose forefathers had chosen martyrdom to avoid baptism, rushed to the font of his own free will. To some, like the German poet Heine (1797–1856), baptism was 'a ticket to European culture', to others it offered hope of economic advantage. Others still may have turned to Christianity as a logical extension of their Judaism, but all remained Jews in the eyes of gentiles, who found their sudden rush to the forefront of European life startling. One minute they were nowhere, an unseen race (though not unseen enough) confined to their ghettos, living their own narrow lives, withdrawn, subdued, the next they seemed to be everywhere, owning huge banks, controlling vast industries, cultivating large estates, editing influential newspapers, running successful practices, prospering and, even less forgiveable, exulting in their prosperity. To gentiles who had not risen far in life, or who perhaps were not interested in rising in the first place, it looked as if the once meek Jews were set to inherit the earth. T. P. O'Connor, an Irish journalist writing of Disraeli in 1878, protested that he was 'moulding the whole policy of Christendom to Jewish aims'. The fact that Disraeli had been baptized as a boy and was a member of the Church of England, and could not have become Prime Minister had he been anything else, was regarded as irrelevant, but in England, at least, Disraeli headed the Conservative Party, and gave eloquent expression to its aspirations and fears. This upstart Jew became the voice of old England. Elsewhere in Europe Jews were at the head of the parties of reform and progress.

This was particularly true of the German-speaking lands. In the Austro-Hungarian Empire, the rural population resented the dominion of Vienna, and within Vienna, Catholic and conservative resented the influence of the Jews. In Austria as a whole, Jews formed some 4.35 per cent of the population in the 1860s. In Vienna, it was over 7 per cent, but these were people who were, so to speak, full, self-confessed Jews. There were also many half-Jews and quarter-Jews and ex-Jews who may have described themselves in census returns as Christians, who may have thought of themselves as such, but who, as far as the general public was concerned, were Jews. If one includes them, Jews possibly formed a sixth or a fifth of Vienna's population, perhaps more, but even then their influence was out of all proportion to their numbers. The mass circulation dailies, or 'boulevard sheets' as they were dismissively called, like the *Neues Wiener Journal* and *Neues Wiener Tagblatt*, were both Jewish owned, as was the liberal *Neue Freie Presse*, perhaps the most influential paper in the German-speaking world. Wickham Steed, Vienna correspondent of *The Times*, had the impression that about three journalists in four were Jewish. All the great names which made the Viennese theatre the envy of Europe, Schnitzler, Hugo Von Hofmannsthal, Max Reinhardt, were Jews or half-Jews. The warmth, the colour, the gaiety, the *gemütlichkeit* that charmed so many visitors to the capital, was largely Jewish, or Hungarian, or Bohemian, but anyhow, not native to the city, and most things alien tended to be regarded as Jewish. What charmed the visitor, however, often offended the native, who saw gay Vienna as *Grosstadt*, the symbol of a crass and materialistic society.

When Hitler arrived in the capital from Linz, he found a place so different from the Austria he knew that he thought he had come to a foreign
city, and it was his experience of Vienna which set him thinking feverishly
on the Jewish question. In Linz there were few Jews, and these, he said,
'had become Europeanized to external appearance and were so much like
other human beings, that I even looked upon them as Germans'. Viennese
Jewry was not in fact any less Europeanized. They were indeed the supreme
Europeans, cultivated, urbane, in touch with German, French and English
culture. But while, in the provinces, Jews had blended into their scene, the
entire scene in Vienna was largely coloured by the Jews, and the colour
was not to Hitler's liking.

In 1897, Karl Lueger, head of the Christian Socialist Party, was elected
Mayor of Vienna on a promise to wrest the city from the Jews, and
retained office till 1910. Lueger, a brilliant demagogue, knew how to
harness the resentments both of conservatives and of the Viennese lower
middle-class. He denied that he was anti-semitic. He made a point of
visiting Jewish homes and synagogues, and retained Jews in his entourage
so that he could claim, not without justice, that some of his best friends
were Jews. But when the Christian Socialists eventually gave way to the
National Socialists, Hitler felt no need to make any such protestations.

One could also discern in some of the anti-Jewish agitation more than a
passing undertone of sexual jealousy. The Jew, as we have seen, was
thought to be in league with the devil and prone to every variety of dark
practice, and what could be darker or more devilish than sex? (The Jew,
in ancient times at least, also had an extravagant idea of the sexual tastes
and aptitudes of the gentile. The Talmud, for example, decreed that one
shouldn't stable one's ass with a non-Jew in case it should be buggered.)

That the Jew had and has a robust sexual appetite is well attested from
even the most cursory reading of the Bible, the Talmud, and more recent, if
less sacred, texts. 'Be fruitful and multiply' is the first commandment in the
Torah and what was traditionally regarded amongst Christians as a sordid
if necessary act was raised by the Rabbis to the level of a holy sacrament.
But as the Rabbis themselves were to lament, it was carried to unholy
lengths. There are still Rabbinic decrees forbidding the consumption of
non-Jewish wines lest they should lead to undue familiarity with non-
Jewish women. They did not, of course, assume that lechery was a peculiarly Jewish vice, yet it was seen as such and there were frequent enactments
forbidding Jews from employing Christian girls in their households. In
nineteenth-century Germany, when Jewish shops grew in number and

size, there were widespread murmurings that Christian sales girls were being debauched by their lecherous employers. Streicher's *Stürmer* seethed with so-called exposés of Jewish depravity. It became an obsession with Nazi leaders which, as we shall see, found its apotheosis in the Nuremburg laws.

If anti-Jewish feeling in central Europe can be explained in terms of Jewish intrusion – the resentment of Jewish influence and ubiquity – it never, at least until the rise of Hitler, assumed the virulence of anti-Jewish feeling in Eastern Europe, where Jews both shunned the outside world and were shunned by it.

There were few Jews in Russia until the several partitions of Poland at the end of the eighteenth century brought the great and historic communities of Lithuania and Poland under Tsarist rule. This did not mean that Jews were allowed to spread across Russia: they were in the main confined to what came to be known as the Pale of Settlement. It may, perhaps, be useful to add that the Pale was not quite as constricted as the term suggests, for it covered an area of about three hundred and eighty-six thousand square miles (about four times the area of the United Kingdom), with about five million Jews in a population of forty-four million. But what gave a sense of constriction was the fact that one could not travel beyond the Pale without a special permit.

The great leap forward which brought western Jewry into the mainstream of European life left the mass of Jewry in the Russian Pale virtually unaffected and in 1841 the Russian Minister of Education, Uvarov, proposed the creation of a network of Jewish day schools. The plan was viewed with the gravest misgivings by most Rabbis, who suspected a scheme to convert Jews to Christianity, and when the schools were established, most Jews shunned them. But gradually, especially after deferment from military service was granted to graduates from secondary schools, they began to find their way into the classrooms. A secular Jewish intelligentsia began to emerge and with it a mood of optimism and, given the spread of enlightenment among the masses and the tolerant policies followed by Alexander II ('The Tsar Liberator'), one could have envisaged, as some did envisage, the gradual emergence of Russian Jewry into the modern world. In 1881, however, the Tsar was assassinated. In the ensuing disorder anti-Jewish riots erupted all over the Pale. In some cases they were tolerated and in others encouraged by the authorities. Commissions established to investigate the causes ascribed them to 'Jewish exploitation'. A new policy of coercion was launched and Jews who had earlier been encouraged to seek places in the school system were now subject to a *numerus clausus*.

Jews had to face increasing discrimination and harassment and Pobedono-stsev, head of the Holy Synod of the Russian Orthodox Church, saw a solution to the Jewish problem in the conversion of a third of Russian Jewry, the expulsion of a third and the extermination of the rest. And then, as if in pursuit of this policy, came the trial of Mendel Beilis.

On 12 March 1911, the mutilated body of a twelve-year-old boy was found in a cave near Kiev. Police investigations suggested that he died at the hands of a local criminal gang, but Shcheglovitov, the Minister of Justice, brushed their findings aside and pressed charges of ritual murder against Mendel Beilis, the thirty-seven-year-old manager of a local brick kiln. The main witness for the prosecution was a lamplighter who said that he had seen the boy playing near the kilns on the night he vanished, and that he last saw him being dragged towards the brickworks by a Jew. A Catholic priest, Father Justic Pranaitis, was called to show that the murder of the boy bore all the characteristics of the sort of ritual murder enjoined by the Talmud and other holy texts, an assertion which was dismissed without difficulty by several authorities, both Jewish and non-Jewish. More crucial, however, was the confession, under cross-examination by the lamplighter, on whose testimony the entire case rested, that he knew nothing at all and that he had been confused by relentless pressure from the secret police. Beilis was found not guilty, but it was remarkable that such a case could have been brought at all, even in Russia.

The ritual murder charge was first directed against the Jews some centuries before Christ, when it was alleged that it was customary for the Jews to kidnap a Greek, fatten him up for a year, then offer him up as a sacrifice and eat his flesh.

The same charge was then made against the early Christians, and Father Tertullian, writing in the second century, protested: 'We were said to be the most criminal of men, on the score of our sacramental baby-killing, and the baby-eating that goes with it.' It was in the twelfth century that the charge assumed what might be called its 'modern form' and from then on it was directed solely against the Jews.

In March 1144, the body of a young boy was found in a wood near Norwich. He was last seen entering a Jewish house on Easter eve and the rumour spread that he was seized, bound, gagged, that his head was tied with cords and pierced with thorns, and that he was then nailed to a cross. No proof was brought to show that any Jew had been implicated in the death of the child, but the belief that they slew him for some dark purpose persisted. The burial place of the boy became the centre of a cult and the boy himself was eventually canonized as St William of Norwich. The charge was soon repeated, with minor variations, in Gloucester, Bury St Edmunds, Winchester, London and Lincoln. The last gave rise to a cult of Little Hugh of Lincoln, who was also canonized, and featured in Chaucer's 'Prioress's Tale':

> O yonge Hugh of Lincoln, slayn also
> With cursed Jewes, as it is notable,
> For it is but a litel whyle ago,
> Preye eek for us.

The charge was raised in France, Germany, Bohemia, Poland, Lithuania, Italy, Greece, Egypt, Syria, Hungary, Spain. Most of the accusations arose on or about the approaches to Passover and the myth assumed two main forms: the one that Jews were accustomed to re-enact the crucifixion of Christ and that they needed Christian blood for their Passover matzoth.

Jewish protestations that the Mosaic law forbade them to taste even the blood of an animal, let alone a human being, were brushed aside. The libel was denounced by bishops and kings. In the thirteenth century the Emperor Frederick II of Hohenstaufen instituted a rigorous inquiry into the whole charge and concluded: 'There is not to be found either in the Old Testament or the New Testament that the Jews are desirous of human blood.' Pope Innocent IV, writing in 1247, declared (totally without effect) that the charge was malicious and false; but in fact, until 1965, the Church still celebrated the beatification of Simon of Trent, who was said to have been martyred by Jews in 1475. That Jews were required to butcher a Christian from time to time, preferably a Christian child, became part of ineradicable European folk-lore, and spread, with the expansion of European influence, into Moslem areas.

Between the disappearance of William of Norwich in 1144 and the Beilis case in 1911, there were about a hundred and twenty instances where the charge of ritual murder was laid against Jews, about a third of them in the nineteenth century alone. If there was progress elsewhere, in this area there were continuing reversions to the darkest superstition. In 1840, fifty-eight leading converts to Christianity, headed by S. M. Alexander, the first Anglican Bishop of Jerusalem, declared:

We, the undersigned, by nation Jews, and having lived to years of maturity in the faith and practice of modern Judaism, but now, by the grace of God, members of the Church of Christ, do solemnly protest that we have never directly nor indirectly heard, much less known among the Jews of the practice of killing Christians or using Christian blood, and that we believe this charge, so often brought against them formerly, and now lately revived, to be a foul and Satanic falsehood.

There were many elements in the Judeophobia which Hitler harnessed to his political machine, but the irrational, the dread of the Jew, the belief that he had recourse to dark and murderous rituals, that he had occult powers, was perhaps the supreme one. The Hitlerite definition of Jews as *Untermenschen* was but a reversal of the fear that they could become *Übermenschen*. His father, an Austrian customs official, stemmed from a class which was particularly resentful of the prosperity and success of the Jewish bourgeoisie, and which had formed the mainstay of Lueger's anti-semitic Christian Socialist Party.

Hitler echoed these resentments and detested the Jewish influence in the life and culture of Austria. He also shared the belief, propagated by the *Protocols of the Elders of Zion* (a forgery emanating from the fertile imagination of the Tsarist secret police), that there was a Jewish conspiracy, involving both bankers and revolutionaries, to control the earth. The extent of the Jewish involvement in the revolutionary movements which shook Europe at the end of World War I had a startling effect even on stable imaginations.

When the Protocols appeared in an English edition in 1920, the London *Times* asked:

What are these 'Protocols'? . . . Are they a forgery? If so, whence comes the uncanny note of prophecy, prophecy in parts fulfilled, in parts far gone in the way of fulfilment? Have we been struggling these tragic years to blow up and extirpate the secret organisation of German world dominion only to find beneath it another, more dangerous because more secret? Have we been straining every fibre of our national body, escaped a 'Pax Germanica' only to fall into a 'Pax Judaica'? The 'Elders of Zion' as represented in their 'Protocols' are by no means kinder taskmasters than William II and his henchmen would have been.

In America the *Chicago Tribune* came out with headlines like 'Trotsky Leads Jew-Radicals to World Rule. Bolshevism only a Tool for his Scheme'.

Henry Ford's *Dearborn Independent* ran a series of articles on the 'Protocols' which later re-appeared in book form under the title: *The International Jew: the world's foremost problem.*

The criticism and fears voiced by Hitler were thus not singular, but he added to them an element of pure fantasy which brought back distant echoes from the Middle Ages the fear of the Jew as a destroyer and poisoner, whose intrusion into the life of Europe was, he believed, polluting the Aryan blood stream. The Nuremburg Laws of 1935 'for the Protection of German Blood and Honour' were but a step from the 'Final Solution'. Here was the blood libel given a new form and a new virulence.

Commenting on the blood libels earlier in the century, the Jewish philosopher, Ahad Ha-am, drew one comfort from them:

This accusation is the solitary case in which the general acceptance of an idea about ourselves does not make us doubt whether all the world can be wrong and we right, because it is based on an absolute lie, and is not even supported by any false inference from particular to universal. Every Jew who has been brought up amongst Jews knows as an indisputable fact that throughout the length and breadth of Jewry there is not a single individual who drinks human blood for religious purposes . . . Let the world say what it will about our moral inferiority: we know that its ideas rest on popular logic and have no real scientific basis . . . 'But' – you ask – 'is it possible that everybody can be wrong and the Jews right?' Yes, it is possible, the blood accusation proves it possible. Here, you see, the Jews are right and perfectly innocent.

The Jew does not believe in original sin, but, especially where tradition has entered into his upbringing, he has a pronounced sense of guilt, instilled in him by endless generations of prophets and preachers. There are, after all, few denunciations more sweeping than those of Jeremiah:

For among my people are found wicked men: they lay wait as he that setteth a snare; they set a trap to catch men. As a cage is full of birds, so are their houses full of deceit; therefore they are become great, and waxen rich. They are waxen fat, they shine: yea they overpass the deeds of the wicked . . .

Jews have not always been helpless or innocent, and not every calamity they suffered has been undeserved. They have, after all, been around for a very long time and scattered among many places, and not all of them could have lived exemplary lives and acted as model citizens. There was also something inherent in their character and circumstances which gave some of them unsocial qualities and which sometimes brought out the worst in their neighbours. Their very belief that they were chosen of God could not but invite the opprobrium of man. Every Jew is familiar with the words of Hillel, and the precept 'love thy neighbour as thyself' is at the heart of Judaism, yet every student brought up on the Babylonian Talmud – and it must be remembered that for many centuries, especially in Poland, the Jew studied little else – is inculcated with a disdain for the gentile which has entered into Jewish lore and into the very expressions of the Yiddish language. It is true that every harassed and persecuted minority will tend to regard its persecutors with contempt – if you can't beat 'em, scorn 'em. It is further true that Rabbis were at pains to explain that the contemptuous references to gentiles in the Talmud were not concerned with gentiles as such, but with idol worshippers, and that the Russians and Poles were not idol worshippers. The attitudes, however, persisted and there is nothing like disdain to breed disdain, and worse.

His religious observances also required the Jew to stay apart. The words of Haman in the Book of Esther – 'there is a certain people scattered abroad, and their laws are diverse from all people' – were to be echoed by persecutors down the ages. And yet where, as in Medieval Italy, Jews felt sufficiently at ease to drop their own usages and draw closer to their neighbours, they were thrown back. The Lateran Council, in 1215, ordered that Jews 'in all Christian lands and at all times, shall be publicly differentiated from the rest of the population by the quality of their garments, especially since this is ordained by Moses'. Rabbi Solomon Schechter (1847–1915) later defined anti-semitism as 'the dislike of the unlike', but it was, on the contrary, when Jews were ceasing to be visibly Jewish, when many of them, indeed, had become practising Christians, as in fifteenth-century Spain and modern Germany, that anti-semitism assumed its most murderous forms.

Jews have shown an eagerness for money which, as we have explained, was partly due to their circumstances, but which also helped to form their circumstances, and certainly the explanation that their commercial aggressiveness was part of their struggle to survive was no consolation to their competitor or victim. Few Mosaic laws have been interpreted by the Rabbis with the open-mindedness and the liberality with which they approached the laws of usury. The golden calf has never been entirely eliminated from the Jewish creed, with results that have often been pernicious and sometimes tragic.

Moreover, the Jew, once adrift from his own traditions, had scant respect for the traditions of his neighbours, and conservative Christians throughout Europe regarded the Jew as inimical to all they stood for. As a constant agent of change, he was creating a universe in which they found themselves out of place.

The Jews were cosmopolitan, aspiring to the general in an age of particularism, so that in the Hapsburg lands, for example, they were the only Austrians at a time when everyone else was German, or Hungarian or Bohemian or Polish, as they were to be the only Czechoslovaks in Czechoslovakia. They also tended to be eclectic and to search out the dominant, richer, more catholic culture. They were generally regarded as a Germanizing influence, incurring the hostility of Hungarians, Poles, Bohemians and Moravians, each of whom were struggling to assert their own individual identity, without however, gaining the appreciation of the Germans.

If the United Kingdom should ever break up into its component parts, it is likely that British Jews will be the last Britons.

Jews have also sometimes been described as persons of doubtful loyalty. At the outbreak of World War I many Jews in the Pale of Settlement were deported into the interior to prevent them collaborating with the Germans or Austrians. Neither the Germans nor the Austrians had to take any such precautions. Nearly three hundred thousand Jews fought in the Austro-Hungarian armies during the four years of war, and nearly thirty thousand fell in battle. A further twelve thousand fell in the German ranks. One is born with a natural loyalty to one's homeland which can quickly atrophy in the light of experience, and Jews within the Pale of Settlement had little cause to be loyal to the Tsar. In central and western Europe it was otherwise – which does not mean, however, that every Austrian, German or British Jew rushed to the colours at the first sound of battle. Many so-called German, Austrian and British Jews were *Ost-Juden* who had only lately arrived from the Pale of Settlement and were disinclined to risk their lives at the moment when they were only beginning to discover the joys of living. There were numerous accounts of Jews shirking their military responsibilities. One could explain them, but the explanations were unlikely to satisfy the many families mourning the loss of sons and fathers. And then, as the fighting died away, one central-European country after another was convulsed by revolutions which were in almost every case led by Jews, often foreign Jews, in the name of the proletariat.

The Jewish apologist could answer charges that Jews were inherent revolutionaries with examples of Jewish conservatism, Jewish disloyalty with Jewish patriotism, Jewish bigotry with Jewish tolerance, Jewish cupidity with Jewish generosity, Jewish exclusiveness with Jewish gregariousness, Jewish lechery with Jewish puritanism. But the troublesome elements in the Jewish character cannot be overlooked. Yet if there is a rational basis for some anti-Jewish feeling, the most virulent hatred and worst excesses of anti-semitism, as we have seen, arose mainly from the irrational, and if the Jew is unable to admit to his failings even where he knows himself to be guilty, it is partly because he has so often been attacked for things of which he was innocent and any lingering private feelings of guilt he may have had towards the gentiles have been assuaged by the holocaust. Whatever wrongs Jews may have perpetrated, whatever errors they may have committed, the account has been settled, and more.

Does the Jew therefore feel more secure? Some do, if only because a new focus has been found for racial hatreds, and possibly next to a Black or a Hindu even the immigrant Jew can feel more like a WASP or an Englishman. In any case few Jews are now immigrants and they are established sufficiently to regard themselves as part of the host society and, indeed, to share its prejudices. If some Jews, as we shall see in a later chapter, were in the vanguard of the movement for racial equalities, not a few have the disdain for the *schwartzes* (Blacks) which they used to have for the Ukrainian peasant and may, indeed, feel the more integrated in the host society for sharing its antipathies.

Others fear that such prejudice is indivisible and if a serious movement should develop to limit the rights and opportunities of any minority, the Jews too would be threatened. Whether he has the foresight to realize this or not, the very existence of bigotry directed at any group tends to stir unhappy memories, so that if, say, the Englishman is troubled by the influx of coloured immigrants, the English Jew is doubly troubled.

There is probably less anti-semitism and certainly less overt anti-semitism in the world today than at any time since the rise of Christianity. Auschwitz is, of course, one reason; another is the decline in religious fanaticism and, indeed, in religious belief in general, and while rampant secularism may be a threat to Judaism it has made life easier for the Jew. A third reason, which is connected to the second, is that the western world has become more Jewish. The commercial drive which was said to characterize the Jew and which was regarded with such disdain by the European (if not the American) bourgeoisie, has become, if not respectable, then at least more widespread and acceptable – while the self-same drive has somewhat abated among Jews. In other words, the Jew has become less Jewish. One will find a growing number of them in callings such as public administration, teaching and the arts, which can hold little attraction to anyone primarily interested in cash.

Which does not, of course, mean that anti-semitism is dead. Where one finds wire screens across synagogue windows it is still alive, and one will find them, for example, on most British synagogues, but it does not amount, as it once did, to a conscious burden, something one goes to bed with at night and rises with in the morning. And if it was not seen in the context of past events few Jews would give it a thought.

Hitler killed five or six million Jews. One does not know how many he created for there are countless individuals of Jewish origin who do not believe in Judaism, do not observe Jewish tradition, who are completely removed from Jewish life and who would admit to being Jews only if someone knocked on their door in the small hours and asked if they were Jewish. One might call them *Hitler Juden*. They will remain Jews for as long as the very fact of being Jewish can incur hatred; they are Jews for the hell of it. The acrid smell of the crematoria still lingers in their nostrils and one doesn't know how many generations will pass before it dies away.

· CHAPTER FOUR ·

Pushers

'All our misery comes from Jews who want to climb too high. We have too many intellectuals. I want to prevent Jews from pushing ahead too much. They should not make such great strides.'

Thus spoke Baron Maurice de Hirsch (1831–96), one of the richest men in Europe and possibly one of the greatest pushers of all time. It is not certain how much money he made in his lifetime, but it is known that he gave away over $100,000,000, and such sums are not acquired through careful husbandry and frugal living.

Hirsch was perhaps the most successful Jewish entrepreneur of his age, and the most munificent, but not the most celebrated. If there was a name which almost symbolized Jewish commercial flair, it was Rothschild – a name which represented not one individual, but a seemingly ubiquitous brotherhood, the sons and grandsons of a Frankfurt money-changer, Mayer Amschel Rothschild, who dominated the money-markets of Europe until World War I, and whose progeny are still a force to be reckoned with.

In 1875, when Prime Minister Benjamin Disraeli heard that a large packet of shares, which would have given Britain control of the Suez Canal, were on offer, there was only one person to whom he could turn for ready cash: Baron Lionel de Rothschild. His secretary, Cory, was quickly sent round to the bank and ushered into the presence of the Baron.

How much money was needed?, he was asked.

Four million pounds.

When?

Tomorrow.

The Baron, fingering a muscatel grape, popped it into his mouth and spat out the skin.

'What is your security?'

'The British Government.'

'You shall have it.'

It was the London Rothschilds who found the £20,000,000 to compensate slave owners after the abolition of slavery in the British Empire in 1833. In 1854 a £16,000,000 loan to finance the Crimean War was launched through the House of Rothschild, and in 1871 they raised £100,000,000 to help France pay her war indemnity to Prussia. Salomon Rothschild, of the Vienna house, financed a large part of the Hapsburg railways; James, of the Paris house, did the same for France and controlled the *Chemin de Fer du Nord*. All loans from France to Russia were financed through the Paris house. The papacy was often dependent on loans from Karl Rothschild, head of the Naples house. In New York the Rothschilds were represented by August Belmont and in Berlin by Samuel Bleichroeder, though both were later to establish their own banking houses. Belmont proved to be of great value in organizing the federal finances in the American Civil War.

There was, by the end of the nineteenth century, hardly a financial centre where Jewish bankers did not enjoy a position of considerable prominence. In Brussels there was the house of Bischoffsheim, and also Errers, Oppenheim and Stern who combined with Sulzbach and May of Frankfurt to form the Banque du Bruxelles, in 1871. In Switzerland Isaac Dreyfus and Sons participated in the formation of the Basler Handelsbank and the Basler Bankverein. In Holland there was Wertheimer and Gompertz and the house of Lissa and Kann. The Hungarian General Credit Bank of Budapest was of Jewish creation as were the Hungarian Commercial Bank and the Hungarian Hypothecary Credit Bank. In St Petersburg the Guenzburg families established the Discount and Credit bank as well as the Bank of St Petersburg. The Warsaw Discount Bank was founded in 1871 by Mieczystaw Epstein, and Leopold Kronenberg took part in the formation of the Warsaw Credit Union as well as the Bank Hadlowy; but it was London, until World War I the banking capital of the world, which saw the largest concentration of Jewish financial talent, and which, besides the Rothschilds, also attracted the Hambro family from Copenhagen, the Speyer brothers, Emile Erlanger, Ernest Cassel and others from Germany, the Sassoon brothers from Bombay, and Hirsch, who was himself the scion of a Munich banking family, and whose wife was a Bischoffsheim.

In England Jewish bankers enjoyed a social prominence which would have been denied them elsewhere. Several of them formed part of the royal circle, and Cassel in particular was described by the official biographer of Edward VII as 'the King's closest friend'.

In America Belmont, the Seligmans and Speyer and Co helped to finance the federal government in the civil war, while Erlanger and Co helped the confederacy. After the war Kuhn, Loeb mobilized the capital for the westward thrust of the railways, while Goldman, Sachs, Kuhn, Loeb and the Seligmans raised large sums to finance the major public utility corporations required by the new industries and growth in population.

All this gave an impression of Jewish omnipotence, but, in fact, when the Jewish banking clans seemed at their most powerful they were already on the decline. State loans were increasingly undertaken by central banks, and private partnerships, even where they were internationally linked, could not always compete with the new financial conglomerations.

There is a cartoon by Max Beerbohm showing five Jewish bankers in the ante-room of Buckingham Palace shortly before the accession of George V, with the caption: 'Are we as welcome as ever?' The short answer was no. It was not merely that George V was less interested in money and had less need for monied friends than Edward VII, but the golden age of the merchant banker was over.

Some of the reasons why Jews were attracted to banking have already been touched on. There were others. Nobility in Europe over many centuries was measured in acres, and where a merchant made money he often converted it into land. The Jew in many countries was, until comparatively recent times, not allowed to own land, and even when he was, he rarely felt sufficiently secure to invest his money in it. He could not risk being tied down by his wealth, and his assets had to be immediately realizable. Jews, moreover, were a close brotherhood, who understood one another and could, until comparatively modern times, communicate with one another through the lingua franca of Hebrew. They knew of one another, were often related, so that their letters of credit had ready currency, and, until they became established institutions, they showed a greater readiness to take risks. They were more open to new methods and new ideas, more adaptable to new situations, and had a keener sense for new opportunities, so that it was not mere chance that Mayer Amschel Rothschild of Frankfurt should seek, amid all the chaos of the Napoleonic wars, to send one of his sons to England, or that Salomon Rothschild of Vienna should have been prepared to invest a fortune in railways at a time when steam propulsion was still in its infancy. It was perhaps Baron

Maurice de Hirsch who best represented the qualities and not a few of the defects which characterized the Jewish banker.

Hirsch, a member of an old-established Bavarian Jewish banking clan, inherited one fortune and married another, but the two or three millions with which he began his career would have been insufficient to cover the outgoings of his many households, and he regarded himself, and was generally regarded, as a self-made man. He was, in the words of a French writer, 'a cheerful *arrivé*' and, on the whole, tended to behave like one.

His paternal grandfather had been ennobled by the Bavarian Crown for public services during the Napoleonic wars, though the Hirsch family bank was of only local significance. His wife's family, the Bischoffsheims, had more extensive interests. His father-in-law, Senator Raphael Bischoffsheim, helped to found the National Bank of Belgium, and was on its board of directors for twenty years, and the family bank, Bischoffsheim and Goldschmidt, with its branches in Amsterdam, Antwerp, Brussels, London and Paris, was one of the foremost finance houses of Europe and was later to be involved in the formation of the Comptoir (Nationale) d'Escompte, the Société Générale pour favoriser le Commerce et l'Industrie and the Banque de Paris et des Pays Bas, as well as the Banque Franco-Egyptienne in Cairo and the Bank of London and San Francisco.

Hirsch joined Bischoffsheim as a clerk, but he never became a partner even after he became a son-in-law, for the family was a little nervous of his audacity and ambition, and in 1862 he founded his own bank, Bischoffsheim and De Hirsch, Brussels, with his brother-in-law Ferdinand as partner. He appears to have displayed only scant interest in the day-to-day business of merchant banking. His main passion was railways and he became involved in financing feeder lines in various parts of Europe, which he was later to sell to the trunk lines at a profit. This provided him with the necessary experience for his largest and most ambitious undertaking – the Oriental Railway.

The great railway boom of the mid-nineteenth century had sent lines in all directions, but they were slow to thrust far beyond Vienna, and the Balkans remained unopened both because of the difficulties of the terrain and because of the hazards of working in the Ottoman Empire.

In 1868 the Turks granted a concession to a Belgian company, Van der Elst, backed by the banking house of Lagrand-Dumonceau, to cut a line from Vienna through Bulgaria to Constantinople. It was too vast an undertaking for the concessionaires and within a year they went bankrupt. Hirsch may have anticipated such an outcome, for when new bidders were invited for the concession in April 1869, he came forward with a complete plan.

Hirsch, while still with Bischoffsheim, had helped place the first Turkish loan in Paris in 1854 and had, jointly with the Ottoman bank, helped to establish the Credit Générale Ottoman in Constantinople, both of which gave him invaluable Turkish contacts. But it is clear that the concession finally came his way because he had a degree of courage lacking among more orthodox bankers like the Rothschilds, who already owned the South-Austrian Railway and who might have been the natural promoters of a Balkan extension.

The plan called for a line from Constantinople via Adrianople, Sofia and Sarajevo, which, with various connecting branch lines to Salonika and elsewhere, involved a distance of over two and a half thousand kilometres, much of it over rough, mountainous terrain. The whole undertaking was expected to cost $40,000 per kilometre over the level stretches and $50,000 per kilometre through the mountains. To ensure an adequate return, the Turkish government promised Hirsch an annual rental of $2,800 per completed kilometre for ninety-nine years to be paid out of a state loan, plus a further $1,600 per kilometre from the operator of the line, which together represented a return of eleven per cent on the entire investment. He was also given the right to exploit minerals, forests and other natural resources along the line of the track on a royalty basis. Once the track was in operation any income beyond $4,400 per kilometre would be divided between the operator (fifty per cent), the government (thirty per cent) and Hirsch (twenty per cent). But Hirsch began to make his money long before the track was built through an ingenious scheme of his own, which acquired the name of *Turkenlose*.

The Turks were in chronic deficit and European markets were saturated with Ottoman bonds which sold at a heavy discount. With the agreement of the Turkish authorities, Hirsch proposed a new bond, paying three per cent over ninety-nine years, but which would offer, along with the interest, a bi-monthly draw with cash prizes of up to $120,000. Such a scheme, more lottery than bond, was not acceptable to the London market, but after prolonged negotiations – which, it was said, involved a payment of $160,000 to the Austrian Chancellor – Hirsch was allowed to launch them through the Viennese stock exchange.

The Ottoman government issued about two million bonds at a nominal value of $80 each, which Hirsch obtained for about $26. He in turn formed a syndicate of underwriters, including several French and Austrian banks with which he was associated through his Bischoffsheim connection, which took up the first series of the issue (about 750,000, at $30), and which in turn offered them to the public at $36. The launching was accompanied by a publicity campaign of unprecedented dimensions, with favourable editorial comment assured by lavish advertising, and although the Franco–Prussian war broke out almost on the launching day, the issue of the first series was a success. The second series, launched two years later, though offered to the public at $34 went rather more slowly and over half the bonds were left with the underwriters. The bonds were to have a chequered history, but Hirsch's own profit was secure.

Hirsch's resilience and resourcefulness were evident at every stage of the project. In August 1869 his entire plan was threatened by the sudden withdrawal of the South-Austrian Railway, which had undertaken to operate the track. The South, as we have seen, was a Rothschild enterprise and the Rothschilds tended to regard Hirsch as an adventurer, and although the Oriental was a natural extension to their own lines, they may have been startled by the unorthodox nature of his funding scheme. As a result Hirsch was suddenly compelled to set up, alongside his finance and construction companies, a new railway company, which he did within months, by hiring the services of Talbot, director general of the Paris–Lyon Railway, as Chairman, and of Von Pressel, builder of the South-Austrian Railway, as chief engineer. Construction began without further delay and within two years 500 kilometres of track were complete, 400 were in operation and a further 660 were under construction. Then came a benign set-back.

The area through which the line was to pass was beset by numerous international rivalries. Austria favoured the route proposed by Hirsch, Russia did not, for it viewed the line as an impediment to its own pan-Slav ambitions and an intrusion in what it regarded as a Russian sphere of influence. After repeated representations, the Turks curtailed the limits of the line to 1,200 kilometres and took over its administration from Hirsch, who by way of compensation was allowed to retain the proceeds of the bonds.

The new order relieved him of building the most costly and treacherous part of the line, that through the mountains of Bosnia. He was, moreover, not particularly happy in the role of operator, which he had assumed only after the precipitate withdrawal of the South-Austrian Railway. Indeed the whole reversion proved so advantageous that not a few observers suggested that it had been instigated by Hirsch in the first place, and there is some evidence that the Grand Vizier, Mahmoud Pasha, was enriched by some two million dollars once the reversion was completed.

The Vienna to Constantinople line was finally finished in 1888 and in the same year Hirsch, after numerous claims and counter-claims, was bought out by the Turkish government.

It is estimated that Hirsch made between \$32m and \$34m from the entire Oriental Railway scheme, but he may have had to pay out more than half of that in bribes.

An historian, G. W. F. Hallgarten, who described Hirsch's part in the Oriental Railway as a story of 'cunning, force, robbery and deceit', conceded at the same time that the line might not have been cut without him. It must be added that it was impossible to transact business of any sort within the Ottoman Empire without resorting to bribery on a massive scale and one sort of corruption tends to breed others.

Hirsch had numerous business interests and was heavily involved in sugar refining and copper, which, though less dramatic than his railway ventures, may have been more profitable. The 1873 Stock Exchange crash, which ruined many a banker, left him virtually untouched. On the contrary! He had sufficient liquid resources to buy up huge holdings at low prices, and, for example, took up a massive pack of Viennese bonds at a very large discount which he eventually redeemed at par.

Like many self-made men, Hirsch needed the reassurance of exalted company. If he was thrusting and restless in his commercial ventures, he bludgeoned his way to social eminence with money-bags and he could speak of Edward, Prince of Wales, the Crown Prince Rudolf, and Ferdinand, King of Bulgaria, as his personal friends. But then all three had extravagant tastes and were often short of money, which does not mean that they were only drawn to him by his wealth, for he had other qualities, but his money, or rather his readiness to part with it, was the supreme one. The Rothschilds were fairly well known for their lavish entertainments in their Piccadilly mansions and their stately homes in the Vale of Aylesbury, but Hirsch could out-Rothschild the Rothschilds at every turn. He had one palace in Paris, another in Versailles, a third near the Rothschilds in Piccadilly, a castle in Moravia, a country house near Sandringham, a shooting lodge near Newmarket and a vast hunting estate at St Johann in Hungary. It was there that, during a memorable fortnight in October 1891, he entertained a large party which included the Prince of Wales, Lady Randolph Churchill (Sir Winston Churchill's mother), Lord Dudley, Lady Wemyss, Lord and Lady Curzon, and Arthur Sassoon. In a five-day shoot the party slaughtered over eleven thousand head of game.

It was the Prince of Wales who introduced Hirsch to Lord Marcus Beresford, an eminent figure in British racing circles through whose agency he built up one of the most remarkable stables in the country and in 1892 his filly, La Flèche, won the Cambridgeshire, the One Thousand Guineas, the Oaks, the St Leger and came near to winning the Derby. Whatever Hirsch took in hand his intention was to win, and win he did, though he donated the prize money to London hospitals.

Hirsch was not a man much given to putting his thoughts on paper or, for that matter, perusing the thoughts of others, and he had a total aversion to intellectual pursuits, but a philosophy of sorts does emerge from his occasional utterances, and it can be seen most clearly in his ambitions for the Jewish people. As in all his undertakings he was never daunted by the matter of scale, and when he familiarized himself with the Russian Jewish problem he proposed to solve it by moving three and a half million Jews from the Pale of Settlement to the New World over a period of twenty-five years – neither more nor less. It proved to be too ambitious a scheme even for Hirsch, for even his wealth and resourcefulness were not equal to it, and he was not spared the years. He turned to the Jewish problem only in 1886 and within a decade he was dead. The Jewish Colonial Association, to which he gave over $100,000,000, acquired vast tracts of land, mainly in the Argentine, and he entertained the highest hopes that given a new start in a new world he would create a new type of Jew.

The Argentine, he said, 'is not precisely a land of milk and honey, but it gives a magnificent return for honest labour ... The predictions of our enemies that Jews would never go back to agriculture have been falsified. The Russian Jew has grit, industry, sobriety. No matter what he has been at home, he takes readily to the spade.'

There was an element of wishful thinking in all this. Like many nineteenth-century philanthropists and social reformers, he believed that the masses could be raised to new heights of endeavour by being moved away from the oppressiveness and corruption of urban life into an agrarian environment of broad acres and open skies; but his utopia fared little better than others. The Jewish Colonial Association acquired over two million acres of land in the Argentine, most of which was cultivated or suitable for cultivation. It also provided homes, agricultural machinery, cattle, sheep and horses and loans at favourable terms, but in all only about three thousand five hundred families, comprising some forty thousand people, made use of the scheme, and in the end most of them drifted back to town.

The Russian Jew may, as Hirsch said, have had 'grit, industry and sobriety', but the isolation and the very nature of farming left few outlets for enterprise. One traveller to the Argentine in 1899 came back with a most discouraging report:

Although the colonists were given free transportation from Europe and found ready-built houses on fenced-in farms with the corrals filled with cows and oxen, and they were supplied with farm implements, ploughs and harvesters, and even some hard cash, some of them abandoned house and farm, sold the implements and livestock and preferred to earn their living as peddlers or cattle-dealers, or moved into Buenos Aires.

But even those who remained tended to apply to farming methods which would have been more appropriate in commerce. The Jewish traveller, Elkan Adler, who was in the Argentine in 1905, observed:

The Jew seems too speculative to make a good agriculturalist even in the Argentine. He is too fond of putting all his eggs in one basket. Lucerne grass paid very well indeed in 1901, and so he devoted himself almost exclusively to Lucerne. The rain spoils the crop and he is down in the dumps, especially if a Roumanian, quite prepared to throw up the game and go to Rosario or Buenos Aires and start a business in town . . .

The colonies established by the Hirsch foundation in North America, though on a much more limited scale, proved hardly more successful. In 1891, for example, forty-nine Jewish families were settled in typical farm houses in the Canadian prairies, with cattle, horses, implements, seed and food for three years, and loans at favourable rates. They were joined shortly after by relatives and friends for whom further farms were acquired, but the whole scheme dwindled to nothing within a few years and the settlers moved into Winnipeg and Minneapolis.

Jews were ready for sacrifices, hard work, application, but they lacked the patience for a calling which would perhaps offer steady returns over many years, but which offered little scope for adventures, or for dreams. Farming was too predictable. A farmer remained a farmer, whereas even a pedlar could dream of becoming a Hirsch, and even those settlers who were prepared to devote themselves to their acres for the rest of their lives hoped for something better for their sons. What perhaps Hirsch did not realize was that he was in many ways the typical Jew writ large, and, as we shall see in another chapter, the Jew could make a supremely successful cultivator, but only in certain prescribed circumstances.

Hirsch gained little satisfaction from the money itself, for he was an abstemious man and his extravagance lay in his lavish hospitality and the extent to which he indulged his guests. He was a restless figure. He usually spent his winters in Paris and on the Riviera; spring in London; summer on his estate at Beauregarde near Versailles; the early autumn in his hunting lodge; October and November in Piccadilly. One is not quite certain about his nationality. He was born a German, became in turn Belgian and French, though it appears that he died an Austrian, and one has the feeling that he sought to plant his co-religionists firmly on the soil because he abhorred the restlessness he found in himself.

He was tall, with iron-grey hair, and an exuberant moustache whose waxed extremities curved upwards towards his ears, an unhappy man, and, one suspects, unfulfilled. His only child, Lucien, a dour recluse who seems to have spent much of his time on numismatics, was a disappointment, but Hirsch still hoped to connect him to one of England's better families. As Lucien himself seemed to have had no ambitions in that direction, Hirsch, possibly without his knowledge, approached Margot Tennant, a woman intelligent, vivacious and beautiful and a member of an old, wealthy and titled family, who was eventually to marry Herbert Asquith, a future Prime Minister. Hirsch, as always, sought nothing but the best.

Mrs Asquith recalled the meeting in her autobiography some fifty years after the event. 'I want you to marry my son Lucien,' Hirsch told her. 'He is quite unlike me, he is very respectable and he hates money; he likes books and collects manuscripts and other things and is highly educated.' Margot mumbled some reservations, but he persisted: '. . . you would widen his interests! He is shy and I want him to make a good marriage; and above all he must marry an Englishwoman.'

Like most Jews of his generation, Hirsch admired, and indeed almost worshipped England, and in England, especially as a friend of the Prince of Wales, he found an acceptance which, in spite of his vast wealth, he did not receive elsewhere. When Margot refused him he turned to Lady Katie Lambton, Lord Durham's sister, but that too proved abortive, and Lucien died shortly after, aged thirty-one. 'My son I have lost,' Hirsch later declared, 'but not my heir; humanity is my heir,' and certainly his largest benefactions date from the year of his bereavement, though his career as a philanthropist began long before that. He had, during his frequent visits to Turkey and the Balkans, been depressed by what he described as 'the misery and ignorance' of the Jewish masses in the Ottoman Empire and the eastern provinces of the Hapsburg Empire, and he gave several million dollars to establish Jewish vocational schools. His efforts were not universally applauded and some of the more Orthodox Rabbis feared that his schools would lead to assimilation. Others dismissed his philanthropies as an attempt to buy status. That Hirsch had an almost pathetic craving for status is beyond doubt and one gets the impression that, for all the fortunes he lavished on his princely friends, he excited derision rather than affection, and even the Prince of Wales, with whom he was on particularly close terms, would make fun of his accent and manner of speech and he was aware that he was not quite as accepted as, say, the Rothschilds, which is perhaps why he disliked them. He stemmed from nobler stock, was richer than them, gave more freely, entertained more lavishly, yet where they moved, he pushed. 'When a Jew becomes rich', he once said, in an obvious reference to the Rothschilds, 'he is no longer a Jew.'

Edouard Drumont, whose *La France Juive* became an anti-semitic classic, regarded Hirsch with rather less disfavour than the Rothschilds:

He does not display the conceited supercilious attitude of the Rothschilds, whom hardly anyone dares to address in company; as a cheerful *arrivé* he shows more frankness and is a better integrated and rounded personality, and is therefore less ridiculous than the other Jewish aristocrats. His arrogance is mitigated by his bad jokes and bonhomie. Of a fresh colour, a bit bloated, he feels happy when not suffering from his liver pains. He likes to play the good-natured one with a tendency to malicious teasing . . .

This behaviour, in contrast to that of the Rothschilds, is easily understandable. Thus they believe themselves to belong to the aristocracy, while Hirsch believes that the aristocracy belongs to him . . . And, indeed, Hirsch did himself create his position in society. He calculates exactly and knows the purchase price of each moral qualm.

Herzl, who met him shortly before his death, found him extremely vain, but 'on the whole a pleasant, intelligent, simple, natural man'.

Hirsch's wealth and munificence put him in a class by himself, but he had many of the characteristics common to the successful Jewish entrepreneur. One was a certain brashness, with perhaps a belief that those qualities which advance one in commerce should advance one in life, yet even with the brashness, there was a touch of diffidence.

Many Jewish bankers found even nominal Jewishness an impediment to economic advance during their struggling years and to social acceptance when they had arrived, and they not infrequently converted to Christianity, as happened with the Hambros in London, with Belmont in New York, with the Bleichroeders in Berlin, and many lesser figures. Others, however, while not being formally religious, saw in their very eminence an obligation to their co-religionists. This was the case with the Rothschilds whether in Frankfurt, Vienna, Paris or London, and it was obviously the case with Hirsch. It may be seen most clearly in the career of Jacob Schiff, who arrived in America as an eighteen-year-old immigrant from Frankfurt, in 1865, and quickly rose to become one of the most influential and respected bankers in the country. Schiff stemmed from exalted rabbinic stock, though his father had been a considerable merchant and an associate of the Frankfurt Rothschilds. He became a partner first in a small brokerage firm, married a daughter of Solomon Loeb, of Kuhn, Loeb, and in 1885 became head of the firm.

The last decades of the nineteenth century were the great years of the American railway entrepreneur, and he was extensively involved in the reorganization of the Union Pacific and the Great Northern Railway and in funding the Pennsylvania, Baltimore and Ohio Railroad systems, as well as in the flotation of Westinghouse Electric, US Rubber, the American Telegraph and Telephone Company, and a $200 million bond issue on behalf of Japan to finance its war with Russia.

Yet with all his vast commitments he found time to concern himself with the affairs of the Jewish community and he became to America what Lord Rothschild (grandson of the founder of the London house) was to England, the virtual head of the Jewish community. There was hardly a major issue affecting world Jewry which was not considered in detail in the board room of Kuhn, Loeb.

New Court, the London Head Office of the Rothschild bank, consisted of brothers and cousins. Kuhn, Loeb, consisted of in-laws. Schiff, as we have seen, married one daughter of Solomon Loeb; Paul Warburg, scion of a celebrated Hamburg banking family, married another, and Felix, his brother, married a daughter of Schiff. Both the brothers, needless to say, became partners. (Otto Kahn, who joined the firm in 1897, also became a partner through marrying the daughter of Abraham Wolff, yet another partner.)

Schiff once declared: 'I am divided into three parts; I am an American; I am a German, and I am a Jew,' and although he gave generously both of his fortune and of his time to Jewish causes, he was nervous of any suggestion that he was perhaps more Jew then anything else. This was true also of the Rothschilds, and like the Rothschilds, he kept his distance from

Zionism, though, like them, he did more for the re-creation of Zion than many, indeed most, avowed Zionists. He helped to create the Haifa Technical College (the Technion) and the Athit Agricultural Experimental Station, and, but for his intervention, what was left of Palestine Jewry during World War I might have perished from hunger. His brother-in-law, Felix Warburg, though not formally a Zionist, was deeply moved by what he saw of the Zionist endeavour in Palestine. During his first tour of the country, wrote Chaim Weizmann, 'he felt like doffing his hat to every man and every tree he saw'. He was a generous benefactor to the Hebrew University and a major investor in the Palestine Economic Corporation, and he served for a time on the enlarged Jewish Agency for Palestine.

Warburg had a deep attachment to the arts and was active in the development of the Juilliard School of Music (in which his brother Paul was also involved), the New York Philharmonic Symphony Orchestra and the Harvard Fogg Museum of Art. Schiff was a generous benefactor to numerous universities, helped to found the Harvard Semitic Museum and gave $1 million to Barnard College, New York. Otto Kahn helped innumerable operas, orchestras, musical academies and art schools, and indeed from the end of World War I to his death in 1934, wherever a group of players or singers struggled for survival, their thoughts turned hopefully to Kuhn, Loeb, and particularly to Otto Kahn.

The sense of public service displayed by Schiff and the Warburgs was also characteristic of Bernard Baruch, who made the first of the many millions he was to acquire before he was thirty. He quickly came to discover how little money meant, and, while not unhappy with his own work, he could not help contrasting it with that of his father, a distinguished doctor. He gave generously to charities, but as he later recalled: 'I still felt dissatisfied with merely making money. I also realized that while giving money to a worthy cause was a step in the right direction, it could not prove as gratifying as the personal efforts I might make on behalf of some cause.' (To which one should perhaps add that his older brother, Hermann, who was also a doctor, abandoned medical practice to join him on Wall Street.)

Baruch, who was born in 1870 and died in 1965 having made a fortune from the reorganization and amalgamation of railways, was first and foremost a speculator, a function which he thought vital to the proper development of a free society, provided it was discharged with intelligence and discretion. There was certainly nothing haphazard about his own operations. He was no gambler. As a young man he said account books were his 'favourite reading', a habit which persisted throughout his life, and he made a particularly close study of commodities such as gold, copper, sulphur, rubber and coffee. In 1916 President Wilson appointed him advisor to the Council of National Defence and Chairman of the Commission on Raw Materials, Minerals and Metals. When America entered the war a year later he became Chairman of the War Industries Board, a function which he discharged with the same foresight and skill which had character-ized his business activities. Thereafter he was frequently in demand as advisor to various public authorities. In 1946 he served as US representative to the United Nations Atomic Energy Commission, and put forward a scheme – the 'Baruch Plan' – for the creation of an international authority to control the uses of atomic energy and inspect all atomic installations. The plan, though widely approved, was vetoed by the Russians. Baruch died in 1965, aged ninety-five, universally revered, a statesman and sage.

Baruch was born about a quarter of a century before Hirsch died, and lived in a different time and different place. In Europe the millionaire still had to convert his money into titles and benefactions to gain social acceptance, whereas in America wealth was a form of nobility in itself. In Europe one almost had to apologize for one's fortunes, in America they were a commendation, a proof of alacrity, foresight, judgment. A tradi-tion developed there of inviting men who had proved their skills in com-merce to adapt them to public life. In Europe the successful businessman had to show compensating qualities if he hoped to attain public office; in America commercial success was enough, and Baruch could therefore enjoy the feeling of acceptance and fulfilment which eluded Hirsch.

Hirsch too speculated on commodities on a large scale and with con-spicuous success, but he would have been dismissive about a man whose enterprise was largely devoted to such business. But then, by the time Baruch came of age, the type of project undertaken by Hirsch, like the Oriental Railway, was beyond the scope of any one individual or, indeed, any one bank.

In his early years, possibly, Baruch might have been classed by Hirsch as the kind of Jew who pushed too hard, but in one's early days one had to push that much harder, certainly in America, to get anywhere at all, to steal a march in the night and strive while others rested. Baruch, in a typical operation, had his first coup when he was twenty-eight, during a July Fourth week-end. He was at home with his parents one Sunday night when news came through that the Spanish fleet had been destroyed at Santiago, signalling the end of the Spanish-American war. It was 3 July.

The next day, Monday, would be the fourth, when the American exchanges would, of course, be closed. But the London Exchange would be open. If he could get to his office before dawn he could make a fortune. But this was 1898, before the age of cars, and trains had stopped running for the night. He therefore rushed to the railway depot, hired a special train, and, hurtling through the night, reached his office before dawn. Baruch recalled the operation with pride:

I was repeating on a smaller scale the financial feat which legend ascribed to Nathan Rothschild at the Battle of Waterloo ... Wellington's campaign in Belgium started badly, which depressed English securities. Rothschild, who had crossed the channel to get first news of events, is said to have been on the field of Waterloo when the tide of battle turned against Napoleon. By getting word of this to London a few hours in advance of the official couriers he enabled Rothschilds to make large purchases before the shares rebounded.

The actual facts did not quite tally with the legend, but it is true that the Rothschilds had a system of couriers which enabled them to act a little ahead of the market. Baruch lacked the couriers but he had the alacrity. He saw his chances and he took them. In England, a national holiday being part of the closed season, this would have been regarded as not quite playing the game; in America this was part of the game. What was opportunism in one place was enterprise in another, though even opportunism was forgiven provided one was successful enough for long enough and shared one's success with society. In English, and perhaps in European terms, an entrepreneur was a successful opportunist, much as a banker was a successful speculator, an attitude which was pithily summed up by Sir Ernest Cassel, who began his business life as a clerk in the London office of Bischoffsheim and Goldschmidt and who rose to be one of the richest and most influential men in England (when he died in 1921 he left over £7½ million):

When as a young and unknown man I started to be successful I was referred to as a gambler. My operations increased in scope and volume. Then I was known as a speculator. The sphere of my activities continued to expand and presently I was known as a banker. Actually I had been doing the same thing all the time.

New lands and new territories had a ready appeal to Jewish entrepreneurs. They were possibly somewhat late on the scene to play a major role in the development of the American West, but they were a crucial element in the development of South Africa during the final quarter of the nineteenth century and a considerable proportion of the 'Uitlanders', whose restiveness under Boer rule was to lead to the South African war, were Jews. Among them was a dapper, myopic, fair-haired Cockney, called Barney Barnato, who, arriving virtually penniless, built up one of the largest fortunes in South Africa and controlled a labour force of one hundred and twenty thousand men.

Barnato, the son of an old clothes dealer, was born in Petticoat Lane in 1852 and attended the Jewish Free School, a local foundation for the children of the poor, financed largely by the Rothschilds. He hoped initially to be a Music Hall performer and had pronounced talents as a clown, but tales of easy fortunes being made in South Africa changed his ambitions, and after acquiring forty boxes of cigars, which he hoped to sell to prospectors, he set off. The cigars remained unsold but he was able to use them as collateral to set up as a small scale diamond-buyer, and within a few years had prospered sufficiently to become a diamond dealer and broker in mining property. Saturday became his most profitable day, for banks closed early and he could pay for stones by cheque and resell them before the banks reopened, a habit which did not add to his stature either among Jews or anyone else. Nor did he wait for prospectors to come into town, but made his way round the mines on foot or pack horse to seek out bargains, and in time he bought up a few claims for himself. When business was slow he turned to other goods, and, as he was later to boast: 'There is nothing this country produces that I have not traded in, from diamonds and gold, right away through wool, feathers and mealies, to garden vegetables.' In 1876 he staked his entire capital of £3,000 on a number of small claims adjoining his own, which, after frantic diggings, yielded stones of twenty carats and a profit of about £2,000 a week. He had arrived.

Hitherto he had enjoyed the help of an older brother, Harry, who had come out to South Africa as a Music Hall artist, and was now functioning as his partner. As his interests grew he brought out his nephews, Woolf, Solly and eventually Jack Joel to assist him. He was semi-literate, with little patience for paper work, all of which he delegated to his relatives. And as he continued to prosper, speculation grew on the source of his prosperity. It was rumoured that he had been handling illicit diamonds, a suggestion which, he later averred, hurt him deeply:

How many times in the years from '76 was I inclined, almost determined, to quit Kimberley and South Africa forever! I was making a pile and gathering power but no one knew, or even can know, how hard I worked for it all. If I have made millions I have worked for them as few men ever can have worked. But I have been blackguarded by men who could neither gain nor work.

South Africa in the 'seventies was a place where fortunes were made overnight, but it was understandable that those who made them were regarded with some suspicion among those who did not. In Barnato's case the suspicions were heightened by the fact that the London Hotel, Kimberley, which was owned by Harry, was virtually the illegal diamond bourse.

As deeper strata were opened for exploitation, more funds were needed for expensive machinery, pumping engines and sifting gear. Several of Barnato's competitors made scrip issues to raise capital, but Barnato himself held back. He had yet to grasp the first principles of company flotations and promotions, and as Mr Stanley Jackson noted in a recent biography: 'Having always dealt in cash or kind, he preferred diamonds, gold sovereigns and banknotes – wealth he could physically see and touch – to the crisp pieces of paper that were called "shares".' But eventually, as his operation grew, he was compelled to go to the market. In 1880 he launched the Barnato Diamond Company with a capital value of £115,000. The issue was over-subscribed within hours and trebled in value in a week.

In the following year his shares, along with much else on the South African market, slumped, but he had sufficient reserves to retain his own large holding and buy up a great many of the claims which were flooding the market, at a discount. In spite of the all-pervading gloom, he had infinite faith in South Africa in general and in the Kimberley mines in particular. On this occasion certainly his optimism seemed well-founded, but his growing prosperity and size brought him on a collision course with another expanding force, De Beers, controlled by Cecil Rhodes. Whoever owned the Kimberley mines could virtually control the price of diamonds. Apart from Barnato and De Beers, there was but one other major concern in the Kimberley region, a consortium known as the French Company. Barnato and De Beers were fairly evenly matched, but if either could control the French Company he would be able to over-whelm the other. In the summer of 1887 Barnato received word that Rhodes was negotiating with Rothschilds of London to raise £1.4 million to take over the French. Barnato's immediate response was to start buying French shares. Rhodes at first tried to bribe him off, and when that proved a disastrous gambit, he changed tactics and suggested that if Barnato did not contest his £1.4 million bid he would resell the company to Barnato for £300,000 plus a fifth share of the combined group. This was too generous an offer to refuse. Barnato did not seem to realize that he was thereby opening his camp to a Trojan horse. Once inside, Rhodes attempted to acquire further Barnato shares. His ultimate aim was a merger and he wanted a majority holding to negotiate from a position of strength. The vulgar, thrusting Cockney was not quite Rhodes' idea of a perfect partner. He confessed that he could not stand 'the sight of that scoundrel', but he recognized a powerful adversary and a commercial genius of almost unfailing judgment whom it would be impossible to buy out. Amalgamation was the only alternative. Rhodes, of course, had larger ambitions, and wanted his Kimberley base secure so that he could turn his attention to his schemes beyond the Limpopo. On 13 March 1888 they finally reached agreement. Barnato's would be amalgamated with De Beer to form De Beers Consolidated Mines, with a nominal capital of 20,000 £5 shares, of which Barnato, with 6,000 shares, had the largest single holding. The new group acquired a virtual monopoly of the world diamond output.

Barnato was now thirty-eight, a multi-millionaire, but still working his eighteen-hour day, smoking, drinking, cursing, enjoying an occasional gamble at cards or horses, but finding his main pleasure in the larger gambles of trade. With the encouragement of Rhodes he stood for the Cape Parliament as a member for Kimberley and fought a campaign so marked by vilification and abuse that for a time Barnato was tempted to withdraw. But, as he later said: 'I stayed and faced it out, and fought that Kimberley election as no election had been fought in South Africa before, and came in at the head of the poll. And no dog barked.'

He diversified and invested heavily in the Rand gold mines and in property in the booming town of Johannesburg. But the boom collapsed after rumours that the gold mines were giving out. Barnato, as before, was unperturbed and laid the foundation stone of Barnato House, which was to be one of the most prestigious buildings in the city, as proof of his confidence in the future. 'Money and patience, money and patience will overcome all difficulties here as they did in Kimberley,' he declared, and he used the opportunity to buy up blocks of shares and parcels of property at knockdown prices. 'I've never been frightened of losses, and that's why I am where I am today,' he said. He invested in the liquor trade, building materials, transport, printing and publishing and, as the depression eased and prosperity returned, his judgment was vindicated. Barnato was by now regarded, with something like awe, as infallible. He became a pied piper among speculators and the market followed wherever he led. He became a figure in London society as well as South Africa. He engaged an architect to build a mansion in Park Lane, and while it was being built, he sought to rent Apsley House from the Duke of Wellington. It was not available so he took a lease on Spencer House in St James's and entertained mixed multitudes of speculators, racing touts, jockeys, trainers and small-time actresses. He had married Fanny Bees, an actress with a small touring company, shortly after he had established himself in Kimberley, but their first child was not born until seventeen years after their marriage. He called her Leah Primrose, after the richest mine in his group. He had a son the following year, and another the year after. He launched both his Johannesburg Consolidated Investment Co., which was mainly concerned in property, and his gold mines, as a public company with a nominal value of £10 million, but such was the scramble to get aboard the Barnato bandwaggon that the shares quickly acquired a market value of over £60 million. Barnato himself was worth about £20 million.

The natural next stop was to launch a bank, which he did, in 1895, with a nominal value of £3½ million in £1 shares. There was a rush for shares and value doubled overnight and then trebled. The new concern was not a bank in any orthodox sense of the word, but a trust company to which Barnato sold shares in his South African enterprise. Shareholders asked no questions while prices rose and dividends were high. 'I make a fiver every minute of my working day,' he boasted, and he had a long working day. He began to share some of his wealth with charities. He endowed hospitals, orphanages, helped in the foundation of the Johannesburg Synagogue (with a theatrical performance as well as cash), but, in spite of the patronage of Kruger, social acceptance eluded him. A Mansion House dinner given by the Lord Mayor of London, in his honour, in 1895, was largely boycotted: 'The Mansion House is not the proper place for glorifying a successful operator in a department of the Stock Exchange,' said *The Times*.

Barnato was in London in October 1885, when within one day – and that appropriately *Yom Kippur* – large blocks of South African shares were suddenly dumped on the market. The value of his companies slumped to less than half while his bank shares, which had stood at £4, fell to 30 shillings. It is still not certain who was responsible for the selling or what had caused it, but Barnato had sufficient reserves to withstand it. He bought heavily to stabilize the market – an operation which cost him over £3 million out of his own pocket.

As the slump continued his usual optimism and resilience faded. The troubled situation in South Africa, and especially the Jameson Raid which was to lead shortly to war between Britain and the Boers, filled him with the direst apprehensions. His whole empire was in danger. His bank was particularly vulnerable, and, in 1896, it was absorbed by one of his other companies on none too generous terms, to save it from collapse. He was attacked in the press, abused in a constant torrent of letters; his life was threatened. He still managed to cheer himself with plans to build a grand hotel and theatre in Johannesburg, but his worries weighed on him. He slept badly, drank heavily, and suffered from bouts of paranoia and hallucinations. A doctor ordered complete rest. His spirits improved and he showed little sign of strain when he embarked on a voyage to England on 3 June 1897. He was to represent the South African Chamber of Mines at the Golden Jubilee celebrations in London and he looked forward to moving into his new Park Lane mansion which was nearing completion. Twelve days later, while the ship was off Madeira, he vanished overboard. He was forty-five.

If Hirsch regarded himself as the self-made man in that he began life with a few million and came to acquire a great many, Barnato began with nothing and came to be among the richest men in South Africa. But he was a parvenu among parvenus in a new world, forcing out new frontiers where everyone was on the make, among others on the make, but rather quicker and more resilient. He died too young to have been civilized by his wealth, though it is doubtful whether he would have mellowed if he had lived much longer. He was, to the last, the cheerful vulgarian he had always been, enjoying a drink, low gossip, low company and cards, and if he had interests beyond business it was in the theatre and racing. He had acquired a share in the Empire,[1] Leicester Square so that he might bring the best from the London West End stage to South Africa, and he had never entirely abandoned his theatrical ambitions. He was no Rhodes and did not see in his growing commercial empire a means towards other things. He felt that his place in the Cape parliament was necessary to a man of his commercial standing, but he was no social or political reformer. On the other hand he used his influence to shorten the hours and improve the working conditions of black labour. He would have liked to keep out of the wider political tangles if he could, but he couldn't – his business interests had grown too large for that. He came to know Kruger, the President of the Transvaal Republic, and used his influence for the release of British prisoners after the Jameson Raid in 1895, but he was never

[1] a music hall, i.e., vaudeville theater

particularly distressed by the fact that he and his fellow 'Uitlanders', though paying about ninety per cent of Transvaal's taxes, had no political rights. As Cecil Rhodes' brother observed: 'The Jewish element is a damper on any political agitation'; while profits were good they were prepared to go without the franchise.

Barnato's main gift was a ready instinct for a bargain. He never quite grasped the basis of company organization necessary to keep his market together, and there he was fortunate in his two nephews, Woolf and Solly Joel, who were able to give an organizational framework to his torrent of ideas.

Barnato and his nephews all married small-time actresses whose attractions were rather more obvious than their talents, and all three had them converted to Judaism, mainly, one suspects, for the sake of the old folks at home, for neither Barnato nor the Joels were in any sense observant Jews, though they occasionally showed their face in synagogue. Barnato had signed over powers of attorney to Solly before embarking on his final journey, and Solly was the last man to see him alive before he vanished.

Most Jewish entrepreneurs were involved in distribution and acquired a special skill in marrying surplus to scarcity, and made good through their own efforts some of the deficiencies of communication. The coming of the railways ruined a great many Jewish carters, as well as thousands of Jewish pedlars. The more enterprising, however, survived to establish general stores, often in lonely outposts, supplying the manifold needs of scattered farmers and peasants. And out of the general stores grew the department store.

The Jews did not invent the large-scale department store – that was pioneered by the French – but they were amongst the first to realize its potential and, by the end of the nineteenth century, of the five major German groups, three, Shocken, Tietz and Wertheim, were in Jewish hands. In America, too, the biggest, and certainly the best known of the groups, tended to be Jewish owned. The Gimbel brothers, the sons of a German immigrant, opened up first in Milwaukee, then in Philadelphia and, in 1910, descended on New York. After World War I they devoured Saks & Co and the Kaufman and Baer group in Pittsburgh and are now represented by large stores in every major conurbation.

The Straus brothers, who were to make Macy's into a national institution, were born in Germany, settling in Georgia in 1852. After the Civil War they moved to New York, and rented Macy's basement to display crockery and glassware imported by their father. From there they gradually moved upwards and took over the store in 1887.

Bloomingdale's, Ohrbach's, B. Altman, and others were likewise founded by German-Jewish immigrants, and that Jewish flair in this field is not extinct may be seen in the rapid growth of the Korvette discount stores (since merged with Spartan industries) founded by Eugene Ferkeuf and a handful of Jewish Korean War veterans. (The name of the company, E. J. Korvette, was an acronym for Eight Jewish Korean veterans.)

In England the Cohen family of Liverpool developed the Lewis's chain of north-country department stores and then moved south to acquire Selfridges, which is to London what Macy's is to New York. Lewis's have since been taken over by Sir Charles Clore's Sears Holdings.

The most celebrated group in Britain, however, is Marks and Spencer, which is the creation of Simon Marks and Israel Sieff, who married each other's sisters, and whose board is still dominated by the family.

Simon's father Michael, who arrived from Russia in 1882, worked as a pedlar and then opened a stall in Leeds market. From there he branched out to open a chain of penny bazaars. His son, who became chairman of the firm in 1917, and remained chairman till his death forty-seven years later, and his son-in-law, converted the chain into something more substantial, at first functioning as a sort of up-market Woolworths. They later narrowed their range of goods and improved their quality. With branches in every major shopping centre they brought about a social revolution. Marks and Spencer – outfitters to the nation; it was impossible to distinguish class from class, for apparel no longer proclaimed the man, and certainly not the woman. 'St Michael', the company brand mark, became a hallmark; a St Michael's article represented the best available quality at the lowest possible price. It also comes with a standard of courtesy and service no longer generally available in Britain, for the company takes as much care in selecting staff as in selecting merchandise. They pay the highest wages, offer the best working conditions, and with their health clinics and dental clinics, and their highly qualified personnel staff, they have virtually operated as a private welfare state. But it has all paid off, for the firm is recognized as the most efficient enterprise of its sort in the country and is regarded with a mixture of affection and awe by its clientele, employees, and, not least, by its investors.

The growth of the department store in Germany – when it was regarded as a peculiarly Jewish phenomenon – was viewed with alarm by the small German shop-keeper. They were accused of unfair competition and every conceivable malpractice. Special taxes were levied on them at the end of the last century, and they were singled out for particular attack by the Nazis. During *Kristallnacht*, in November 1938, when most of the synagogues in Germany were razed, many Jewish department stores were set ablaze and looted.

In America, competitors were expected to be competitive and in the post-Civil War years few virtues were ascribed to being small, and none to staying small. Bigness and growth were what America was about, and the large department stores were among the symbols of free enterprise.

In England the department stores were created initially for the carriage trade and it was the Jews who, after World War I, brought them to a wider public. In England smallness is a virtue and bigness a form of original sin, but there has never been the agitation against the department stores that one found in Germany, if only because the benefits they offered made them cherished national-institutions.

The mail-order firm was in a sense an extra-mural extension of the department store, but again, as in the department store, the Jews, though not among its pioneers, were amongst the first to realize its possibilities. In a way, it was also an enlargement of peddling, for like the pedlar it depends, or at least initially depended, on the isolated customer and, in particular, the agrarian communities, and like the pedlar it did not wait for the customer to come to the shop, but brought the shop to the customer.

When Richard W. Sears founded Sears, Roebuck in Minneapolis in 1888, he had limited ambitions and limited stock and the company did not really get off the ground till it moved to Chicago, where it was incorporated in 1895 with a capital stock of $159,000. About a quarter of the stock was acquired by Julius Rosenwald, son of a German Jewish immigrant. Rosenwald had worked for a time with an uncle who owned Hammerslough Bros in New York and had moved to Chicago at the age of twenty-two to manage the family wholesale clothing firm of Rosenwald and Weil. He joined the board of Sears, Roebuck and when it was incorporated on the New York stock exchange about a decade later it was capitalized at $50 million. In 1910, on the retirement of Sears, he became President of the company. By the time he died in 1932, at the age of seventy, Sears, Roebuck was one of the biggest enterprises in the country, with an annual turnover of about half a billion dollars.

The scale of his enterprise enabled him to dispense with many of his suppliers and manufacture his own goods. It enabled him both to lower prices and maintain quality. But perhaps his main stock in trade was a reputation of reliability backed by his celebrated 'money-back-if-not-satisfied' guarantee, now fairly commonplace, but then virtually unknown. The Sears, Roebuck catalogue, which, by the time of his death, appeared in editions of 40 million, was to be found in most American homes, and studied with greater avidity than the Bible. The successive editions of the catalogue almost form a social history of America, its developing tastes, the aspirations which Sears, Roebuck in part reflected and in part antici-pated. Within thirty years Rosenwald's initial investment of $37,500 was worth $150 million.

Intelligent anticipation was one of the secrets of Rosenwald's success; the other was the creation of a constant and loyal work-force through numerous fringe benefits, such as health and dental clinics, recreation centres, long-service bonuses, as well as sickness and death benefits, offering a sense of security then almost unknown in American commerce. His attitude was benign and paternal at a time when paternalism was not yet a bad word, and it extended beyond his work-force to the community at large. He subsidized YMCA and YWCA centres for Blacks in twenty-eight cities, gave generously towards the establishment of rural schools in impoverished areas of the American south, and spent $2.7 million on a model housing development for Blacks in Chicago. He also gave $5 million to the University of Chicago and a further $5 million to the Chicago Museum of Science and Industry. In 1917 he established the Julius Rosen-wald Foundation with a capital of $30 million, directing that both the capital and interest be spent within twenty-five years of his death.

He was, like most leading Jewish businessmen of his generation, anti-Zionist, but like them could not entirely dismiss the claims of Zion, and gave modest sums towards educational and agricultural institutions in Palestine, and a massive $6 million to promote Jewish agricultural colonies in the Soviet Union. There could hardly have been a more emphatic demonstration of his belief that the Jew should stay put where he was. He also gave half a million each to the Hebrew Union College, which trains clergy for the Reform movement, and the Jewish Theological Seminary, fountainhead of the Conservative movement, which suggests a liberality of mind as well as money, or perhaps a hedging of bets.

Rosenwald married twice and had five children, including two sons, the oldest of whom, Lessing, joined Sears, Roebuck as a dispatch-clerk at the age of twenty, became chairman on the death of his father, and retired at the age of forty-eight to devote himself to philanthropy and public service. Now in his eighties, he is a zealous collector of rare books, manuscripts and prints. In 1943 he donated some 25,000 engravings, etchings, lithographs, mezzotints and woodcuts to the National Gallery, Washington. He has also given some two thousand rare books, many of them dating from the first days of printing, and manuscripts to the Library of Congress and one rare-book dealer has described him as 'the most unsung hero in American culture . . . one of the greatest patrons the people ever had'.

In 1943 he was instrumental in the formation of the American Council for Judaism, and became its first president. The Council sees Judaism as 'a religion of Universal values' and 'not a nationality' and has been critical of what it calls 'the Israel–Zionist domination of American Jewish life'. It claims to have some twenty thousand followers, but its shrill hostility towards Israel has alienated some of its own staunchest supporters, and in spite of the prestige, to say nothing of the money, given to it by Rosen-wald, it has never been more than a marginal element in American Jewish life.

His anti-Zionist views are not shared by his younger brother William, an investment banker and head of the American Securities Corporation, who is not only a generous donor to Zionist causes but appears as an effective speaker on Zionist platforms and has served as Chairman of the United Jewish Appeal.

The Sears, Roebuck of Britain is Great Universal Stores, headed by a Scottish Jew, Sir Isaac Wolfson. Wolfson, who was born and brought up in the Gorbals district of Glasgow, left school at fourteen and worked for his father, for a time, as a picture-frame salesman. He joined GUS in 1932, became chairman in 1946 and set out on a course of expansion which made the mail-order business at the core of the company but a minor part of a vast commercial empire comprising some 3,000 retail shops, as well as interests in banking, insurance, property, shipping and road transport. In 1955 he established the Wolfson Foundation, which in the past twenty years has given away over $45 million, mostly to educational institutions. He has been showered with honorary degrees by universities and colleges. He likes to tell the story of the man who asked:

'This fellow Wolfson. He's an FRCS and an FRCP and a DCL, Oxford and an LL.D Cambridge, and a doctor of this from the University of that, but what does he *do*?'

'He's a writer.'

'A writer? What does he write?'

'Cheques.'

Scots complain that he gives more to English causes than Scottish ones, Jews that he gives more to Christian causes than Jewish ones. It is, as he will explain, one of the drawbacks to giving.

The Wolfson legend has been snowballing in recent years and Sir Isaac gives the impression that he is not sure what it's all about. 'I'm just an ordinary Yiddisher *baalehbos*', he will explain, 'like my father *olavhasholom* (peace be upon him). He was a kind man, a simple man, very *frum* (Orthodox), a *heimisher Yid* (a homely Jew). I've always tried to be the man he was.'

He has built *Heichal Shlomo*, the Chief Rabbinate centre in Jerusalem (and, incidentally, one of the ugliest buildings in the Near East) as a memorial to his father, and some fifty synagogues in various parts of Israel. He is a man of deep, almost simple piety, who begins and ends his day with prayers, and who will take inquiring visitors aside to show them the *tzitzit* (a ritual undergarment) under his shirt. He does not travel on the Sabbath or festivals and has thus always lived within easy walking distance of a synagogue. When he and Lady Wolfson were guests of the Queen in Windsor Castle they were provided with kosher food. His piety is at the source of his generosity, for it would not be too much to suggest that he regards God as a sleeping partner, if not controlling shareholder, of Great Universal Stores, and the millions he has been scattering in all directions as part of His dividend.

This does not mean that Sir Isaac is, even now, at eighty, a soft touch in business. Charity, as far as he is concerned, has no place in business, even if he will allow that business has a place in charity. He is a believer in free enterprise in its freest form and he would argue that where a businessman needs charity, he should not be in business. He would ascribe his own success to hard work, clean-living and luck.

Luck has been the main ingredient in the fortunes of a company whose name is insinuating its way into the English language, and whose product is well on the way to becoming an international currency – Levi Strauss.

The origins of the firm have passed into lore. Levi Strauss was a 'fiftier', who arrived in California too late for the goldrush but found gold in 'them there twills'. He had brought a roll of canvas which he hoped to sell to a tent-maker. There was no call for tents but there was for hard-wearing trousers, and the first of Levi's jeans was born. The copper rivets came a decade later to reinforce the pockets and Levi's have been making substantially the same garment since. Hundreds of other firms have, of course, also got into the act, but Levi's remains supreme. They sell about ten million garments a year and have a turnover of about half a billion dollars.

Old Levi Strauss, a bachelor, died in 1902 aged seventy-two, and left the company to the four children of his only sister. It became a public company in 1971, but it is still run by their descendants, or their in-laws.

In the course of its growth the company branched out into drapery, and sold socks, towels, sheets, bedspreads and underwear. These, by the end of World War II, accounted for about half its turnover. But in 1946, Walter Haas Jnr, a great-grand-nephew of the founder, decided to sell off the other interests, whether profitable or not, and to devote the entire resources of Levi Strauss to denims, which are patented as a 10-ply No. 3 cord made specially for the company. Mr Haas would not claim to be a visionary, and he did not anticipate a social revolution. It was less a business decision than a colossal gamble, which has paid off colossally well.

Charles A. Reich, in *The Greening of America*, has ascribed the ubiquity of jeans to the fact that they 'make one conscious of the body', but then so does a truss. It is more likely that they represent what is perhaps America's main contribution to the well-being (some might say the ill-being) of mankind: informality. Jeans were to the American 'fifties what Oxford 'bags' were to the English 'thirties, except that the bags, though indeed informal, were unsightly, uncomfortable, not hard-wearing, and not inexpensive. Jeans, like the bags, were possibly a revolt against the trouser-crease. Had they come after the permanent crease they might never have made it, but once they survived from the 'fifties into the 'sixties they became the uniform of Interyouth and were adopted by the worshippers of youthfulness and the young and those anxious to show that they were young-at-thigh. It also represented numerous other fashionable trends. The mass-produced garment trade had enabled the dispatch-clerk to dress like the company chairman; jeans reversed the process and enabled the company chairman to dress like the dispatch-clerk. The garment no longer proclaimed the man, or indeed the woman; jeans were unisexual. It wrought secondary revolutions. The fact that it hugs the figure made the pockets useless, so that the man who wears jeans also needs accessories like a handbag – and this to a garment which probably broke through to the wider public because it was almost a symbol of virility. Its supreme quality is that it is cheap, but it has all the defects that go with cheapness: it shrinks, it fades, it frays. Yet so entrenched is it in popular affection that its very defects are part of its attraction and there are shops which will sell their jeans ready-faded, ready-frayed and ready-patched to make them look even shabbier than they naturally are.

Levi Strauss have not created the revolution; they have fed it and have thrived on it. What they have done is to provide a consistent product at a reasonable price, which, taken over a century, is no mean achievement, and they have resisted the temptation to put a premium on their mark. Their jeans are exclusive, the original product, but still competitive.

Can their luck last? It could, of course, happen that the young could turn to Brooks Bros. suits, and if they do the old would almost certainly follow, but it is more likely that Brooks Bros. will turn – if, indeed, they have not already turned – to denims, and one may reasonably presume that Levi Strauss, now in its second century, will survive into its third. There are enough nephews and cousins and brothers-in-law and sons-in-law about to ensure that it does.

If there is anything as Jewish as the garment trade it is perhaps the drink trade, which may seem surprising in a people as sober and as abstemious as the Jews. But their abstemiousness (from drink at least – if a Jew becomes intoxicated it is usually on food) was no doubt one of the reasons for their prominence in the trade; they never felt tempted to consume their own stock.

From the sixteenth to the nineteenth century, when many Jews acted as lessees of the Polish landowners, they often established breweries and distilleries to increase revenues (these were among the first industries in Poland), and other Jews, though not direct lessees, became tavern keepers. When Poland was dismembered in the latter years of the eighteenth century, about fifteen per cent of Jews in the towns and about eighty-five per cent of those in the country were engaged in the manufacture, distribution or sale of alcoholic beverages. It is, in the circumstances, not surprising that the largest liquor empire in the world, Seagrams, should be controlled by a Jewish family whose very name, Bronfman (which in Yiddish means Brandyman), declares their trade. (The second biggest, Schenley, is likewise Jewish owned.)

The founding father of the dynasty, Yechiel Bronfman, was not however a distiller but a miller, who left Odessa in 1889, in the aftermath of a pogrom, and settled in western Canada. There he set up as a firewood salesman, and soon prospered sufficiently to buy a hotel. He had four sons, of whom the ablest and most astute was Sam, who was in the hotel business on his own by the time he was twenty, branched into the liquor trade and within a few years prospered sufficiently to set up a distillery near the confluence of the St Lawrence and Ottowa. Two years later he established a link with the mighty Distillers Company, Edinburgh, which assured him a regular supply of the finest quality Scotch whiskys.

In 1927 he heard that one of his principal competitors, Joseph E. Seagram, was in difficulties. He arranged a merger, as a result of which Distillers Corp-Seagrams came into being, with Seagrams shareholders receiving twenty-five per cent of the joint stock, William Ross, head of the Distillers Company, in Edinburgh, becoming Chairman of the whole, and Sam Bronfman as Vice-Chairman.

Bronfman was what American papers sometimes called 'peppery', that is to say he had a volcanic temper which, once activated, could be subdued only with difficulty. A natural autocrat, he was unfitted by temperament to be Vice anything. His relationship with Ross was not always equitable and in 1934 he bought DCS out.

In that year he entered into negotiations with Lewis Rosensteil of Schenley for a possible merger. The Bronfmans owned about twenty per cent of Schenley, so he thought that the deal was as good as through, but in Rosensteil, he encountered an entrepreneur every bit as wilful and bloody-minded as himself. The deal foundered and a feud ensued which has become part of the liquor-trade lore.

Growth of the company in its early years was sluggish, and American prohibition laws might have been almost specifically designed to advance it. Bronfman was more than vaguely aware that much of his output found its way across the border, but as he later said, he was not around to count the empty bottles. There was no marketing cost involved, no advertising; the situation was the answer to a distiller's prayers. The trade was, however, suddenly threatened, in 1930, when the Canadian authorities closed the border to liquor traffic. Through its boot-legging subsidiary, Atlas Shipping, Seagrams set up a further subsidiary, Northern Export, on the tiny French-owned St Pierre and Miquelon island group, off the coast of Newfoundland. In 1931 enough Canadian whisky was landed in St Pierre to provide every man, woman and child with ten gallons a week.

With the ending of prohibition in 1933 Seagrams was well-placed to meet the pent-up demand and by 1937 it overtook Schenley into first place in the American market. When during World War II the production of grain whisky was stopped by government order, Bronfman refused to follow his competitors into the production of alcohol made from fruit, potatoes or sugar-cane. He used the occasion to upgrade taste. With whisky in any case in short supply, there was something to be said for offering the best and, as Bronfman explained: 'Lower-price blends pay a little overhead. Deluxe products are where you make the money.' By 1948 sales topped $738 million, with net profits after tax of nearly $54 million. In the past few years sales have consistently topped the billion mark, the family's fortune is estimated at well over $400 million, a substantial part of which however comes from outside the liquor trade, for the company has for some time now been engaged in a policy of diversification with the acquisition of interests in oil, property, films, publishing, banking, and tourism. And Seagrams are not only the largest liquor empire in the world, but the largest private land-owners in Canada. Drink, however, is still at the heart of Seagrams. When Sam died, in 1971, the company owned thirty-nine distilleries and eighteen wineries, scattered throughout the world and the United States, and producing about 114 different brands of beverages including America's most popular brands – Chivas Regal, Seven Crowns and Seagram's V.O.

Sam had three brothers and three sisters and more nephews than he cared to count, and he kept nepotism within manageable limits by restricting the succession. He was prepared to scatter largesse round through the length and breadth of his family but arranged things so that effective control remained in his own hands, and then, as he grew older, in the hands of the oldest of his four children, Edgar. His schemes were not enforced without friction; he was rarely on speaking terms with all of his brothers at once, and not infrequently spoke to none. Nor was his relationship with his own four children unmarred by conflict, but he drew reassurance from the fact that his son Edgar had all of his determination and not a little of his drive.

Edgar, a history graduate at McGill, at one time contemplated taking up law, or going into Wall Street, and even, though a little improbably, becoming a Rabbi, but eventually entered the family business. 'Nobody told me I had to go in,' he recalled, 'but a kid gets the feeling early that joining the business is his natural destiny . . .' He was head of the Canadian subsidiary of the company by the time he was twenty-four. In 1955 he moved on to head office in New York and in 1957, when he was only twenty-eight (and his father sixty-five), he put it to his father that it was about time he took over. Sam, without actually standing down, gave way. A further eight years were to pass before Edgar was not only nominally, but effectively, in control, and then, as if to assert his authority, he launched a programme of changes which increased the advertising budget from $2 million to $7 million and introduced bottled cocktails, Hawaiian,

Puerto Rican and Jamaican rums, four new liqueurs, a gin and a vodka, and several new brands of Scotch including A Hundred Pipers and Passport.

A tall, lean figure, with the appearance and bearing of a film-star, Edgar has always had an interest in showbusiness and has backed several Broadway shows, including *The Apple Tree* and *1776*, and he made futile attempts to gain control first of Paramount and then MGM.

In 1953 Edgar married his first wife, Ann Loeb, whose father, John, was a partner in the banking house of Carl M. Loeb Rhoades. John became a member of the board and was instrumental in negotiating several major deals, including the acquisition of the Texas Pacific Coal & Oil Co. Edgar's sister Minda married Baron Alain de Gunzburg, a Paris banker and distant cousin of the Rothschilds, and through him the Bronfmans have invested heavily in French property, a fleet of gas tankers and the Club Mediterranée. Another sister, Phyllis, a keen student of art and architecture, urged her father to hire Mies van der Rohe to build the company's new headquarters in Park Avenue. The bronze-coloured edifice, which is possibly van der Rohe's masterpiece, eventually cost $41 million.

Edgar has never been blind to the burden of his inheritance and once said ironically: 'To turn a hundred dollars into a hundred and ten dollars is to work; to turn a hundred *million* dollars into a hundred and ten million dollars is inevitable.' He has struggled to assert himself as a Sam Bronfman in his own right without quite succeeding, nor is he too sanguine about the future. As he once observed: 'You've heard about shirt-sleeves to shirt-sleeves in three generations. I'm worried about the third generation. Empires have come and gone.'

Sam Bronfman was, for much of his life, the lay head of the Canadian Jewish community and as President of the Canadian Jewish Congress (an office he held for over thirty years) he tried, without much success, to rescue Jews trapped by the advance of Hitler. After the war he organized a flow of arms to the Haganah, the underground Jewish army in Palestine. He set up a supermarket chain in Israel, and tried to produce an exportable Israeli liquor, which looks and tastes a little like a chocolate mousse which has failed to set. In all the family contributes about $1½ million a year to charities, including about half a million to the Combined Jewish Appeal (most of which goes to Israel).

His benefactions, which extended to Jewish and non-Jewish causes, though Israel perhaps had a particular place in his affections, have sometimes been described as an attempt to buy respectability and live down his bootlegging past (in so far as bootlegging, given the nostalgia which now surrounds it, may be thought of as something to be lived down), but such contrition was foreign to his character. He saw his chances and took them and would not have thought much of anyone who did not. His generosity arose more out of a sense of obligation. It was not merely that he was very rich, but he traded in a quality product in which he took some pride, and which he liked to think was consumed mainly by quality people; bene-factions went with such quality. It is unlikely that he was trying to impress anyone but himself. His generosity to Israel may be explained in simpler terms. There was the residual adhesion to Judaism, inherited from his father (which in itself imposes emphatic obligations on the rich), but what was probably more important was the memory of his frantic pre-war efforts to rescue Jewish refugees, when he found almost every door closed.

Jews have been fairly prominent in newspaper publishing, though less so now than at the beginning of the century. We have already noted their dominant role in Vienna. Their dominance was hardly less marked in Berlin where from 1877 until the rise of Hitler, the Ullsteins were king. The company was founded by Leopold Ullstein, a Bavarian paper mer-chant who acquired the failing *Neues Berliner Tageblatt* in 1877, revamped it and reissued it as an evening paper, the *Deutsche Union* which, after a merger with the *Berliner Zeitung* and the *Berliner Burgerpost*, claimed a circulation of forty thousand. He then launched the *Berliner Morgenpost*, which built up a circulation of six hundred thousand, the largest in Germany, but perhaps his most dramatic breakthrough came with the *Berliner Illustrierte Zeitung* which by 1894 had a circulation of two million.

Leopold Ullstein had five sons, all of whom developed different branches of his enterprise. By the 'thirties they were not only the biggest newspaper group in Germany, but they also published books, magazines, dress patterns and music. They also had their own news agency, picture service, film studio and even a zoo to serve their children's papers.

The Ullsteins returned to Germany after World War II, but did not thrive in the new climate and in 1960 the group was taken over by Axel Springer.

In Britain there has been limited Jewish interest in press ownership. In the last century both the *Sunday Times* and the *Observer* were at one time owned and edited (with no conspicuous success) by Rachel Beer, a member of the Sassoon banking clan, and the *Daily Telegraph* was owned until 1928 by the Levy-Lawson family. The *Telegraph* was originally picked up as a bad debt by Moses Levy, a printer (who for a while also owned the *Sunday Times*), but it was his son, Edward, who put new life and zest into it, and who, in 1871, joined with the *New York Herald* to sponsor Stanley's successful search for Livingstone. The paper, which began as a mouthpiece of Liberalism, moved to the right as it prospered and became what it is still today, the mainstay of British Conservatism.

The *Daily Herald*, the *People*, and numerous other publications belonging to the Odham group, were owned for a time by Julius Elias, the son of a Polish immigrant, who began as a jobbing printer, built up Odhams into one of the largest printing and publishing organizations in the country and was elevated to the peerage as Lord Southwood. He died in 1946 and since then no national or even major British provincial paper has been in Jewish hands.

Perhaps the most celebrated name in American newspaper publishing is that of Joseph Pulitzer, a Hungarian immigrant who began his journalistic career in 1868 as a reporter on the German St Louis language daily *Westliche Post*. Ten years later he bought the St Louis *Despatch* for $2,500 and merged it with the local *Post* to create the prestigious St Louis *Post-Despatch*. In 1883 he turned his attention to New York, bought *The World* from Jay Gould and two years later launched the *Evening World*.

He introduced numerous innovations in illustrations and typography, showed consistent sympathy for labour and was not afraid, when occasion demanded (and even when it did not), to resort to sensationalism, spent heavily on promotion and pushed circulation and profits to what had been thought of as unattainable heights. He died in 1911 and while the St Louis *Post-Despatch* continued to prosper under his sons, his New York papers went into a prolonged decline and were sold in 1931 to the Scripps-Howard group.

Pulitzer did much to enliven journalism but little to elevate standards and the munificent endowments with which he established the Pulitzer Prizes for journalism and the Pulitzer School of Journalism at Columbia University were possibly an act of atonement.

The Pulitzer of our own time is perhaps Samuel Newhouse who acquired his first paper at the age of twenty-seven when he bought the Staten Island *Advance* for $98,000. During the depression, while others were contracting, he acquired numerous other papers, including the St Louis *Globe-Democrat*. In 1955, in what was described as the biggest transaction in US newspaper history, he paid over $18 million for a number of titles, including the Birmingham (Ala.) *News*, and several radio and television stations. Four years later he took over Condé Nast and

Street and Smith, two major magazine houses whose publications include *Vogue, House and Garden* and *Mademoiselle*. In 1960 he donated $2 million to establish the Newhouse Communications Centre at Syracuse University.

Of the 1,800 or so daily papers in the United States, about fifty are owned by Jews, of which twenty-two are part of the Newhouse group. The rest include, or rather included (for it was sold last year) *The New York Post*, owned and edited by Dorothy Schiff, a daughter of Jacob Schiff, the *Washington Post* and the *New York Times*.

The *Washington Post* was picked up at an auction in 1933 by Eugene Mayer, a banker, who merged it with the *Washington Times-Herald* and produced out of the ailing pair a paper worthy of its setting. But it was his daughter, Katherine Graham, who brought it into the very first rank of journalism, though it was, of course, Watergate which pushed it into the realms of lore. Not every paper would have understood the significance of Watergate. Few would have had the staff with the necessary investigative skills and fewer still would have given them their heads without recoiling from their discoveries. It after all calls for more than passing courage, even in a free country, to take on the head of state. Mrs Graham kept her hand on events at every stage of the affair and followed them through with unfailing judgment.

The *New York Times* was founded by Adolph Ochs, the son of a German lay-Rabbi, who settled in Knoxville, Tennessee. At eleven, young Ochs was an office boy with the *Knoxville Chronicle*, at seventeen a compositor on the *Louis-Courier-Journal*. By the age of twenty he owned the *Chatanooga Times*, which he had bought for $250 and which he converted within a few years into one of the south's leading papers. By 1896, when he was thirty-eight, he had prospered sufficiently to descend on New York and acquire the *Times*. Its circulation was 9,000. When he died in 1935 it had a daily circulation of 466,000 and 730,000 on Sundays.

The largest selling paper when Ochs came to New York was Pulitzer's *World*. In 1895 Hearst bought the *Morning Journal* and the unrelenting circulation war between him and Pulitzer led to a deterioration of standards, which had never been of the highest, and gave rise to the expression 'yellow journalism'. Ochs was determined to stay above the fray and to find, and if necessary create, a market for quality journalism and to give his readers not merely what they wanted but what he thought (and what he hoped they would think) was good for them. He was helped immensely by the acculturation of the Jewish immigrant masses, their hunger for the written word, their inherent didacticism and their ability to suffer boredom gladly, and if they did not always turn to the *Times* the moment they had a grasp of English, their sons often did. One did not read the paper merely to be amused or informed, but to be instructed. It was a sort of Home University.

Ochs' son-in-law, Arthur Hays Sulzberger, and his grandson, Arthur Ochs Sulzberger, have kept his traditions intact so that one still turns to the *Times* out of a sense of duty rather than pleasurable anticipation. When in the 'sixties an attempt was made to produce a West Coast edition, it failed, possibly because California has a more relaxed attitude to life. It is high-minded rather than brilliant, as if good writing might arouse a suspicion of shallow thinking, if not flippancy. It may not have *all* 'the news that's fit to print', but it sometimes reads as if it does.

It has often been said that Jews were rarely involved in primary production and that their genius lay mainly in organizing the marketing and distribution of goods and in banking and finance. It has been suggested that Barnato, for example, who headed innumerable mining concerns, didn't know a mine from a hole in the ground. But, as Sir Monty Finniston, the Chairman of the British Steel Corporation, observed, there comes a point in the growth of almost any enterprise when finance becomes the chief preoccupation and the Chairman becomes a banker almost in spite of himself. One can, in fact, find many Jews engaged in primary production both as managers and entrepreneurs. In the eighteenth century, for example, the beginnings of Polish industry were largely the work of Jews, who leased the great estates of the nobility, and opened mines, built roads, set up flour milling, distilling and food-processing industries.

If they were not as conspicuous in primary production as in other fields it is partly because such enterprises take time to develop and time means stability, continuity and at least a passing sense of security, something which few Jews enjoyed until modern times.

In 1848 Meir Guggenheim, then twenty, came to America from Switzerland and after establishing a successful stove-polish and embroidery business, turned, when well into his fifties, to mining, and acquired an interest in the Leadville mine, Colorado. The mine was water-logged and unusable, but he drained it and it proved to be the source of his fortune. He had seven sons, most of whom went into different branches of mining, and he acquired mines and smelters in the American South West, Mexico and South America. In 1901 he merged his interests with that of the American Smelting and Refining Company. His second son, Daniel, by now head of the company, opened up new mines and refineries in Bolivia,

Chile and West Africa, while the eldest, Isaac, headed the Guggenheim Exploration Company which developed new areas in different parts of the globe. The Guggenheims were involved in every stage of the production of non-ferrous metal as well as chemicals and even diamonds, and the company, while it was still largely a family concern, was at one time worth over $500 million.

There was no Jewish industrialist in Europe to compare with the Guggenheims, but then few industrialists have sons as able as the seven sired by Meir. Yet one could still find very substantial enterprises engaged in primary products, such as the Hirsch combine of Halberstadt, Germany. The firm was established on a small scale in 1806 by Aron Hirsch. It grew steadily under the capable management of his son, but it was his grandson, Aron Sigmund, who revolutionized the enterprise through a series of dramatic mergers with the Ilsunburg and Harz copper company and the Eberswalde Messingwerke, and the construction of new foundries and processing works.

Ludwig and Isidor Loewe, the sons of a penniless Thuringian teacher, built up a small machinery-vending company into a major armaments combine which, by the end of the century, after a merger with the Mauser company and the formation of the Deutsche Waffen-und-Munitionsfabrik, was supplying half the armies of the world with rifles.

Ludwig died in 1886 at the age of forty-seven and it was the younger brother, Isidor, who was the main driving force in the company, and who gradually diversified into tramcars and motorcars. He was examining the possibilities of aircraft production when he died in 1910 at the age of sixty-two.

The biggest Jewish industrialist in Germany was possibly Emil Rathenau of the General Electric Company – which gave Germany its first telephone system and which, by the time he died in 1915, had more than seventy thousand employees.

His son, Walther, who succeeded him as head of the company, sought to diversify its interests, but with the outbreak of World War 1 he was called into government service and became virtual controller of the German economy. He continued after the war as economic adviser to the Weimar Government and became first the Minister of Reconstruction and then Foreign Minister.

Nearly all Jews of any prominence in Germany during this period were subjected to ceaseless slander. Isidor Loewe was accused of producing faulty 'Jew rifles' which, it was said, were a greater hazard to the user than the enemy. His attacker, Hermann Ahlwardt, a notorious anti-semite, was eventually imprisoned for libel. Rathenau, as industrialist, statesman and political thinker, was more prominent, and the attacks upon him amounted to outright incitement to murder. In 1922, at the age of fifty-five, he was assassinated by a right-wing extremist.

Ludwig Mond, who was born in Cassel in 1839, and who was to build up one of the largest chemical companies in the world, was fortunate in making his home in England.

Mond, who as a student had worked with Bunsen in Heidelberg, discovered a means of extracting sulphur from alkali waste. He brought the process to England, where, after encountering several rebuffs, he found a company in Widnes, Lancashire, willing to take him into partnership to develop the process. His patent proved profitable and it was adopted under licence by various other concerns in Britain and Europe and he felt tempted to establish a chemical concern of his own.

He had for some years been following the efforts of the Belgian chemist, Solvay, to convert salt into carbonate of soda through the use of ammonia. Attempts to apply his method had not proved commercially viable, but Mond continued to have faith in it. In 1872 he bought the right to develop the process and acquired a site at Winnington, Cheshire, not far from the Liverpool docks and with a good rail link to the limestone deposits of Derbyshire. However his plans were greeted with hostility in the neighbourhood, which feared, not without justice, that the establishment of a large chemical works would destroy the character of the surrounding countryside. Local labourers refused to work for him and he imported Irishmen. Hills were flattened and woodlands felled and towers and chimneys rose in their place. He was on site daily to supervise the building operations and spurred the labourers on with threats and curses. 'Don't call me "Sir",' he would roar, 'I am not a gentleman.'

Solvay obtained carbonate of soda through the reaction of ammonium bicarbonate on sodium chloride, a method which had two main drawbacks. The first was that the sodium chloride solution contained calcium sulphates and magnesium alloys which, reacting with the ammonia and carbon dioxide, encrusted the pipes and choked the process. A further defect was the tendency of the pipes to clog during the secondary stage when the ammonia was recovered from the residue. Mond believed, more through instinct than theoretical calculation, that both these tendencies could be checked. His first experiments suggested the contrary. He bedded down in his laboratory, and by working on the problem day and night, managed, through an intricate process of trial and error, to solve it. But even then he feared something might go wrong, and though his home at Winnington Hall was but a few hundred yards from the works, he had a long bell rope suspended from his bedroom window in case he should be needed at night.

By 1874 the plant was fully in commission, but orders were few, prices were low and he lost about £5 per ton of carbonate of soda, which spurred him on to even greater effort. He drove himself, and drove others furiously, as a colleague later recalled:

Gifted with a powerful determination, he could never contemplate his own failure, and had little sympathy for such as admitted theirs.

A friend was once asking him not to be too hard on a man who had failed to achieve a successful result in a task which had been allotted to him, and urged that the man had done his best, when Mond said: 'Heaven help the man who does his best and fails; there is no other hope, and I have no use for him.'

He continued his struggle to improve his process, reduce costs and find new markets, and in 1880 his breakthrough was complete. Output was trebled, costs were reduced and each ton of soda brought a profit of a pound instead of a loss of five. He expanded, and instead of buying his liquid ammonia from nearby gas works (where it was obtained from the reduction of coal), he established his own gas works.

The Solvay process was by then used by several companies, but as Mond was first in the field he had obtained his licence at preferential rates, paying a royalty of 8/- per ton, against the £1 paid by others, with the result that he could undercut them, and in 1881 he bought out a nearby rival at Sandbach.

His main partner in all this was John Brunner, a former clerk in the Widnes factory who had joined him to set up the Winnington works. In 1881, after the amalgamation with Sandbach, they formed a limited company, Brunner, Mond and Co., with nominal capital of £600,000. There were five partners, but Mond and Brunner held a controlling interest with the right to remain managing directors for life. New land was acquired, new plant installed and within a few years Brunner Mond was the biggest alkali producer in the world. Mond, who had married shortly after he moved to England, and who by now had two grown-up sons, acquired an elegant town house in St John's Wood, London.

Brunner Mond introduced changes in industrial relations which were, in their way, more revolutionary than their chemical processes. They were among the first employers in England – certainly of any size – to give their workers a full week's annual holiday with pay, though they had to earn it with 'good service' (which forty-two per cent of them did), but they still worked the usual eighty-four hour week. In 1889 they introduced an eight-hour day, a startling innovation, which was, however, justified by the fact that the workers were producing as much in eight hours as in the previous twelve. Brunner Mond came to be regarded as model employers. Cheshire labourers, who had resented his intrusion into their quiet countryside and had refused offers of work on his building site, now clamoured for jobs in his factories. A job with Brunner Mond offered a life-time's security, and more. It was something which a father could hand down to his sons, like a family inheritance.

Mond was now a very rich and very successful man and honours were showered upon him from every direction. Heidelberg, where he had begun his chemical researches, awarded him an honorary degree. He was made a Doctor of Literature at Oxford and a Doctor of Science at Manchester. He became President of the Society of Chemical Industry (which he had helped to form), a Fellow of the Royal Society, the Prussian Academy of Science and of the Royal Society of Naples. He was given the Grand Cordon of the Crown of Italy.

He did not rest on his laurels. He expanded his output of commercial gas. He developed a new means of extracting nickel – which was in growing demand for steel alloys in a much purer form than hitherto available – without losing its accompanying chemicals. The drawback to his process was that the nickel initially emerged in gaseous form as nickel carbonyl, which was lethal, but he was confident that if handled with sufficient care, it was safe. He financed the scheme from his own resources and built a plant at Clydach, near Swansea, which, employing a continuous process, reduced Canadian ores to produce nickel, copper sulphate and numerous other substances. It was opened in 1897 and Mond was on the Riviera resting from his exertions when news reached him that three men had been poisoned by an escape of nickel carbonyl. He at once decided that the plant must close, but his younger son, Alfred, who had worked closely with him on every stage of the scheme, persuaded him to continue in operation. The first results were disappointing and Mond had to pay preference shareholders out of his own pocket, but within a few years Mond Nickel, as the company was known, became highly profitable and grew to be one of the largest nickel producers in the world.

Mond acquired a country seat at Combe Bank, near Sevenoaks, and a

Roman palazzo which, with its Titians, Tintorettos and Filippo Lippis was more of a museum than a dwelling place. When he died in 1909 he bequeathed most of his collection to the National Gallery.

He had two sons. The eldest, Robert, a scientist by training, became a noted archaeologist and was associated with the discovery of the Elephantine papyri. His younger son, Alfred, a lawyer, who showed ready administrative skill and business acumen, succeeded his father as head of Brunner Mond, and in 1926 he was largely responsible for bringing together his company with Nobel Industries, British Dyes and United Alkali to form Imperial Chemical Industries, one of the largest and most successful combines in the world.

There are some parallels between the careers of the younger Rathenau and the younger Mond. Both were heirs to great empires and both found themselves drawn into politics and high political office. In 1906 Alfred Mond entered Parliament as Liberal MP for Swansea and he became Minister of Works in 1916 and Minister of Health in 1921, an office which he held till the collapse of the Lloyd George coalition in 1922.

Alfred Mond was not brought up as a Jew but became aware of his origins through the anti-semitism he encountered in the course of his political career. World War I had given rise to a fierce outburst of anti-German feeling, which was followed by a wave of anti-semitism, such as England has not experienced before or since. Alfred had been to Cheltenham and Cambridge and had been brought up, certainly to the satisfaction of his father, as an English gentleman, but not perhaps to the satisfaction of his political opponents. The mass circulation *Daily Mail* took pains to refer to him as Alfred *Mortiz* Mond.

After the outbreak of war, a Brunner Mond soda factory in the East End of London was converted to the manufacture of TNT. The factory was in a densely populated area and the company warned the government of the possible consequences. In 1917 the factory exploded, killing forty people, injuring hundreds of others and rendering some two thousand homeless. Alfred was hardly to blame but one can imagine what would have been made of such an incident in Germany. He did not remain totally unscathed even in Britain, but the worst onslaught came when he sought to defend his Swansea seat in the 1918 elections. He was denounced in different publications as a Jew and a traitor and accused of trading with the enemy, of spying for the enemy and of endangering the lives of his workmen. He had converted his country home into a hospital and had opened his London home to Belgian refugees. His only son, Henry, had been wounded in action, and he himself had been one of the ablest and most hardworking Ministers in His Majesty's government. It did not answer his critics and he had to take one libel action after another to clear his name, and even then the attacks continued. He found himself driven back slowly towards the Jewishness he had virtually renounced. He became an active Zionist, gave generously to Zionist causes and appeared frequently on the Zionist platform. His son and daughter, who had been brought up as Christians, converted to Judaism after the rise of Hitler.

In the past few decades a great many companies have been launched upon a career of spectacular growth less through expanding the output of any particular product than through a series of take-overs and mergers, a process which has been much encouraged by tax laws which penalized incomes more than capital, and by limitations on dividends which left many companies under-valued and, therefore, vulnerable to take-overs. The most dynamic exponent of the process was Charles (now Sir Charles) Clore, who, through a series of dramatic coups in the 'fifties, brought together within a period of seven years a commercial empire which included, among many lesser items, some of the largest shoemakers and retailers in England, a major shipbuilding concern, a Scottish bus company, and a vehicle distributor. And he did so mainly by approaching share-holders over the heads of the management which, though perfectly legal, was not quite cricket, for managers had, over the years, worked out certain lines of conduct, to make life easier for one another, and Clore had disturbed them. He then consolidated his holdings for a period and launched out again in the mid 'sixties with a $150 million bid which gave him control of the Lewis's group, including Selfridges, one of London's largest and most prestigious stores, owned by the Cohen family of Liverpool.

There was no common link between his different acquisitions other than the fact that they held out good prospects at a favourable price – prospects which, more often than not, he was able to realize through the introduction of improved methods and new management and the thawing of capital tied up in valuable sites.

Many others followed his example, albeit on a more limited scale, and for a time take-overs became something of a Jewish industry.

Sir James Goldsmith has been a comparative newcomer to this field. The son of a moneyless branch of a moneyed family, he launched his business career in the early 'fifties with the acquisition of a small French pharma-ceutical firm for £200. He built it up into a substantial business, but understood little about cash-flow and found after a few years that although he was still making a profit over the fiscal year, receipts could at any one time fall so far behind expenditure that he was unable to carry on trading. So in 1957 he sold his firm for £200,000 to stave off imminent bankruptcy. He promptly reinvested his money in another company, diversified into dietary foods and general food products, became a manufacturer as well as a distributor, and within a decade his company – which adopted the name of Cavenham – had a turnover of £6 million. Within a further decade this total grew to £1,658.5 million, and Cavenham, with assets worth £330 million, profits of £45 million and a labour force of seventy-seven thousand is the third biggest (after Unilever's and Nestlé's) food group in Europe, the tenth biggest company in the United Kingdom. It is no loose collection of enterprises, but is exclusively engaged in the production, marketing and distribution of foods. The earlier interest in pharmaceuticals, on which the firm was originally based, has been sold off and there is diversification in territory rather than products. The company owns shops, supermarkets, warehouses and factories in Britain, North America, France, Belgium, Luxembourg, Denmark, Sweden, Germany and Spain. About half of the workforce is employed in Britain, which yields about twenty-seven per cent of the profit, the rest being divided almost equally between Europe and North America, so that while operations might be sluggish in one country, they are usually profitable in others. In 1976, for example, difficult trading conditions in the United Kingdom were more than offset by booming returns from North America.

In the meantime, Sir James, who was knighted in 1976, has been able to acquire the banking expertise necessary to handle a multi-million pound concern, which is perhaps not surprising in one who is related to both the Goldshmidt and the Rothschild banking clans (a grandfather, in fact, went by the name of Goldshmidt-Rothschild and Sir James is on the board of Banque Rothschild).

The mishap in the early part of his career has given Goldsmith something of an obsession with hard cash. New acquisitions are thus paid for as far as possible with shares and long-term loans, while sales are generally made for cash, so that the company is always ready to tackle new opportunities and unforeseen commitments.

As Chairman of the company he is mostly concerned with financial problems and is more banker than manufacturer. The goods made by Cavenham include household names like Bovril and Marmite and he has taken an interest in the very technology of production, in the creation of new lines and in marketing, so that, for example, when Bovril recently produced a beef cube to challenge Oxo, the leading brand in the market, he concerned himself intimately with every detail of what has proved to be a highly successful operation.

Jews have a recognized instinct for the market, for what can sell and what can't, what yields a small margin and what a large one. They are less well known for their managerial skills and the take-off point for many a Jewish entrepreneur comes when he is successful enough to hire a non-Jewish manager. Goldsmith has always been his own manager and prides himself on the efficiency of the organization he has created. Its head office, with its panelled walls, leather furniture and the aroma of good cigars, has the relaxed atmosphere of a very expensive, very exclusive gentlemen's club.

Goldsmith left Eton at sixteen after winning £8,000 (on a £20 investment) in a betting shop, and he takes some pleasure in gambling, but he does not carry it into the board room. All business is by its very nature a gamble, and it is unlikely that he would have made a career of it if it was not, but he tries as far as possible to eliminate the element of chance in his transactions by careful calculation and detailed market research, and he attributes the dramatic success of Cavenham to such commonplace factors as good organization and planning, a careful study of trends, the selection of the right men for the right jobs and, he would admit, luck. He is a strong believer in selection by merit. 'The best, no matter what their background, must reach the top,' he once declared. That has been the guiding principle in his own organization, though he will admit that his own rise to the top as one of the most dynamic and successful figures in European business, was not due entirely to merit. Though he had no money, it was useful to have been at Eton, to be related to the Rothschilds and to be an accepted and familiar figure among the most moneyed families in Europe. But he nevertheless regards himself as a self-made man for he built himself up through his own effort, playing his own hunches, learning from his own mistakes, and continually ploughing back the money derived from one enterprise into others.

Goldsmith's mother was of French Catholic peasant stock so that technically he is not a Jew. When he was much younger he accompanied his father to synagogue once a year – on *Yom Kippur*. After his father died even *Yom Kippur* fell away. His own Jewishness is attenuated in the extreme and it was hardly a matter to which he gave any thought. As he rose to prominence he found himself singled out for attack in the gossip columns of the daily press. These attacks were not as explicit or vicious as the defamation which Alfred Mond had suffered but they have had substantially the same effect. They have not, or at least not yet, made Goldsmith a Zionist, but they have made him dwell upon matters, such as his own antecedents and identity, to which he had not given much thought before. He had never, either at prep school or at Eton, or in the army (where he was commissioned in the Royal Artillery), or in his early business dealings, ever experienced anything which might be construed as anti-semitism, and the attacks have, in a sense, helped him to rediscover himself.

They have not – as sometimes happens in such cases – added to his determination, for that is a quality in which he has never been deficient. There was an outcry in the spring of 1976 when news leaked out (something that had never happened before) that Goldsmith, Joshua Kagan, George Weidenfeld, Sigmund Sternberg, Bernard Delfont and Lew Grade, all of them entrepreneurs in different fields, all of them self-made, all of them successful and all of them Jewish, were to be knighted or ennobled in Prime Minister Harold Wilson's retirement honours list. Goldsmith, who was to receive a knighthood, was not entirely surprised by the reverse reactions, for success and achievement, he believes, are bad words in contemporary England, suggesting an excessive eagerness, a thrusting brashness, a tendency to jump the gun. And if they come together with Jewishness, they amount almost to a social misdemeanour. They are sometimes forgiven when they are obtained with reticence and obscurity and, perhaps, a sense of guilt which might take the form of public benefactions. Goldsmith is neither reticent, nor obscure, nor apologetic. He glories in his role. Hirsch would have disapproved of him.

CHAPTER FIVE

There's No Business Like . . .

– show-business and, with the exception of the diamond and fur trades, none which is so overwhelmingly Jewish. One can explain the Jewish involvement in diamonds and furs, for both offer a promise of sufficiency if not plenty. Show-business offers only a promise of bankruptcy. To be sure, not everyone who embarks on a show-business career ends in the hands of the official receiver. Some remain solvent, others become very rich, but for everyone who rises sufficiently to enjoy some fortune and acclaim, there are a thousand who remain unsung, unknown and in penury. There are few businesses which offer such high rewards to the successful, but few in which it is more difficult to succeed. It is a gamble and far more so than – to take another Jewish calling – the gambling trade, where one can, after all, make a fairly accurate reckoning of the odds. There is no such reckoning to show-business entrepreneurs. They play their hunches and if they pay off they triumph, and if they don't they fade away, or get a job with a relative whose hunches have paid off. But the very fact that it's a gamble is one of the reasons why show-business is so attractive to the Jew.

Another is that show-business is by its very nature open to the talents, and one of the reasons why it is so open is that it has never been regarded as a respectable calling. If it has attained some respectability in our time it is because there is more money in it than there was before and money counts for more than it did before. Actors, and all involved in their performance, were 'merely players', vagabonds, which, to an extent, they still are, even if they are moneyed and cossetted, and it was for long regarded as undignified to write for the stage, let alone appear on it. It was thus more open to the immigrant than other callings, which may partly explain why Jews and Irish have been so conspicuous in the entertainment trade. Both have a natural aptitude for it, and both have been less hesitant to make use of their aptitude.

What is particularly paradoxical about the Jewish role in show-business however is that, if everyone frowned on the theatre, Jews frowned on it most of all, and thought of it, not without justice, as a place of low resort. Where Rabbis spoke of it at all it was to fulminate against it. The theatre, apart from the nature of the spectacles it provided, was, in early days, associated with religious rites and theatre-going was condemned as a form of idol worship. The attitude is summed up in the words of the first Psalm:

Blessed is the man that walketh not in the counsel of the ungodly, nor standeth in the way of sinners, nor sitteth in the seat of the scornful.

The Hebrew, *Moshav Letzim*, 'the seat of the scornful', was often used as an expression for the theatre, and *letz*, or 'scorner', as the synonym for performer. All, especially Jewish womenfolk, were urged to shun such places, as one may gather from the admonition of Naomi to her Moabite daughter-in-law, Ruth: 'My daughter, it is not the custom of the daughters of Israel to frequent theatres and circuses.' In later centuries, when Judaism found itself embattled against Hellenic culture, it regarded the theatre as the intrusion of an alien creed and warned against it, but with imperfect success. One finds Jews eminent in the theatre in the time of Nero, and one third-century sage, Rabbi Simeon ben Lakish, was, in his youth, a circus strong man.

The one occasion in the year when a certain amount of lightheartedness and even ribaldry was tolerated among Jews was during Purim, a minor festival, which commemorates the triumph of Persian Jewry over their adversaries. It takes place in March and is in some ways akin to the pre-Lenten carnival of Catholic Europe. In the Middle Ages, it was customary to provide satirical entertainment, often to the accompaniment of music in the form of a *Purim-shpiel*. The very expression indicates its German origin. It initially took the form of family entertainments, but grew in scale, and by the sixteenth century one reads of public performances and professional performers. But as Purim only lasts one day it could not have provided a particularly lucrative outlet for dramatic skills.

In Italy, however, where the Jews, in spite of being confined to ghettos (the very word ghetto is of Italian origin), tended to mix fairly freely with the surrounding population, one finds them participating in the dramatic entertainments provided in the ducal courts during the sixteenth century.

The first Jewess to win any eminence on the English stage was Hannah Norsa, the daughter of a Mantuan Jew who kept a tavern in Drury Lane. In 1732 she enjoyed a great success as Polly Peachum in John Gay's *Beggar's*

Opera, but she left the stage to become the mistress of the Earl of Orford. (Her sister, Maria, became the mistress of his brother, Sir Edward Walpole. In those days actresses did not aspire to be the wives of noblemen.) Rachel, and Sarah Bernhardt, two of the greatest names in the French theatre, were both of immigrant stock, the former the daughter of an impoverished Swiss pedlar, the latter the illegitimate child of a Dutch Jewess. Similarly, many of the stars of the German and Austrian theatre in the late nineteenth and early twentieth centuries, like Bugomil Dawison, Sigwart Friedmann, Maximilian Pol and Adolf Von Sonnenthal (for many years the reigning star of Vienna's Hofburg-theatre), were all Polish or Hungarian Jews.

In eastern Europe, a number of small theatrical companies came into being which derived their inspiration mainly from the *Purim-shpiel*. Some were, in effect, small travelling circuses, including jugglers, trapeze artists, and weight-lifters, who introduced the occasional word or song into their act, and who sometimes found that their songs were rather more appreciated than their acts. Condemned as *letzim* (scoffers) by the Rabbis and as vagabonds by the police, they led a furtive fly-by-night existence. It was Abraham Goldfaden (1840–1908), a gifted dramatist and song-writer whose *rozhinkes mit mandlen* ('raisins and almonds') became a classic, who gave a stability, if not respectability to the theatre. Goldfaden launched his company with a performance in a wine-cellar in Jassy, Romania, and its success prompted him to establish other groups which toured the major cities of the Pale. There was, even among Jews who had ceased to go to the synagogue, a love of synagogue music as rendered by *Chazanim*, who wore clerical garb, and who were regarded, in Yiddish, as *klay kodesh*, holy vessels. Goldfaden brought together ex-*Chazanim*, singers, actors, whose talents were evoked through scenarios cobbled together to fit the audience. Other companies sprang up, and they multiplied to the point where the Tsarist authorities began to fear a subversive influence. In 1883 the Yiddish theatre was banned. This would not normally have put it out of business, for Russian Jewry had evolved ways of getting round bans, but Jewish life in the Pale had been unsettled by the pogroms. Half the population seemed to be in motion and the other half were preparing to move and the Yiddish theatre followed its audience to New York, Philadelphia, Boston and London.

Among the things which nearly all the Yiddish groups had in common were certain pretensions to grandeur and style. Managers aimed for the highest form of theatrical endeavour which was, of course, the opera. In

1884 the 'Russian Jewish Opera Company' descended on New York with a 'company dramatist' and nine players including Madame Sonya Heine, who would play feminine leads, Madame Esther Silberman, as supporting 'soubrette', and Morris Heine as 'chief comic'.

In London too there was a Russian Jewish Opera Company which staged everything from not-so-grand opera to vaudeville. The most ambitious effort witnessed by the immigrant community was, however, a performance of *King Ahzaz*, by the Jewish composer, Samuel Alman, in Feinman's Yiddish theatre, a large hall with accommodation for one thousand five hundred. The company then went on to stage a Yiddish version of Rigoletto. 'Nowhere except in grand opera at Covent Garden', wrote the *Daily Chronicle*, 'could one hear in England a company of such brilliant talents as in this Yiddish theatre in the East End, which has been founded by the subscriptions of rich and poor Jews, and has been built to fulfil a great racial ideal among the people.' Alas the theatre folded in the year it was founded.

The life of the London Yiddish theatre was short and inglorious. Immigration virtually stopped with the outbreak of World War I. The sons of the immigrants assimilated rapidly and preferred the more robust entertainment available in the English music hall and the cinema, and the Yiddish theatre gradually faded out of existence.

In New York, where the prospective audience was, of course, much larger, the shows were sometimes more ambitious and there were frequent attempts to stage Shakespeare – *farzetst and farbessert*, which is to say, translated and improved. One performance of *Hamlet* drew such applause that according to Bernard Gorin, the historian of the Yiddish theatre, the audience called for the author.

Jacob Gordin, the writer and journalist, who, until his arrival in America in 1891, had never seen a Yiddish play, found the Yiddish theatre 'far removed from Yiddish life', and 'vulgar, false, immoral', and he combined with such theatre idols as Jacob Adler and David Kessler to reform the Yiddish stage, mainly through the quality of his own plays, specially written for the Yiddish theatre, with virtuosi parts tailored to the styles of the leading performers. His most successful play was the *Yiddisher Koenig Lear*, the Jewish King Lear, but there, at least, he acknowledged his sources. He also borrowed heavily from Gogol, Gorki, Victor Hugo, Ibsen, Lessing and others, without always making such acknowledgments, but if he was guilty of systematic plagiarism, he introduced his audiences to a quality of drama to which they might otherwise have remained strangers and, as one of his detractors put it, 'better second-hand Shakespeare than first-hand Gordin'.

Gordin in fact brought in improvements at all levels, not only in the material available for production, but in the quality of the production itself, in the removal of back-stage anarchy which often invaded the front in the standard of performance, and in artistic integrity, though the realism he aimed for bore little relation to Jewish reality.

The new order he created hardly survived its stars, for by the 1920s immigration virtually came to a halt. The older generation of immigrants was beginning to fade out, their sons had learned English and there were cinemas beckoning on every corner. The Yiddish theatre lost its audience long before it lost its personnel. Maurice Schwartz, the last of the great Yiddish actor-managers, brought together a company – the Jewish Art Theatre – as late as 1918. Its performances of Yiddish translations of European classics and of new plays, such as I. J. Singer's *Yoshe Kalb*, got respectful attention from respected critics, but they were like the last of the hand-loom weavers, living a penurious, hand-to-mouth existence trooping to every corner of the globe where Yiddish was still spoken and incorporating about one hundred and fifty plays in their repertoire so as to have something for everyone. Some Yiddish actors, like Moni Weisen- freund (Paul Muni), were young enough and adaptable enough to make the transition to the English stage; most faded into oblivion.

By the late 'twenties the best talents to emerge from the immigrant community, like the director, Harold Clurman, and the playwright, Clifford Odets, were beginning to find their way to the American stage. In 1931 Clurman and Odets founded the New York Group Theatre, one of the few significant repertory companies to have flourished in America for any length of time. Clurman was much influenced by Stanislavsky, and the belief that the theatre had to reflect the realities of day-to-day life. The work of Clifford Odets was almost tailor-made to fit both his theory and style. They had some remarkable successes with *Waiting for Lefty*, about a New York cab-driver's strike, and *Awake and Sing*, about the conflict within a poverty-stricken Jewish immigrant family. The whole atmosphere they engendered went well with the mood of post-depression America, but they were somewhat stylized for later taste and Clurman is perhaps better known today as a theatre critic.

The work of Clurman and Odets was almost an extension of the Yiddish theatre. It shared its didacticism. It too spoke of *der heim* (the home- land), but a *heim* which had, by then, been firmly transplanted to America, and as it was there to be seen and experienced, it was more difficult to romanticize so that the realism it portrayed was more realistic. It introduced a discipline and professionalism which Gordin sought but never attained. Apart from anything else, the level of writing was more disciplined and professional. The star system, which had been the bane of the Yiddish theatre, was abolished, so that there was no longer any need to tailor scripts to particular histrionic talents. The Yiddish actor was like other actors, but more animated so that he flailed with his arms and boomed with his voice and could not utter an adieu without suggesting that the end of the world was nigh. If Odets' plays cut life down to lifesize, Clurman did the same for the actors.

His younger contemporaries, like John Houseman, co-founder with Orson Welles of the New York Mercury Theatre, who staged a memorable *Hamlet* (with Leslie Howard in the title role), merged into the mainstream of the American theatre.

In Europe the Yiddish theatre, even within the great centres of Jewish population like Poland, never had the sort of flowering it enjoyed in America and did not establish a sufficient tradition or body of talents from which there could be, as there was in America, an evolution into the mainstream of Western drama. Jews like Otto Brahm (born Abrahamson) and Max Reinhardt were both major influences on the European and especially the German-speaking theatre, but they owed little, if anything, to their Jewish origins.

It was Brahm who introduced Ibsen, Gerhart Hauptmann and Hugo von Hofmannsthal to German audiences and made the Deutsches Theatre Berlin the home of *avant-garde* drama, and Berlin itself a major theatrical centre. In 1894 he brought over the young Max Reinhardt, who was assistant director at the Salzburg State Theatre, to work with him in Berlin, and in 1905 he put him in charge of the Deutsches. The style of the two men differed considerably. Brahm had a rather didactic approach and his preferred plays tended to be social commentaries. Reinhardt was more concerned with the classics and brought the works of Shakespeare, Schiller, Goethe and Molière to a wider public. Yet he sought to give them contemporary relevance. 'Our standard must be not to act a play as it was acted in the days of its author. How to make a play live in our time, that is decisive for us.' His range was catholic and he introduced new works by Wilde, Synge, Shaw, Ibsen and Strindberg, but his particular genius lay in the spectacular. He did not allow himself to be cramped by the technical limitations of the theatre, and introduced all manner of innovation, like the revolving stage (which he first used for a production of *A Midsummer Night's Dream*) to make it more flexible. In 1911 he transformed the chilly spaces of London's Olympia into a Cathedral for a performance of *The Miracle*, a wordless spectacle. In 1920 he produced *Jedermann* ('Everyman') for the Salzburg Festival (which he founded), where it was to be an annual event until the rise of Hitler. When the Nazis came to power his reign over the German theatre was brought to an immediate end, and he moved to the West Coast of America, where his production of *A Midsummer Night's Dream* (which he later made into a film) at the Hollywood Bowl attracted nightly audiences of sixteen thousand. He was in his sixties by then, too late to transplant himself on to foreign soil, too much a part of German culture to flourish away from it. But his influence lingered both through the school for actors which he established in America towards the end of his life (he died in 1943) and through such disciples as Otto Preminger, who had worked at his Josefstadt Theatre in Vienna for a time, but came to America in his early thirties and adapted himself with sufficient speed to become one of Hollywood's foremost directors, and one who showed an interest in the Jewish predicament which his master had rarely displayed.

If there was a Jewish element in Reinhardt's work it lay in his love of extravagance; but it was always a controlled extravagance and it may be said that he disciplined spectacle into an art form.

Extravagance at its most extravagant, which is to say, extravagance for its own sake, was to become the property of Broadway and Hollywood, where it assumed a classic form in the work of Florenz Ziegfeld (1869–1932), a showman who began his career at the Chicago World Fair in 1893. In 1907, after a visit to Paris, he launched *Ziegfeld Follies*, a theatre spectacle which continued, with frequent changes of material and cast, until it was taken over by Hollywood in 1931. Ziegfeld brought together many talents, including Eddie Cantor, Will Rogers, and Jerome Kern, and beautiful women by the train-load. He worked on the principle, which was to have its apotheosis in Hollywood, that one cannot have too much of a good thing, and that if there was nothing like a dame, there was certainly nothing quite like a thousand dames, bejewelled, be-feathered and be-sequined. The effect was curiously un-erotic, and it showed that a thousand half-naked girls did not quite add up to five hundred naked ones; they were scintillating rather than titillating. Show-business had not yet discovered sex, but it discovered a near substitute called 'glamour', which might be defined as sex trapped in aspic.

Billy Rose (1899–1966) worked on Ziegfeldian principles, but on a more limited scale. He began life as a shorthand writer and was for a time an assistant to Bernard Baruch, but he turned to popular song writing and by 1924 was earning $100,000 a year as a composer. He perfected his craft after analysing existing 'hits' and discovering that the simpler the lyrics and the more commonplace the tune, the greater was the likelihood of success (and where the tune was already known a hit was almost certain). Rose is, however, best remembered as a pioneer of night-club entertainment. He opened in 1924 with a small club for people of modest means, and he remained only modestly successful till he built up the Diamond Horseshoe, which became the largest, plushiest and most celebrated establishment of its type and which was decidedly for people of immodest means and of even less modest taste. Here too the accent was on glamour, with successive arrays of splendid women splendidly semi-attired. Yet for all the scale of the enterprise it retained intimacy, geniality and warmth. Here was *gemütlichkeit*, American style. He did not quite make the night-club respectable – he would have been ruined if he had – but it became the sort of place to which – if one's income ran to it – one could take one's wife or even one's daughter.

Rose was also an enterprising Broadway producer and was responsible for several long-running successes, the best remembered of which is perhaps *Carmen Jones*, and he acquired both the Ziegfeld Theatre and the National Theatre (which was re-named the Billy Rose theatre).

A small intense man with a large nose and large glasses, Rose liked to surround himself with magnificent sculptures, including works by Rodin, Epstein and Daumier. These he donated, together with his collection of English masterpieces (including a Romney, a Reynolds, a Gainsborough and a Turner), to the Israel Museum, Jerusalem, in 1965, a year before his death. He married five times. His first wife was Fanny Brice.

As a name on Broadway Rose was perhaps second only to the Shuberts, a theatrical dynasty who became to Broadway what the Rockefellers were to oil and who achieved their eminence with about the same finesse. There were three brothers involved, Sam, Lee and Jacob, born between 1875 and 1877, the sons of a Syracuse pedlar. Their first acquisitions were in up-state New York but they moved rapidly on to Manhattan and by 1956 they owned or controlled about half the major theatres in the country, including seventeen on Broadway itself, until forced to dispose of some of their holdings by anti-Trust legislation.

They were among the early backers of Ziegfeld and among the many talents they introduced to American audiences were Al Jolson, Eddie Cantor and Fanny Brice. Their long drawn-out battle with the aptly named Klaw and Erlanger syndicate (in which they eventually out-clawed Klaw) for control of Broadway was an epic worthy of a Broadway musical itself and, indeed, it became one. 'When they tear down a theatre it's like someone in the family dying,' said Jacob, the last surviving of the brothers but they were perhaps more property men than show men.

It might be thought that the involvement of the Jews in the theatre naturally brought them into the cinema, but few of the Jews who came to dominate Hollywood in what has been called its golden age, which is to say from the late 'twenties into the early 'forties, began life in show-business. Samuel Goldwyn, of Metro Goldwyn Mayer, was a glove salesman. Carl Laemmle, of Universal, was a clothes salesman. William Fox, of Twentieth Century Fox, was in dry-cleaning. Harry Cohn, of Columbia, was a bus-conductor. The Warner Brothers owned a bicycle shop. Marcus Loew, another of the founding fathers of MGM, was a furrier. Adolph Zukor, of Paramount, was likewise a furrier. Nearly all were immigrants, yet between them they possibly did more to determine American attitudes and tastes than the churches or even the schools.

The Jews were not the pioneers of the new medium, which is to say, they were not the technical innovators, but they were amongst the first to see its possibilities, and they vested both faith and money into it when it was still a flickering novelty in amusement arcades and fun-fairs. They also owned theatres, which, once the length and quality of the films improved, they promptly converted into cinemas. A continuous process of integration began whereby cinema-owners who wanted to assure a regular supply of films became producers, and producers who wanted to assure an outlet for their films became exhibitors. Thus, for example, MGM came into being largely through the efforts of Marcus Loew, who owned a large cinema and theatre chain on the east coast, and wanted to control his film supply. A New England distributor, Louis B. Mayer, had already moved to Los Angeles with a similar intention. They brought in Sam Goldwyn, an independent producer, who, in 1913, had made the first full-length motion picture in association with his brother-in-law, Jesse Lasky (who first brought him into films) and Cecil B. De Mille, and the result was MGM (it is not quite certain who brought in the lion).

The other groups grew in similar fashion until the entire industry was dominated by the big five, MGM, Paramount, Warner Bros., RKO and

Twentieth Century Fox, all of which were owned and controlled by Jews. And of the not-so-little three – Universal, Columbia and United Artists – two were in Jewish hands. One met the occasional gentile, like the Skouras brothers, who were Greek, or Winfield Sheehan, who was Irish, but the whole *ambience* was Jewish and even the gentiles acquired Jewish mannerisms, expressions, and habits of speech. As the Scottish director, John Grierson, observed after a stay in Hollywood: 'After a few years in the place, your foreskin falls away.'

In 1926, when Adolph Zukor, a Hungarian immigrant and one-time furrier, opened the magnificent Paramount theatre in New York, he declared that the building should be dedicated to America: 'To think that a country could give a chance to a boy like me to be connected with an institution like this!'

It was a sentiment which could have been echoed – and frequently was echoed – by some of his most eminent Hollywood contemporaries. What distinguished America was not merely that it gave such opportunities, but that one was forgiven for taking them, and if the makers of Hollywood have not been elevated to the pantheon of national heroes, there is, in the many studies of them, a tone of grudging admiration. For they had made it to the top, and had, even when pushed down, tarried long enough to have left lingering mementoes of their stay.

The primary quality they brought to their work was a ruthless determination. In addition to this they had plain brute stamina, and an instinct for what the public wanted before the public wanted it. In the early days of the cinema the mere display of moving figures was in itself sufficient to excite an audience, but as the novelty became less novel, the public began to expect something more for their money and Hollywood gradually assumed its role of a dream factory. If the Goldwyns and the Mayers and the Cohns and the Warners showed an unerring instinct for what the man in the street wanted, it was because they were not all that far off the street themselves. Coarse, untutored and unread, almost to a man, it is doubtful if they would have been so successful had they been anything else.

One of the exceptions was Sam Goldwyn, who was born in Warsaw in 1882, and who, after a short stay with relatives in Manchester, moved to New York. There an immigration official, unable to cope with his mouthful of a name, dubbed him Goldfish, and Goldfish he remained until he moved to Hollywood. He was too independent an individual to remain long within the MGM combine and left in 1924 to set up on his own. He then joined with Charlie Chaplin, Douglas Fairbanks, and Mary Pickford, to establish United Artists, as a distributor for their films, but here too his personality proved too dominant, and he bought his partners out.

He was the complete autocrat, and was regarded with awe rather than affection. Films were his life. He was familiar with every stage of the product and insisted on nothing but the best. This was something he had in common with most Hollywood tycoons, but he knew the best when he saw it, and gathered round himself the most talented actors, technicians, directors and writers (whom he treated with a decorousness unknown in Hollywood), paid them the biggest salary, and somehow managed to bludgeon the best out of them. He only made two or three films a year, but each – *The Little Foxes* and *The Best Years of Our Life* are but two examples – was a landmark. He somehow managed to rise above his origins and, indeed, above Hollywood, and brought to Hollywood something one does not readily associate with it: class. And so, to an extent did Carl Laemmle (pronounced Lemlee), a genial, diminutive figure who looked like a toothy leprechaun. Laemmle came from Germany in 1884 at the age of seventeen, and after being many things in many places, including a furrier's apprentice in New York, an errand boy in Chicago, a spearbearer in *Julius Caesar*, a farm-hand in Dakota, a clerk in a jewellery shop, a book-keeper in a stockyard, a manager in a clothing store, he acquired a Chicago theatre, which, though profitless as a live theatre, proved very profitable when converted to films.

With ample money at last in hand he acquired other theatres and established a film exchange to improve the supply of films. When that proved insufficient, he did what others were to do after him and moved to California, where he established Universal Studios. He was amongst the first to realize the potentialities of the star system (without fully realizing its dangers) and signed up several of the leading names in the industry, supreme among whom was Mary Pickford. He applied himself to his work with a consuming zest and collapsed in 1930 at a business conference. 'I never knew how tired I was,' he confessed. 'I found I was completely worn out, not sick, just worn out.' But to be worn out in Hollywood was to be sick enough and a few years later he was ousted from his post. He died in 1939. Laemmle was one of the very few Hollywood tycoons who was spoken of with warmth even by his employees, and he was known affectionately as Uncle Carl. The expression was not entirely metaphorical, for Universal, during his hey-day, was full of relatives, a fact which gave rise to Ogden Nash's famous couplet: 'Uncle Carl Laemmle has a large famlee.'

Hollywood, the place, as it was said, where 'the son-in-law also rises' was the last redoubt of nepotism, but nepotism was perhaps one of its saving virtues, for it indicated, if only at a crude level, that it was not wholly devoid of charity.

Laemmle was deeply moved by the plight of Germany after World War I and devoted much time and money to relief and reconstruction, but he took a somewhat exaggerated view of the importance of his efforts and his place in history. He commissioned John Drinkwater to write his auto-biography, and entertained hopes of winning the Nobel Peace Prize. Few of his colleagues aimed so high.

William Fox was born in Hungary and came to America as a small child and worked for a time in the garment trade and eventually set up his own small cleaning business. From there he branched out into films and within a few years owned a sizeable chain. By 1912 he entered into production and in 1915 established the Fox Film company which eventually became part of Twentieth Century Fox. Like Laemmle he almost worked himself to a standstill. 'I avoided carrying a watch,' he said. 'I never wanted to know what time it was. My day ended when my day's work was completed. Again and again I did not go to bed at all during the twenty-four hours.' And like Laemmle he was eventually ousted from his post. In 1936 he became bankrupt, and, unlike others in the trade, more or less stayed bankrupt. In 1942, when already in his seventies, he spent a year in jail for attempted bribery.

Harry Cohn, or King Kohn, as he was sometimes called, head of Columbia, directed his company with the arbitrariness of a Caliph. So many legends have accumulated round his barbarity that one almost suspects that he consciously set out to play a part. He was born on the east side of New York, the son of recent immigrants, and worked as a bus-conductor, soft-shoe dancer and song-plugger before getting a job as secretary to Laemmle. In 1920, with his brother Jack and others, he formed a film sales company which four years later became Columbia Pictures. His working relationship with his brothers, or indeed anyone else, was not a happy one and Jack remained in New York to look after the business side of the organization while Harry took charge of production in Hollywood. In spite of frequent attempts to oust him, he remained President of the company, as well as head of production, till his death in 1958. Though paranoiac, foul-mouthed and illiterate, he had a nose for talent and when he found a director in whose judgment he could trust, like Frank Capra, or Sam Spiegel, he gave them a completely free hand, something not commonly available in Hollywood. What kept him at the top, however, was a combination of cunning, ruthlessness and flair. His most human quality was perhaps his awareness of his own deficiencies. When one of his nephews left Hollywood for New York, he said: 'One bastard in the studio is enough.' He was, in spite of his power and influence, a friendless, cheerless individual. When, towards the end of his life, he was urged to give up the presidency of Columbia, he retorted:

No, I won't do it. Sitting behind this desk, I can always press a buzzer and get somebody to talk to me. If I wasn't head of a studio, who would talk to me? Who would come to my house for dinner? No, I won't do it.

The Warner brothers, Harry, Albert, Sam and Jack, the sons of a Polish cobbler, worked in a variety of trades before combining their resources to open a bicycle shop. In 1904 they acquired a film-projector and gave travelling shows with their sister at the piano and Jack, then twelve, as a boy soprano. They prospered sufficiently to join a film exchange and become distributors and exhibitors. In 1912 they moved to California and after a number of false and rather expensive starts, they finally succeeded in launching the Warner Bros. Company. They were readier to experiment than their rivals and pioneered talking films with Al Jolson's *The Jazz Singer*. Sam, who was most intimately concerned in the experiment, died of a heart attack twenty-four hours before the première. A few years later they opened their permanent studio at Burbank, outside Los Angeles. Harry and Albert stayed in New York to look after the business and Jack headed the studios.

The company introduced a degree of realism in its treatment of crime stories which was followed with misgivings in some quarters. For although the good guys always triumphed and the bad invariably came unstuck, the latter were often more attractive than the former, especially if played by Humphrey Bogart, James Cagney and Edward G. Robinson. In the postwar years Warner's made its mark with musical extravaganzas like *My Fair Lady* and *Camelot*, both personally produced by Jack Warner.

'The film Moguls', as they were frequently called, were a diverse and even eccentric collection of individuals; but they had one thing in common, that they were inclined to play safe, to offer what would be most acceptable to most people, or, to quote a character in one of their more famous films, *Cover Girl* (with Rita Hayworth and Gene Kelly): 'Once you start playing to the long hairs you're finished.' They played to the short hairs, but as the short hairs were perhaps in more need of entertainment than the long, they fulfilled a necessary function. Moreover, they not only provided the dreams, they, as exhibitors, provided the *ambience* in keeping with the scene on screen, hence the palaces built by 'Roxy' Rothafel (whose edifices gave a word, first to the American and now the English language), Sid Grauman, of Grauman's Chinese Theatre, MGM, Paramount, Warner Bros., and others, in which the patron was enthroned as king. There were the thick carpets, the heavy upholstery, the crystal chandeliers, baroque extravaganzas, with ushers and usherettes like flunkeys of some great estate, and front-of-house staff in gold braid like admirals. And, it must be added, amid all the empty glitter, the expensive ephemera, there was work of such quality and merit as to almost outweigh the trash, such as *On the Waterfront*, for example, or *Gone With the Wind*, or *All Quiet on the Western Front* and *Twelve Angry Men*. But their most notable contribution was perhaps the musical, which sought nothing more elevating than to please, and to please abundantly, and which succeeded. MGM in particular kept up a flow of musicals like *Meet Me in St Louis*, *Annie Get Your Gun* and *Gigi*, which kept half the world singing and dancing.

At first Hollywood was content with perpetuating European successes, like Louis B. Mayer's 1925 adaptation of *The Merry Widow*, followed in time by Sigmund Romberg's *Student Prince*. Although Romberg, who was born in Vienna, had made his home in America as a very young man, he worked within the traditions of the European operetta. Hollywood accepted that all romance, drama and intrigue happened abroad, if not in central Europe then – as in Romberg's *Desert Song* – in the 'mysterious east'. But in time they turned to discover that there was drama to be found even on their own doorstep and thus one had a succession of home-based musicals beginning with Jerome Kern's *Showboat*, continuing with Gershwin's *Porgy and Bess*, and on through *Oklahoma!*, *Carousel*, *Annie Get Your Gun*, to what is perhaps the apotheosis of the American musical, Bernstein's *West Side Story*.

Now, although most of the talents that went into these musicals, from the backer with the eye for a winner, to the composer were Jewish (as, for example, were or are Romberg, Kern, Gershwin, Irving Berlin, Richard Rodgers, Oscar Hammerstein, Lerner and Loewe, Leonard Bernstein), it was a long time before anything noticeably Jewish was discernible on stage. One found a hint of it in *Pins and Needles*, a 1937 revue, with music by George Gershwin presented by the International Ladies Garment Workers, which then had a predominantly Jewish membership, and again in Frank Loesser's *Guys and Dolls*, which, being based on Damon Runyon's Broadway tales, touched on an area where show-business, the gambling trade and the underworld met, and as such had an oddly Jewish flavour. It is only with the production of Sheldon Harnick's and Jerry Brock's *Fiddler on the Roof*, however, that one comes upon an intrinsically Jewish work, with the Jew finally accepted in his own right. One of course found echoes of old Jewish strains in numerous songs of Irving Berlin, Gershwin and Kern, Loewe and Loesser, but it now swelled forth with a resonant, full-bodied confidence. Gershwin had written a Negro folk opera, *Porgy and Bess*, in 1935, and in the post-war years Irish themes were treated in *Finian's Rainbow*, Scottish in *Brigadoon*, Italian in *Fiorella* and Puerto-Rican in *West Side Story*, so that there was something mildly inevitable about the advent of *Fiddler on the Roof* in 1964. It came as part of the great Jewish boom, when America, at least, evinced a new interest in Jews, possibly because the Jews had discovered a new interest in themselves. American literature not only came to be dominated by writers who happened to be Jews, but by Jewish writers – Bellow, Malamud, Roth and others – writing on Jewish themes. But while the books dealt with the troubled here and now, *Fiddler on the Roof*, like those splendid evocations of an earlier and trouble-free America, *Oklahoma!*, *Carousel* and *Annie Get Your Gun*, dealt with the innocent past. Now and again there was a hint of some external menace, the pogroms which caused the Tevye of the Pale to flee to America, but it was kept well to the background and among the many pleasures it brought to Jewish audiences was a glowing nostalgia undimmed by personal memories of hardship.

The Fiddler could never have reached the screen, or got within sight of it, while the Mayers and the Cohns were kings. The product which was closest to the heart of Louis B. Mayer was the Andy Hardy series with Mickey Rooney. This was small-town America at its most affable and endearing, without its Sinclairish exposés and before it turned into *Peyton Place*. If a trifle sentimental and stylized, it was no more remote from the real small town than the Fiddler's Anatevke was from the actual Pale of Settlement. It was the sort of America to which Mayer, who left Russia at the age of two, would have liked to belong and perhaps even felt that he did belong. He would have fled from Anatevke as his parents had fled from the original.

If there was little intrinsically Jewish in the output of the Hollywood

tycoons, there was something particularly Jewish to their style. The elder
Selznick once told his son David (producer of *Gone With the Wind*): 'Live
expensively! Throw it around! Give it away! Always remember to live
beyond your means. It gives a man confidence.' This was not, in fact, far
from the principles on which Hollywood operated, where the very cost
of a film – 'this multi-million dollar epic' – was often used by the publicity
department as a commendation. It also explains the frequent conflicts
between producers and bankers, in which the bankers not infrequently
won, which raises one of the many paradoxes of Hollywood. If there is
one thing that is almost universally expected of the Jew, it is business
acumen, and it is the one thing which the rulers of Hollywood most
obviously lacked. Perhaps a person who takes business seriously does not
go into show-business in the first place, and possibly the sort of qualities
necessary to capture the imagination of the public are the sort to darken
the eyes of one's auditors, but the fact remains that when a real professional
businessman, the banker Joseph P. Kennedy, entered the industry (to the
dismay of Marcus Loew, who is said to have remarked: 'A banker? A
banker? I thought this business was just for furriers'), he cut through
Hollywood like a scythe, merged some companies, re-grouped others,
and left after about a year and a half the richer by several million
dollars.

The Hollywood tycoons may have been incautious in their investments,
in the way they threw their money about, and in their utterances. They
may have behaved like uncaged lions in the studios, but if they were
otherwise cautious, and the caution is discernible in much of their output,
it was because they were vulnerable, or at least, felt vulnerable. They were
foreigners almost to a man. Some still spoke with foreign accents.
Goldwyn used the English language as if it was some Yiddish hybrid,
which gave rise to the Goldwynisms, some of which were later created
on Goldwyn's behalf, but the best of which, such as 'include me out',
issued straight from the horse's mouth and which one historian of the film
industry, Philip French, has described as an 'immigrant's adventures with
the English language, part mixed metaphor, part malapropism, part
illiteracy, that have a power and pungency of their own'.

They were chary about touching on their Jewish origins. When Ben
Hecht, one of the most talented writers in Hollywood, sought to mobilize
support for a Jewish brigade to serve as part of the British Army in World
War II, not one of the leading producers would give their name to it,
and David Selznick told him:

I don't want anything to do with your cause for the simple reason that it's a Jewish political cause. And I am not interested in Jewish political problems. I'm an American and not a Jew.

This was not a complete delusion. An essential part of Jewishness is the feeling that one is an outsider, not part of the crowd. In Hollywood the entire crowd was so Jewish that non-Jews felt outside. Nor did they have to feel strange whenever they moved east to confer with the New York end of the business, for that too was Jewish.

It is even more so today, as one can see from a complaint of Truman Capote, in a recent issue of *Rolling Stone*:

The truth of the matter about it is, the entire cultural press, publishing ... criticism, television ... theatre ... film industry ... is almost ninety per cent Jewish oriented. I mean, I can't count on one hand five people of importance – of real importance – in the media who aren't Jewish, I can't.

In New York, however, Jews lived with their Jewishness, in Hollywood they did not, and until well after World War II the general tendency was to de-Judaize and Americanize, so that even though many of the tycoons stemmed from intensely Orthodox homes – some were the sons or grandsons of Rabbis – they, so to speak, returned to the faith of their fathers only on their burial and sometimes not even then, and any Jewish actor or actress hoping to be built up as a star had to be processed and turned into an all-American boy or girl before they could be exposed to the public. Marian Levee had to become Paulette Goddard; Bernard Schwartz had to become Tony Curtis; Judith Tuvim, Judy Holliday (here, at least, there was an approximate translation of her name); Danny Kaminsky, Danny Kaye; Joseph Levitch, Jerry Lewis; Shirley Schrift, Shelley Winters (the most ingenious conversion was that of Lee Jacob, who changed his name to Lee J. Cobb). Jewish actors and actresses who have aspired to stardom since the 'sixties have, one may add, had it easier, so that Dustin Hoffmann could retain his outlandish name, and Barbra Streisand has retained both her name and her nose: it is unlikely that she would have been allowed to hold on to either during the hey-day of the Mayers or the Selznicks, or, indeed, whether she would have been able to rise to stardom at all.

Jews were good actors, that was well known, but they were, until comparatively recently, thought to be deficient in those heroic and romantic qualities necessary to a major romantic role. Paul Newman, for example, who is Jewish but doesn't look it, did not get his first film break till 1955, when he was thirty.

What also kept Jewish actors out of films was that from the mid-'twenties onwards a sizeable proportion of Hollywood output took the form of Westerns, and there were years when it did not seem to produce anything else. The Jew may have owned the general store, or kept a brothel, but otherwise the West, certainly as depicted by Hollywood, was not part of his scene – he was not even the smart-alec lawyer. Jews did not ride horses, or carry guns, or hold up stage-coaches, or rob banks, and to have had a Jew in a leading role, whether as sheriff or villain, might have introduced elements of subtlety from which the genre was mercifully free. When Jews were finally brought into a Western – as in *Blazing Saddles* – it was an inspired joke, and part of the joke was their incongruity, that they were so much out of place. It would have been like introducing Irishmen into *Fiddler on the Roof*.

Here was the free and open America of lore, uncluttered by the sophistries of the big cities – which was another reason why the Jew would have been out of place, for no one was more associated in the public mind with the big cities than the Jew. The Western was a physical experience, brisk, racy, galloping horses, thundering trains. The agility of the Jew was limited to the mind. The West, for all its malefactors, brutality and violence, was an innocent world, where the simple qualities of manhood lifted one person above another and where the good eventually triumphed over the bad. It was a rude Camelot, as removed from reality as Camelot itself, and it was largely the creation of sedentary men with plump hands and manicured fingernails. The Westerns, to an extent, answered to qualities they missed in themselves. They were, like Andy Hardy, their contributions to Americans, which, like jazz and Coca Cola, represented an uniquely American product. But the myths they created and perpetuated have added to public confusion, for life is not as simple as that, the good and the bad are not so clearly defined, and even where they are, the bad are sometimes more applauded because they generate more novelty and drama and because they are not infrequently more successful.

The one area where one could get away with being Jewish, where indeed it helped to be Jewish, and where one might be taken to be a Jew even if one was not, was comedy, and with the exception of Charlie Chaplin (who is generally thought to be Jewish, partly because he is the supreme master of his craft), Buster Keaton, W. C. Fields and Bob Hope, nearly all the American comedians and comediennes whose names have lingered, from Fanny Brice to the Marx Brothers, and from Jack Benny to Lenny Bruce, have been Jews. If Hollywood was a Jewish industry, no part of it was so exclusively Jewish as laughter.

It has often been suggested that the stance of the Jew as outsider gives him a view of society not available to others and that he can notice aberrations and quirks not readily discernible to others. But America is a nation of outsiders and even if the Jew used to be a little more outside than others, he is today, certainly in America, almost part of the ruling caste. It is, however, true that the history of the Jew has given him a natural scepticism which he has not been slow to articulate, a certain congenital world-weariness which adds a touch of wryness to his language. There is also a *badinage* in the very use of Yiddish, which is, in some cases, carried over by the sons of Yiddish-speakers into English, or at least into American, so that it has come to infect even non-Jews. Damon Runyon was not a Jew nor the son of Jews but there is the sound of Yiddish to his English, possibly because so many of his characters inhabit the outer fringe of show-business. Several of the comedians (Woody Allen is the most obvious example) assume the role of a character familiar to Jewish lore, that of the professional *nebbich*. The Jew has enlarged the familiar 'if you can't beat 'em join 'em', to read 'if you can't join 'em laugh at 'em', to which the *nebbich* has added, 'and if you can't laugh at 'em laugh at yourself'.

It must also be added that comedy and clowning, possibly with a song and dance thrown in, in fact the stage generally, offered the hopeful, ambitious but undisciplined young Jew a way to the top. The Jew was nature's own Samuel Smiles and, since the flight from the ghetto, a fairly routine pattern of ascent had been established. The father worked and scraped to give his son the opportunities he didn't have, and the son worked hard to justify the hopes of his father and also to fulfil his own ambitions, so that he went on from school to university and into the professions. One lived through a constricted today for a more spacious tomorrow. That was the common, though not the invariable pattern, and even in *der heim*, there was the occasional dropout or tearaway, or, as he was called by his despairing elders, the *yungatz*, or *paskudnick*, who had no love of books, spent his evenings, and sometimes even his days, at play, but in *der heim* if one dropped out, one stayed out. The *Kehilla*, or organized community, had no place for irregular talents or irregular ways. The comedian was at best a *badchan*, who might ease the tedium of a drawn-out wedding celebration with a few jokes, or at worst a *letz*, a scoffer: neither was a recommendation.

THE JEWS

The *Kehilla* system, for good or ill, never took root in America and, as Professor Irving Howe has observed in his brilliant study of immigrant life, *World of Our Fathers*: 'the *grober yung* found himself with prospects he would have been denied at home.'

Ill-lettered Jews, those condescended to in Yiddish as *di proste*, had been held in check too long by the repressiveness of old-world moralism and the system of 'respect' for learning. Now, in America, it was their turn, still more the turn of their sons and daughters. Full of sap, excited by the sheer volume of street noise, letting loose sexual curiosities beyond the clamp of Jewish shame, these kids became taxicab drivers, bookies, hoofers, comics, sometimes prize fighters. A long-contained vulgarity, which had already come to form a vital part of Yiddish culture in eastern Europe, now broke through the skin of immigrant life. It was a vulgarity in both senses: as the current juicy thirst of desire, intent on seizing life by the throat, and as the cheap, corner-of-the-mouth retailing of Jewish obscenities. It may be easy to separate these kinds of vulgarity when talking about them, but in life it was not. The budding comics and entertainers, eager to make the 'big time' and impatient with customary refinements of taste, were ready to employ either kind of vulgarity – since they were themselves a compound of both – in order to hold audiences, first on the stoops and sidewalks, later in vaudeville and legitimate theatre.

And later still in films and on television. And once they made it to the top, they were forgiven the heartaches they caused while floundering at the bottom.

The Jewish dominance of Hollywood did not, of course, pass without comment. By the end of World War I it became clear that the cinema was becoming, if it had not already become, the supreme influence in the cultural life of America, affecting its tastes, its habits, its outlook. There was a growing clamour – to quote the words of one influential pressure group – 'to rescue the motion pictures from the hands of the Devil and five hundred un-Christian Jews'. To defend themselves against such criticism, Mayer, Laemmle, Goldwyn and the other un-Christian Jews grouped themselves into the Motion Pictures Producers and Distributors of America Inc., and invited Will H. Hays to preside over them. In doing so they were not merely attempting to buy-off criticism, they were buying respectability, for in the words of Philip French, Hays was everything they were not, an exalted product of middle-America, lean, abstemious, Presbyterian, well-educated. He had been chairman of the 1920 national convention of the Republican Party, which had stage-managed the election of President Harding, who, in turn, had made him Postmaster-General.

Hays forestalled attempts to establish state censorship by forming his own censorship code, strictly applied, so that bosoms were kept out of sight and extra-marital sex was, as far as possible, kept out of mind. For a time he was able to disarm some of the industry's most voluble critics, but he and his successor, Eric Johnston, proved fairly helpless when, after World War II, the form of the criticism changed and Hollywood came under attack from the House of Representatives Un-American Activities Committee as a place of dubious loyalty.

A historian of the film industry, Mr Terry Ramsaye, wrote in 1926:

> It is not an accident but rather a phase of the screen evolution which finds the American motion picture industry, and therefore the screens of the world, administered rather largely by our best and most facile internationalists, the Jews, with those of Russian extraction slightly predominant over the Germans.

This impression remained, and internationalism was no recommendation in post-war America. The many war films in which the Soviet ally was shown in a favourable light were now recalled against Hollywood and there were dark mutterings about Jewish-Communist conspiracies. To some American minds Jews and Communists were one.

The Hollywood tycoons themselves, in so far as they had any political sympathies, tended to be towards the right; Louis B. Mayer, for example, was active in the Californian Republican party. There were certainly among the writers, directors and artists a number of people with left-wing sympathies and not a few were confessed Communists. But there was certainly no proof that even avowed Communists had allowed their views to intrude upon the character or content of their pictures. Unfortunately the heads of the industry who formed the Motion Picture Association of America, the Association of Motion Picture Producers and the Association of Independent Motion Picture Producers, panicked, and when ten employees – one producer, two directors and seven writers – refused to answer questions put to them by the Un-American Committee, the producers declared:

> We will forthwith discharge or suspend without compensation those in our employ and we will not re-employ any of the ten until such time as he is acquitted or has purged himself of contempt and declares himself under oath that he is not a Communist.
>
> On the broader issue of alleged subversion and disloyal elements in Hollywood, our members are likewise prepared to take positive action. We will not knowingly employ a Communist or a member of any party or group which

advocates the overthrow of the United States by force or by any illegal or unconstitutional means.

In pursuing this policy, we are not going to be swayed by hysteria ...

But the whole statement was the result of hysteria, the action of frightened men unsure of themselves or what they stood for.

These were the years too when television began to topple the cinema as the prime source of public entertainment and Hollywood was in no condition to meet the challenge. They had, during their golden years, shown no inclination to put aside any substantial sums for research and development to examine new processes and techniques, and it was only when television was supreme that they produced a whole spate of innovations, three-dimensional cinemas, Cinemascope, Todd-Ao, Vistavision. The quality of films improved too, but if the cinema survived, albeit in a much attenuated form, the Hollywood of lore was no more.

The British film industry was a minor backwater compared to Hollywood, but it went through a brief golden phase in the immediate post-war years, the Ealing years, as they have sometimes been called, when Sir Michael Balcon, presiding genius of the Ealing studios, produced a series of comedies – like *Whisky Galore, Passport to Pimlico* and *Kind Hearts and Coronets* – which, though typical of English humour at its most English, delighted audiences well beyond the British Isles. One remembers the films rather better than their stars. The comedy arose out of the situation and dialogue rather than through the virtuoso performance of any particular individual. They were comedies without comedians, and if they employed any Jewish talent at all it was that of Balcon himself who, even if alien in origin, had reached under the skin of England. His Ealing films did for England what Louis B. Mayer had tried – through his Andy Hardy series – to do for America.

Jews are almost as numerous in television as they have been in the cinema trade, but the leaders of the industry, such as Paley and Sarnoff, have not yet descended into legend as have the Goldwyns, the Mayers, the Laemmles and the Cohns, nor are they likely to do so, for their power is not as arbitrary, nor has television got the same hold on the public imagination that films had in their hey-day. Moreover there isn't the tradition of selling the names of the heads of production as part of the finished product.

William Paley, the son of a Chicago cigar maker, became interested in radio as a means of selling his father's products, and in 1928 he paid $400,000 for a group of semi-defunct stations which he renamed the

Columbia Broadcasting System. Some forty years later his investment was worth about $70 million.

Paley began on the east coast and branched out westwards till he had a coast-to-coast network to rival that of the two other giants, ABC and NBC. With the growth of television after World War II, he pulled ahead to make CBS the premier network in the industry.

His main rival, the National Broadcasting Company, is the creation of a Russian immigrant, David Sarnoff, who began his business life as an office boy with the Marconi Telegraph Company in 1906 at the age of fifteen. Thirteen years later, when the Radio Corporation of America took over Marconi, he became commercial manager of the combined group and rose to be president in 1930. He set up NBC as an RCA subsidiary in 1926.

Unlike the film tycoons, both Paley and Sarnoff have shown a consistent interest in Jewish affairs. The latter was for many years on the board of the Jewish Theological Seminary in New York, and both he and Paley have been generous supporters of the Weizmann Institute of Science.

Paley revolutionized the television industry by removing programming control from the hands of the advertising agencies and placing it with the production companies, but the revolution was never carried far enough. The dominion of the sponsor remains, and with it the pandering to the lowest common denominator in public taste.

There is great professional slickness but little originality or depth or even distinctiveness of character. As in films there is the occasional memorable 'prestige' product, but the overall impression is one of triviality; glossy matter with little content, and anyone watching American television for any length of time begins to feel as if he has been subsisting on a diet of grape-nuts and Coca Cola.

In Britain, until 1955, radio and television were a state monopoly, and the quality of the output was of the highest. In 1955, however, commercial television was launched and in time comprised three networks and several smaller regional companies. The networks, Associated-Rediffusion, Associated Television and Granada were headed by Emil Littler, Lew Grade and Sidney Bernstein respectively, all of whom had spent a lifetime in show-business (Mr Bernstein, now Lord Bernstein, had a photo of Barnum, like some icon, placed in virtually every room in the company), and all three were Jewish. The head of one of the smaller commercial companies, a Canadian newcomer called Roy Thomson, later described a commercial television franchise as 'a licence to print money', and there was a scramble to get on to the television band-wagon. But that was after the breakthrough. The early days were painful and expensive, and one needed steady nerves and considerable capital to continue.

Although the system was different (programmes were not sponsored, and advertisers could only buy time without any say in the character or content of the programmes), the search for high ratings meant that at first the quality was not much above the American level (many of the most popular programmes, indeed, were American imports, which they still are). But the fact that franchises were periodically reviewed meant that the programme contractors had to show discernment and caution, and one programme company in particular, Bernstein's Granada TV, set a standard of excellence which the other companies felt compelled to follow and which, at its best, compared favourably with the best from the BBC, and this while maintaining high profits. Here, perhaps, was an example of the ultimate in enterprise, the ability to make money even from culture.

We have examined why so many entertainers are Jews, but why are so many hard-headed Jewish businessmen drawn into a calling whose ways are so unbusinesslike, whose nature is so demanding and whose rewards are so uncertain?

As a purely business venture it does not compare with, say, banking, insurance, the diamond trade or the fur trade, but then neither does publishing, and it too attracts many Jews. The very fact that show-business is not businesslike in its attitudes in itself attracts the type of entrepreneur who is not particularly well-organized or efficient, but has a ready eye for opportunities. Showmanship in itself is a creative function, for the marshalling of the disparate talents necessary to produce a musical or an opera, or even an orthodox stage-play, calls for more than mere organizational abilities. Moreover, showmanship answers to an inherent streak of flamboyancy in the Jew. The greatest good, says the Talmud, is to study oneself, the second greatest is to enable others to study. The greatest joy is to be there out front, an artist in actual touch with the audience; the second greatest is to be behind the scenes, the king, the producer, the impresario, the angel. If one is even several stages removed from the actual show, something of its effect reverberates back, and half a loaf in show-business is eminently more satisfying than a loaf in say, the fur trade, though when one can get a whole loaf, as some do, it is more satisfying still. The show-business entrepreneur is a player *manqué*.

And finally there are women. Show-business has always attracted a great many young women who have much to show and who, moreover, are prepared to show it, and the Jewish business man has never turned a blind eye (a furtive eye sometimes, but never a blind one) to such attractions. The Rabbis have always been aware of a lascivious streak in the Jewish character. Of all the laws in the Torah, said the twelfth-century sage, Maimonides, those demanding sexual abstinence are the hardest to observe. Yet they were widely observed within the ghetto, and they did not lapse even without. The Jewish immigrants to New York and London left their Rabbis behind, but they were followed by Rabbinical strictures and restraints and the theatre was the one place where one could escape them. Show-business, therefore, offered less of a career than the possibilities of self-emancipation. It was a calling where even in puritan times a certain amount of licence was always expected, if not always forgiven. It has never been a profession for gentlemen or, indeed, ladies. Which brings one to our final paradox: the craving for respectability in the least respectable of callings. Hollywood tycoons would dress in the sober hue of bankers and line their office walls with signed photographs of public figures far removed from their calling. 'Don't tell your friends your father is in the cinema business,' William Fox cautioned his children.

A large slice of British show-business is in the hands of the brothers Winowgradsky, born in the East End, the sons of penniless Polish immigrants. One took the name Bernard Delfont and the other Lew Grade. Both began life as entertainers, soft-shoe dancers, jugglers, clowns; both became theatrical agents, acquired theatres, then branched out into films and television. Both were active in the Grand Order of Water Rats, the show-biz charity, and gave generously to other charities, such as the National Playing Fields Association, of which the patron is Prince Philip. Both were knighted. Delfont is sleek and debonair and looks like the head waiter of an expensive restaurant. Grade, with his bald head, underchin, paunch and long cigars is so representative of the popular idea of what show-biz tycoons look like that one sometimes suspects he plays the part. Both are now in the House of Lords.

Is it possible that a nemesis may have overtaken show-business? The work ethic, the idea that endeavour is worthwhile in itself, and will in the long run bring its due reward, is fading from Western life because, apart from anything else, the young have come to regard the due reward as part of their birthright. One does not feel compelled to struggle for what one has never lacked. The average factory-hand with his forty-hour week and his five weeks paid holiday enjoys more leisure than the average landed gentleman of a century ago, and show-business has moved from the margins of society towards the centre. Indeed those elements of society which are necessarily at its very centre, namely the politicians, work so closely with show-business and mingle so frequently with show-biz folk that one cannot always tell one from the other. Show-business not only generates millions at one end of the scale, but receives millions from the public purse at the other. It is becoming, if it has not already become, part of the ruling establishment, which does not necessarily mean that it has become respectable, though it possibly suggests that the ruling establishment is not what it was.

CHAPTER SIX

Herr Doktor

In Judaism, studiousness is not merely next to Godliness, it is part of Godliness. No religion, certainly no major religion, has ever put such stress on study. 'Whoever labours in the Torah for its own sake', said the Talmud, 'merits many things; and not only that, but the entire world is indebted to him; he is called a friend, beloved, a lover of the Omnipresent; it clothes him in meekness and reverence; it induces him to become just, pious, upright and faithful; it keeps him far from sin and brings him near virtue; through him the world enjoys counsel and wisdom and under-standing and strength.' Good in itself, it is the source of all goodness.

Maimonides, the twelfth-century Jewish philosopher, declared:

Every man in Israel is obliged to study the Torah, whether he is firm of body or infirm, whether young or old and feeble. Even a pauper living on charity and obliged to beg from door to door, and even a breadwinner with a wife and family to support, must set aside a period for study by day and night . . .

The effect of this doctrine was to establish a tradition of near universal literacy so that even if not all were equipped to study, nearly all felt com-pelled to try. There were great academies in Palestine long before the birth of Christ, but the greatest centres of learning were in the cities of Sura, Pumpeditha and Nahardea in Babylon, which flourished from about the third century until the eleventh century AD. As Jews migrated west-wards other academies were established in North Africa, Spain and the Rhine Valley, and then, after the sixteenth century, Poland and Lithuania became the main centres of Jewish learning. The field was narrow. Maimonides, who was a polymath,* with interests ranging from mathe-matics and medicine (he was said to be physician to the Court of Saladin) to Greek philosophy, was an exceptional case. Generally there was a fear that non-Jewish subjects could lead the student astray and certainly the

* person of encyclopedic learning

Polish and Lithuanian academies closed their eyes to the world beyond the Talmud.

Towards the end of the eighteenth century there came a revolt against both the tradition of scholasticism and the dominance of the scholars. This was the Hassidic movement, which argued that a man could also reach the kingdom of heaven through piety and prayer, and that good deeds were more important than great learning. But there was never any serious threat to the old ideal, for the Hassidic masters in time succumbed to the scholastic tradition, and instead of arguing that piety brought one to a higher plane than study, the belief spread that one could not have one without the other, which is to say the scholar, even if not pious by instinct, would be induced to piety by his learning, and that the pious would be pushed to study by their piety.

It was, on the whole, a benign tradition, especially where the Jewish population expanded while employment opportunities narrowed. It kept many young minds occupied which might otherwise have turned to less wholesome interests and when the universities finally opened, as they did in western and central Europe after the Napoleonic wars, Jews rushed towards them like water through the crack of a dam. It does not mean that the Talmudist immediately abandoned his Talmud (though some did), but it did mean that the tradition of study *lishmo*, as a sacred duty for its own sake, had now assumed a secular form. Jews crowded the schools of medicine, and the science schools. They flowed into the departments of law. They studied ancient languages and obscure cults. They poured into the conservatories. At first it was only the sons of the prosperous merchants who could afford the privileges of an education, but as the doors remained open the less prosperous raised their aspirations and scraped and saved to give their sons a step up in life. Sometimes the sons paid for their education by acting as tutors to the wealthy. Tuition, indeed, became a form of out-door relief for the ambitious sons of the Jewish lower middle-class (few Jews ever thought of themselves as being anything less, though Jews rarely thought in class terms).

The universities opened new avenues to advancement. Jews were sub-ject to many disabilities and even where there were no formal restrictions on their entry to various trades or crafts they were still kept out by tacit understandings. In commerce, for example, they had to offer better service or lower prices than their competitors or engage in trades which the more established businessman shunned, like money-lending, or the old-clothes trade. The professions, however, offered the prospect of both solvency and respectability, not to mention the opportunity of deriving gratification from one's occupation as well as an income. And they gave scope to the original mind.

It was perhaps natural that Jews should excel most obviously in medicine. Every stricken minority will show a natural preoccupation with health, and in Jews this amounts almost to an obsession. When one Englishman greets another with 'How are you?' he will be answered with an almost automatic, 'Fine, thank you', or, at worst, 'could be better'. Among Jews the short retort is often, 'don't ask', for if one does ask, the answer will be a medical bulletin. Among Jews in Eastern Europe the parting greeting was not the meaningless 'cheerio' or 'goodbye' or even 'au revoir', but 'zei gezunt', 'stay well'. If a man should complain that his wife was extravagant, his children unruly, his servants dishonest and his business in ruins, he might always be comforted with the words, 'abi gezunt', 'as long as you're healthy', a precept which has not prevented many a Jew from working himself into an early grave. (If the Jewish expectancy of life is high it is mainly sustained by widows.) A large part of the Torah is concerned with the laws of hygiene, quarantine and cleansing and among the most fundamental duties which a Jew has – which is on a par with helping the needy – is visiting the sick. The expression zei gezunt, therefore, represents not merely a benign wish, but is tantamount almost to a positive commandment.

Today most major Jewish congregations will employ two full-time officials – a Rabbi and a Cantor. Until recently many had a third, a physician. Among Jews, as among other peoples, medicine and faith have always been intermingled and it is difficult to establish where the one finishes and the other begins. The priests were the first doctors, and the brass serpent held aloft by Moses so 'that if a serpent had bitten any man, when he beheld the serpent of brass he lived', was to become the symbol of the medical profession. Later, after the destruction of the Temple, when religious leadership devolved to the Rabbis, Rabbis too turned to medicine, gaining their skill through apprenticeship to established practitioners, which did not mean that they went in for faith healing or miracle cures. The high reputation which Jewish doctors were to acquire even in the non-Jewish world arose precisely from the fact that their treatment was based on careful scientific observation. The study of medicine formed part of the curricula of the ancient Talmudic academies, though the main stress was on social hygiene and on preventive medicine rather than cures. 'Bodily cleanliness,' said the Talmud, 'leads to spiritual cleanliness.'

Moreover, the very mobility of Jews, the fact that they were well versed in many languages, including Latin, Arabic and Aramaic, meant that they were well placed to transmit scientific knowledge from one area to another, and during the many centuries when Jews were confined to their own ghettos, Jewish physicians (like Jewish financiers) were to be found even in the royal courts – in spite of numerous papal enactments forbidding the treatment of Christians by Jews.

Many were Marranos, secret Jews, such as Roderigo Lopez, court physician to Elizabeth I (he was executed in 1594 on a charge of conspiracy: Tudor courts were a hazardous place, especially for a stranger from Catholic lands) and Antonio Sanchez, court physician to both Elizabeth of Russia and Catherine the Great. Other Marrano physicians held royal posts in Denmark, Sweden, Spain and the Ottoman Empire.

In the seventeenth century a Bohemian barber-surgeon called Israel Baer Teller published *Be'er Mayim Chayim* (the Well of Living Waters), which was perhaps the first home-doctor and which, though critical of both amulets and the astrological devices common to folk medicine, enjoyed a wide circulation. Written in Yiddish, it was, he said, intended to help poor people who could not afford doctors' fees.

In 1782 Joseph II's Act of Toleration threw open the universities of the Hapsburg lands to the Jews. His example was followed in the aftermath of the French Revolution in Germany and France, but even with open access to the universities it was still no advantage to be a Jew, and in the nineteenth century a baptismal certificate could be as useful as, if not more useful than, a doctorate. Not a few of the most honoured figures in European science, though of Jewish origin, were at least nominal Christians.

Friedrich Gustav Henle, a pioneer both in German anatomical studies and in pathology, was born Jacob Henle, the grandson of the Rabbi of Fuerth. He was baptized in 1820 at the age of eleven and studied medicine at Bonn, where he was the outstanding student of his generation. He then went on to become Professor of Anatomy and Physiology, first at Zurich, then at Heidelberg and finally at Goettingen. His life's work is summed up in the classic *Handbuch der Systematischen Anatomie*, but his researches were catholic in scope and ranged from the cornea of the eye to the human nail, and at least a dozen microscopic structures in anatomy were named after him. His studies in pathology led him to conclude that infectious diseases were caused by specific micro-organisms, a theory which, while not accepted during his lifetime, was confirmed by the researches of his pupil, Robert Koch. The very language of medicine, with Henle's loop and

Henle's membrane, Henle's warts, Henle's fissures, and Henle's sphincter is a memorial to his achievements.

Henle was outstanding not only through the originality of his vision but the very range of his inquiries, for in the main the Jewish speciality has been specialization. Discrimination in the established fields made the new areas more attractive, though the novelty itself offered greater scope for experiment and discovery and a greater challenge.

It is not quite certain why skin ailments should have become a Jewish speciality, but the number of Jewish doctors they attracted was so high that at one time dermatology was referred to in Germany as *Judenhaut* and numerous dermatological disorders, as well as remedies, carry the names of Jewish physicians, such as Kaposi's sarcoma, Unna's disease (seborrhoeic eczema) and Schamberg's disease (progressive pigmentary skin eruptions). Lassar's paste, which, until the discovery of cortisone, was the most widely used unguent for a host of skin ailments, was named after a Hamburg dermatologist, Oscar Lassar, who won the Iron Cross for bravery in the Franco-Prussian war and became Professor of Dermatology at the University of Berlin in 1902.

One possible source of interest in dermatology may be in the attention given by Mosaic law to skin ailments. Whole chapters of Leviticus are devoted to the subject with detailed provisions for quarantine and cleansing (no actual cure is prescribed, though the Talmud suggests that such ailments were unknown in Babylon 'because they eat turnips, drink beer and bathe in the Euphrates', an early instance of preventive medicine).

Their interest in dermatology placed Jewish doctors in the forefront of the battle against venereal diseases. An early pioneer was Antonio Sanchez, court physician to Catherine the Great, who introduced mercury salts in the treatment of syphilis. Lassar carried out some important experiments in the same field, but the scourge was finally contained largely through the efforts of August Von Wassermann, a bacteriologist, Paul Ehrlich, a chemist, and Ernest Chain, a biochemist.

Wassermann was born in Bamberg in 1866 and worked at the Berlin Institute for Infectious Diseases under Henle's pupil, Robert Koch. In 1906 he became head of the Serum Department at the Institute and in that same year he published, together with Albert Neisser and Carl Bruck, a method for the sero-diagnosis of syphilis which came to be known as the Wassermann test. It was left to his colleague, Paul Ehrlich, to devise a cure. Ehrlich, who was born in 1854, perfected a system for the evaluation of anti-toxic sera which placed the whole practice of immunology on a more scientific base. He was particularly interested in chemical compounds which would attack micro-organisms without harming the body cells, and it was as a result of researches in this field that, with the help of Hatta, his Japanese assistant, he developed compound '606' or 'Salvarsan', which was the greatest breakthrough in the treatment of syphilis since the disease reached Europe in the fifteenth century.

Ehrlich's work on immunology won him the Nobel Prize in Medicine and Physiology, shared with Elie Metchnikoff, a Russian-Jewish bacteriologist, who, among many other discoveries, introduced calomel (mercurous chloride) in the early treatment of syphilis. It was the discovery of penicillin, however, which brought the most dramatic results.

Penicillin was developed principally through the efforts of three men, Alexander Fleming, who made the initial discovery, and Howard Florey and Ernest Chain, who isolated the compound and made it available for clinical use.

Chain, the son of a Russian industrialist who made his home in Berlin, was born in 1906, and worked as a biochemist in the Pathological Institute of the Charité Hospital, Berlin until Hitler came to power. In 1933 he moved to Cambridge, 'not because I thought Hitler was here to stay', he later recalled, 'I regarded Nazism as a passing madness and thought it would all be over in six months', but to pursue research under Sir Frederick Gowland Hopkins, one of the foremost biochemists of his day. In 1935, on the recommendation of Hopkins, he joined Dr Florey at the Sir William Dunn laboratories at Oxford and in the following year he came upon a paper published by Fleming on the mysterious compound he had found forming on a mould and which displayed pronounced anti-bacterial properties. Chain thought it was worthy of further investigation. He received Florey's support and with the help of a grant from the Rockefeller Foundation they were able to set the project in motion. By 1943 the drug was available for field use by the allied armies, with dramatic results. Infections which had hitherto led to permanent disablement or death were eliminated in a matter of days. In 1945 Fleming, Florey and Chain were awarded the Nobel Prize.

After the war Chain carried his researches further as scientific director at the International Research Centre for Chemical Microbiology in Rome and developed an improved semi-synthetic penicillin which was at once more potent than its predecessor and showed fewer harmful side-effects. He returned to England in 1961 to take up the Chair of Professor of Biochemistry at Imperial College, London.

Penicillin, especially in its improved form, is the nearest thing to a panacea known to medicine. It has revolutionized the treatment of many infectious diseases and it has virtually eliminated venereal disease as a serious danger to health.

Professor Chain, who was knighted in 1969, has suggested that biochemistry is an area of science that has attracted more outstanding Jewish talent than any other, and it is certainly true that a significant proportion of Jews who have won Nobel Prizes in Medicine and Physiology were, like Chain, biochemists. They include Fritz Lipmann, who worked as a biochemist at the Kaiser Wilhelm Institute in Heidelberg till the rise of Hitler, when he joined the Biological Institute of the Carlsberg Foundation in Copenhagen. In 1939 he moved to America, where he eventually became Professor of Biological Chemistry at Harvard. In 1953 he shared the Nobel Prize with Hans Krebs for his discovery of the co-enzyme A and its importance for intermediary metabolism.

Krebs was born in Hildesheim and worked at the Kaiser Wilhelm Institute for Biology, Berlin and later at Freiburg, where he traced the cyclic process for urea synthesis in the liver. After the rise of Hitler he moved to England, working first in Cambridge, then in Sheffield, and finally in Oxford, where he became Professor of Biochemistry in 1954. Krebs, who was knighted in 1958, has given his name to the 'Krebs cycle', which is the process whereby foodstuffs are converted in the living cell into carbon-dioxide, water and energy, a discovery which takes one almost to the roots of human existence.

The work of Arthur Kornberg, an American-born biochemist,* who headed the enzymes and metabolism department of the National Institute of Health for a number of years, carried the process further through discovering the mechanisms of biological synthesis of ribonucleic acids and DNA, which gained him the Nobel Prize in 1959. (DNA – or deoxyribonucleic acid – forms the genes which transmit hereditary characteristics in all living cells. His discoveries enabled scientists to prepare a completely synthetic form of the substance.)

Yet another biochemist to win the Nobel Prize for Medicine was Otto Loewi, who was born in Frankfurt in 1873 and, after holding various posts in Strasbourg, Marburg and Vienna, became Professor of Pharmacology in Graz. He experimented with frogs to show that the frequency of heart-beats was related to the release of various chemicals, particularly acetylcholine, in the nervous system, and in 1936 he shared the Nobel Prize for Medicine and Physiology with Sir Henry Dale. Two years later

* '37 B.S. at CCNY.

the Nazis marched into Austria and he was deprived of his post and possessions and held in prison for some months before being allowed to leave for England.

Otto Meyerhoff, a little improbably, combined the disciplines of biochemistry and psychology and was author of *Contributions to a Psychological Theory of Mental Diseases*. In 1918 he became Professor of Physiological Chemistry at Kiel and four years later he shared the Nobel Prize with A. V. Hill for work on 'the fixed relationship between the consumption of oxygen and the metabolism of lactic acid in the muscle', which explained the causes of fatigue. In 1929 he became head of the physiology department at the Institute for Medical Research, Heidelberg. The Nazis forced him out of his post and he worked first in France and then in America, where he became Research Professor at the University of Pennsylvania medical school.

Konrad Bloch, a biochemist, who won the Nobel Prize in 1964 for 'discoveries concerning the mechanism and regulation of cholesterol and fatty acid metabolism', was born in Neisse, Germany, in 1912 and moved to America shortly after graduating from the Munich Technische Hochschule, to join the staff of Columbia University. In 1954 he became Professor of Biochemistry at Harvard.

Bloch was immensely helped in his researches by the use of the carbon-14 isotope, a method pioneered by an American-born biochemist, Melvin Calvin, who became a Professor of Chemistry at the University of California at Berkeley in 1947. Calvin used the carbon-14 isotope to study the way in which living plants convert the carbon-dioxide in the atmosphere into sugar through the absorption of sunlight and chlorophyll, a discovery which gained him the Nobel Prize in Chemistry in 1961. He also worked on the Manhattan Project, which led to the creation of the first atomic bombs, and was a member of the US delegation to the 1955 General Conference on the peaceful uses of atomic energy.

When Krebs was at the Kaiser Wilhelm he worked under Otto Heinrich Warburg, scion of a famous German-Jewish banking family whose members showed skills in many other directions. One distant cousin was Aby Moritz Warburg, a noted art historian, another was Otto Warburg, a distinguished botanist. Otto Heinrich's own father, Emil, was a well-known physicist, who converted to Christianity. Otto was also baptized and worked for a time at the Physikalische Reichanstalt, Berlin, of which his father was president. He joined the Kaiser Wilhelm Institute for Biology in 1918 and in 1930 was appointed head of the Kaiser Wilhelm

Institute for Physiology, where he directed fundamental research in several areas, including the metabolism of tumours. In 1931 he received the Nobel Prize for his discovery of the nature and mode of action of the respiratory enzyme. In the following year he isolated the vitamin now known as riboflavin.[1] He also designed an apparatus for measuring the respiration of cells and tissues which is still widely used by biochemists. After 1945 he turned his attention to ways of improving the productivity of soil. He died in 1970 at the age of eighty-seven.

After the rise of Hitler, the Kaiser Wilhelm, which could probably have claimed the greatest confluence of scientific talent in the world, was quickly cleared of all Jews, semi-Jews and ex-Jews. Otto Warburg alone was left unmolested throughout the Nazi years, which is in itself a measure of his importance to German science, but there was no evidence that he was moved to any act of protest by the Nazi treatment of his Jewish colleagues.

Fritz Haber, who won the Nobel Prize in 1918 for his synthesis of ammonia – a discovery crucial to the German war effort – became the director of the Kaiser Wilhelm Research Institute in 1911 and reorganized it after World War I to make it the leading physical chemistry centre in the world. He, like Warburg, had abandoned the Jewish faith, and like him, might have been left unmolested, but when, after the accession of Hitler, he was required to dismiss his Jewish staff, he resigned and went into exile.

Richard Willstaetter, a German organic chemist whose research into plant pigments won him the Nobel Prize and who familiarized the world with the properties of chlorophyll, also made a major contribution to the German war effort, and was awarded the Iron Cross for his work on gas-masks. After the war he became head of the State Chemical Laboratory. He was also Professor of Chemistry at Munich, but in 1929 he resigned his chair in protest at the virulent anti-semitism which he encountered. In 1939, after his house had been ransacked by the Nazis, he was expelled from Germany and made his home in Switzerland, where he died in 1942. 'Of genius there is no dearth,' he said, 'but character is a rare article.' His words might almost have been specifically directed at Warburg.

If penicillin is one of the most important medical discoveries of recent times, another which can almost rank beside it is streptomycin, a product derived largely from the work of Selman Waksman, a microbiologist, who was born in Russia in 1888 and was brought to America as a small child. He invented the term antibiotic to refer to the substance produced

[1] B₂

by one micro-organism engaged against another. His first antibiotic, streptothricin, proved too toxic for therapeutic use, but further experiments, some of which made use of discoveries he had made as early as 1916, led to streptomycin, which had the power of streptothricin without its toxicity. It proved to be a broad spectrum antibiotic and was particularly useful in the treatment of tuberculosis. In 1952 he received the Nobel Prize for his work.

The incidence of cholera was dramatically reduced through a vaccine developed by the Russian bacteriologist, Waldemar Mordecai Haffkine, who studied under Elie Metchnikoff at Odessa, but left Russia when he saw there was no prospect of employment without converting to Christianity. He worked for a time at the Pasteur Institute in Paris and then, on the invitation of the Marquis of Dufferin and Ava, a former Indian Viceroy, he moved to Calcutta, and applied his anti-cholera vaccine with excellent results. In 1896, he developed a further vaccine to cope with an outbreak of plague in Bombay and in the following year Queen Victoria made him a Companion of the Order of the Indian Empire. Five years later, however, when the plague struck the Punjab, nineteen people died of tetanus after inoculation with the vaccine and Haffkine was charged with negligence. He eventually cleared his name and in 1925, a few years before his death, the Plague Research Laboratory which he founded in Bombay was renamed the Haffkine Institute.

In recent years an increasing number of Jews have found themselves involved in geriatrics. This may in part be ascribed to the traditional Jewish veneration for age and the aged, and a tendency to strive officiously to keep alive. 'Never say die' may not be a Jewish expression but it does represent a Jewish attitude, and no matter how old a patient, how depleted his faculties and diseased his organs, he will continue to receive treatment. It is not enough for him to give up the ghost; the ghost will have to give him up before he is written off.

There are, of course, other factors. Recent medical discoveries have eliminated some familiar killers and reduced the virulence of others (such as pneumonia). As a result geriatrics has become one of the major growth areas in medicine. New prospects naturally attract newcomers and Jews have done much to relieve the many crippling disorders which come with old age. Thus, for example, cortisone, corticosterone and cortisol derive mainly from the researches of Tadeus Reichstein, a Polish-born and Swiss-educated organic chemist who, with E. C. Kendall and P. Hench, won the Nobel Prize in 1950 for 'discoveries relating to hormones of the adrenal cortex'. Reichstein was also the first man to produce a completely synthetic vitamin (ascorbic acid, or vitamin C).

Poliomyelitis ('polio') has been brought under control largely through the efforts of two Jewish scientists working in distinct areas who, within a few years of each other, developed effective vaccines. First in the field was Jonas Salk, a young, New York-born epidemiologist, who had been working on an influenza vaccine for the American army. In 1949 he became Research Professor of Bacteriology at Pittsburgh University where, after prolonged field trials, he developed the anti-polio vaccine which bears his name.

The Salk vaccine, prepared by inactivating the polio virus with formalin, has been largely superseded by the Sabin vaccine, which employs a live, though attenuated virus, and which, taken orally, has almost wiped out the disease.

Albert Sabin was born near Bialystock, Poland in 1906 and came to America at the age of fifteen. He began his research career in the bacteriology department of the New York University College of Medicine, and worked at the Lister Institute, London and the Rockefeller Institute for Medical Research before joining the Cincinnati Children's Hospital Research Foundation. His polio vaccine, which became available for general use in 1961, was the result of thirty years' work on the mechanism of immunity to viruses, and the impact of viruses on the nervous system.

An area of medicine which Jews have made almost their own is psychiatry, though it is perhaps still too early to say whether it constitutes a positive advance in human welfare. Its founding father was, of course, Sigmund Freud, whose immediate disciples, with the exception of his biographer Ernest Jones, were all Jews. Jones himself ascribes this fact to the inherited Jewish capacity to stand their ground in the face of all opposition, and for many years Freud encountered nothing less.

The true pioneer in the field was perhaps a Viennese physician, Joseph Breuer, who taught at Vienna university and specialized in diseases of the nervous system. Breuer originated the theory of equilibrium through his researches on the role of the semi-circular canals in the ear, and developed the catharsis method in the treatment of neuroses by encouraging patients to relate circumstances of their neurosis while under hypnosis. The celebrated case of Anna O, which he related to Freud, led Freud to conclude that many of the things festering in the mind never attain consciousness and can be brought to light only by psychoanalysis. In 1895 he collaborated with Breuer on their epoch-making *Studies in Hysteria* but their collaboration ended over Freud's insistence that sex, and especially infantile sex, was at the source of many, if not most emotional disturbances. Freud, who had hitherto used hypnosis, turned to free association as a method of psychoanalysis. A great deal of neurosis, he believed, arose from the suppression of unacceptable instincts in the subconscious, which then sought other means of gratification which, in turn, could result in hysteria and other disorders. In this we may see why psychiatry had such a ready appeal to the Jew and why so many psychiatric patients were Jewish, for apart from the normal standards of behaviour which made some instincts unacceptable was the Mosaic standard which rendered them absolutely taboo. The instincts of the Jew had more to wrestle with, and they were more likely to be suppressed, which in turn, or so Freud's disciples argued, gave rise to a greater incidence of hysteria.

Freud, who was born in Moravia in 1856 and studied medicine in Vienna, limited himself initially to neurological research. In 1885 he went to Paris to work under the famed neurologist Jean Charcot at the Salpêtrière mental hospital. He studied the clinical symptoms of organic diseases of the nervous system and paid particular attention to the pathology of hysterical paralysis. It was these observations which convinced him that in many cases repression was the cause of the hysteria, and he argued that psychotherapy could allow normal judgment to take the place of conditioned response. His theories on the importance of sex from earliest infancy and on the Oedipus complex were published in *Three Essays on the Theory of Sex* in 1905. He also, through self-analysis, studied dreams, which he defined as the disguised fulfilment of a repressed wish.

His ideas, especially on sex, were rejected by most of his colleagues but he managed to draw round himself a core of devoted followers who spread his gospel. He was perhaps at the source of the sexual liberation, but possibly his most important influence was on social policy, for as a result of his work it came to be gradually accepted that even a so-called normal person was not entirely responsible for his actions and that the delinquencies of a delinquent often arose out of his circumstances.

Freud, though not a practising Jew, never disowned his Jewishness. 'Because I was a Jew,' he wrote, 'I found myself free of many prejudices which restrict others in the use of their intellect: as a Jew I was prepared to be in opposition and renounce agreement with the compact majority', including, he might have added, the Jewish majority. He denied the material truth of religion, and in his *Moses and Monotheism*, which he wrote at the age of eighty, he argued that Moses was an Egyptian, that the

Children of Israel had rebelled against him and killed him and that this act of patricide had burdened the Jews with eternal guilt-feelings. But more than his excursions into theology and history, his theories were a complete negation of everything that Judaism – with its stress on individual responsibility – stood for.

Yet, there is something intensely Jewish about the very nature of Freudianism. Traditional Jewish scholarship was never content with deriving the obvious from the evident. Things are not always what they seem, words do not always mean what they say. One was trained to read between the lines, and between the words, and indeed, within the words, for hints, clues and hidden meanings, so that it was almost inevitable that if someone was to force the subconscious to surface it would be someone like Freud. His very definition of the Id, the Ego and the Super Ego correspond in many ways to the three different gradations of spirit – the *nefesh*, *ruach* and *neshamah* – outlined in the Kabbalah, which does not mean that Freud was himself a Kabbalist, but something of the Kabbalistic tradition of inquiry seems to have affected his outlook.

That psychiatry has become a Jewish speciality may derive from the fact that it is concerned with a type of disorder fairly common among Jews. Jews may or may not be more neurotic – and they could be forgiven if they were – but they are certainly less content to live with their neuroses. They believe that there is, or that at least there should be, a cure for everything, hence their eternal quest for a second, third, or even fourth opinion. There is a Talmudic saying that every malady carries its own remedy, so that even during the centuries when it was common to incarcerate the mentally ill, Jews still rummaged for a cure. And sometimes, with the help of this doctor, or that soothsayer, they even found one. But until the coming of Freud there was a disinclination to lay down the rules, for one was touching upon the anarchy of the human spirit. Which brings one to the final reason why psychiatry has such a ready appeal to the Jewish practitioner: each patient represents a new challenge.

The emergence of chemistry as a science, which is to say, its escape from alchemy, is almost contemporary with the emergence of the Jews from the ghetto and they are well represented among its early pioneers, though most of the more notable figures were half-Jewish or converts to Christianity. Adolf Von Bayer (1835–1917), who established organic chemistry as a distinct science, made his first chemical discovery – a double carbonate of sodium and copper – at the age of twelve. In 1860 he became professor at the Charlottenburg Technische Hochschule, Berlin, where he perfected a synthetic indigo which eventually replaced the natural product. His researches on alizarin had a similar effect and he laid the foundations of the vast German dye-stuffs industry. In 1905 he won the Nobel Prize for his work on organic dyes and hydro-aromatic compounds.

Heinrich Caro, who was born in Posen in 1834 and brought up in Berlin, made some of his most important chemical discoveries while working for Robert Dale of Manchester, where he developed several synthetic dyes including Manchester Yellow. He eventually returned to Germany, and in 1868 he became technical director of Badische Anilin und Sodafabrik, which later became the main component of the gigantic I.G. Farben. The compound monopersulphuric acid is still known as 'Caro's acid'.

Henry and Camille Dreyfus, who were born in Basle in the 1870s, introduced cellulose acetate to the textile industry and demonstrated its versatility by applying it as a thin film on the bodywork of British aeroplanes in World War I. After the war they discovered a method for spinning this film into a fibre which they called Celanese. Henry became chairman of British Celanese, while Camille headed the American and Canadian branches.

Adolf Frank was among the pioneers of the German potash industry and devised new means for the manufacture of bromides, ammonia and chloride. Though he built up a major concern he is perhaps less remembered than his son, Albert (1892–1965), who eased Germany's fertilizer famine during World War I through his discovery of calcium cyanamide. He also developed the use of acetylene black for dry batteries and held numerous other patents. In 1938, however, he was forced to flee Germany and for the next twenty years worked with the American Cyanamide Company.

One of the greatest names in chemistry was Fritz Haber (1868–1934), who was born in Breslav, the son of a prosperous chemical merchant. In 1906 he became Professor of Physical and Electro-chemistry at the Karlsruhe Technische Hochschule, where he developed the process of carbon bonds which bears his name. His most important work, however, which began in 1904, was the synthesis of ammonia from hydrogen and nitrogen.

Among the many outstanding scientists who worked with Haber at Karlsruhe was a young Hungarian, George Charles De Hevesy, who was working on radioactive isotopes, or 'labelled atoms', as they were then called, which became major tools in chemical and biological research and which gained him the Nobel Prize. After World War I De Hevesy joined Niels Bohr at Copenhagen for a time and together with Coster discovered a new element, number 72, or hafnium, and in the following years showed how isotopes could be used in biology and animal physiology. In 1926 he became professor at Freiburg and there developed X-ray fluorescence for the analysis of trace materials in minerals, rocks and meteorites. He left Germany after the rise of Hitler and returned to Copenhagen. In 1943 he fled with Bohr to Sweden.

Victor Meyer (1848–97), one of the most brilliant young scientists of his generation, was, among other things, an accomplished musician, but he made his career in organic chemistry. He obtained his doctorate *magna cum laude* at eighteen. At nineteen he became assistant to the great Bunsen. At twenty-three he became Professor of Chemistry at the Stuttgart Poly-technicum, and at forty he succeeded Bunsen at Heidelberg. Though dogged by dark bouts of depression and recurring ill-health, he applied himself ceaselessly both to his teaching and to research. He pioneered the new science of stereo-chemistry and made important discoveries in benzine derivatives. The very fervour with which he applied himself in so many fields suggested a fear that his time was short and he killed himself while at the height of his career at the age of forty-nine.

Chemistry is a comparatively old department of science, and it has attracted fewer Jews than a comparatively new one, like physics. Physics offers infinite scope to the theoretician, which is a further attraction. Jews, indeed, were drawn to theoretical physics – which is but an extension of mathematics – in such numbers that the Nazis spoke of it dismissively as *Judenphysik*.

Sir Rudolf Peierls, a Fellow of the Royal Society, himself a distinguished physicist, examined the reasons for the Jewish interest in physics in a recent volume called *Next Year in Jerusalem*:

The suggestion has been made that the intricate arguments of modern physics have some resemblance to Talmudic studies, and that people who grow up in an environment in which such studies are traditional find this mode of thought natural.

It is not an argument which he himself finds convincing, partly because he doubts if there is any such resemblance and partly because 'a large proportion of twentieth-century Jewish physicists came from families in which religious customs have not been observed for generations'.

There would, however, seem to be a connection between the Jewish pre-eminence in the most abstract of the abstract sciences, mathematics, and the Talmudic tradition, for although the study of the Talmud began as careful consideration of Jewish canon law it moved further and further from reality until it became an intellectual exercise almost for its own sake. The study of the Talmud, moreover, preserved a habit of mental agility, and a belief in academic excellence has persisted even where the tradition of Talmudic study has lapsed.

There were certain areas of study which the Talmudist shunned and there was always an inherent suspicion of what was known as *Chochmas Yavan*, Greek wisdom, which was regarded as pagan and likely to lead to idol worship. There was, however, no such fear, even among traditionally-minded Rabbis, of Islamic wisdom, so that Jews could turn to mathematics with a clear conscience. The Talmud itself, it must be added, is not too scientific in its method. For example, it used a verse in Kings 7:23 where the 'sea of Solomon' is said to be ten cubits in diameter and thirty in circumference as proof that pi equals three, and goes on to make numerous calculations on that basis. Rabbinic mathematics never in fact progressed beyond an elementary stage, partly because of the deficiencies of Hebrew numerals, which are based on the alphabet and which have no symbol for zero. Moreover, the fact that certain words added up to certain figures was in itself given significance so that, for example, the Rabbis concluded that a pregnancy lasted for two hundred and seventy-one days because the Hebrew term for pregnancy added up to that figure. The Jewish contribution to mathematics therefore dates from comparatively modern times and consisted initially in the introduction of Arab trigonometry and mensuration to the West. It was only with the opening of the universities in the nineteenth century that Jews assumed the role of innovators and one encounters figures like Karl Gustav Jacobi (1804–51), who made important contributions to the theory of homogeneous functions, spatial functions, calculus of variations, elliptical functions and the theory of numbers, and George Cantor (1845–1918), who established the mathematics of infinity and thus brought a new dimension to the science.

James Sylvester was Second Wrangler at Cambridge in 1837, but as a Jew could not matriculate. He was nevertheless elected a Fellow of the Royal Society and in 1841 he became Professor of Mathematics at the University of Virginia. His outspoken sympathy for the slaves, however, made it impossible for him to remain and he returned to England where he eventually obtained a chair at Oxford. Sylvester was possibly the greatest English mathematician since Newton, and his collaboration with Arthur

Cayley on the Theory of Invariants left a lasting influence on mathematical studies. The Royal Society struck a special commemorative medal to mark Sylvester's contribution to science, and its first recipient was George Cantor.

Karl Schwartzschild, who became director of Potsdam observatory in 1913, and Professor of Astronomy in the University of Berlin, was a child prodigy: he published a paper on celestial mechanics at fifteen. He was a polymath* who made fundamental discoveries in optics, electricity and atomic theory, and developed the new science of astrophysics, while his work on gravitation helped to confirm Einstein's Theory of Relativity.

Albert Einstein, who was born in Ulm in 1879, had never imagined himself as a scientist or theoretician: his laboratory was in his own head. His father, who owned a small electrochemical business, moved first to Italy and then to Switzerland, where Einstein graduated in mathematics from the Zurich Polytechnic and took a job at the patent office in Berne.

He remained in Berne for the next ten years and would have been quite happy to stay there for the rest of his life. He found the work congenial and undemanding and it left him with sufficient time to pursue his own researches. It was there that he produced three epoch-making papers. The first was on 'Brownian motion', the second – which won him the Nobel Prize for Physics – was on 'photoelectric effect'. The third, the 'Special Theory of Relativity', revolutionized thinking on such fundamentals as space, time and matter. Einstein was immediately pulled at from all sides with offers of professorships, and after holding posts in Prague and Zurich, he became a professor at the Royal Prussian Academy of Science. It was there that he developed his Special Theory into the General Theory of Relativity, which suggested, among other things, that large masses produce a gravitational pull which can warp the underlying field so that planets, for example, could be deflected from their paths, a theory which was confirmed a few years later by the expedition set up to observe the 1919 solar eclipse. From then on he was, a little to his dismay, no longer an obscure scientist, but a public figure and a household name.

Einstein, a small, frail being, with a large head, large careworn eyes and a white mane, conformed to the popular idea of the absent-minded professor. He was a trifle hazy in his ideas of what constituted proper dress, but he was very much alive to the world about him and infinitely saddened by it. When Hitler came to power in 1933 he immediately resigned his post in Berlin and made his home in America, where he became a

* person of encyclopedic learning

professor at the Institute for Advanced Studies, Princeton and where he remained till his death in 1955.

He was troubled about the misapplication of the discoveries of science. During World War II he alerted President Roosevelt to the feasibility of an atomic bomb. His own discoveries on the relationship between mass and energy indicated the possibility of such a product, but it was Leo Szilard, a Hungarian nuclear physicist who had worked in the Kaiser Wilhelm Institute until the rise of Hitler, and a fellow Hungarian, Eugene Wigner, who were aware how far the process had been carried, and who feared that Germany could soon be in a position to produce a nuclear explosion. They had tried to awaken the American authorities to this danger without effect. They then approached Einstein, whose intervention galvanized the authorities into action. A vast research plant was established at Los Alamos in New Mexico for the development of 'Tube Alloys', the code name for the atomic bomb.

The central figure in the operation was Niels Bohr, a Danish physicist, born in Copenhagen in 1885, the son of a Christian father and a Jewish mother (the daughter of David Adler, an eminent Danish banker and politician). Bohr studied in Manchester under Rutherford and in 1916 he became Professor of Chemical Physics at the University of Copenhagen. Six years later he won the Nobel Prize for his work on the release of nuclear energy. In 1920 he became head of the newly-formed Copenhagen Institute for Nuclear Physics, which in time became a place of pilgrimage for atomic physicists from all over the world. Among his co-workers was a brilliant young Italian Jewish physicist, Enrico Fermi. After the rise of Hitler, Bohr was joined by several refugees from Germany, including Lisa Meitner and her nephew, Otto Frisch, who had worked in the Kaiser Wilhelm Institute in Berlin on the bombardment of the uranium atom. Both were later to make their way to England, and Frisch went on to Los Alamos. Bohr himself fled from the Nazis in a fishing boat in 1943 and escaped to Sweden. He was brought to England in the bomb bay of a Mosquito, to act as consultant to Tube Alloys.

At Los Alamos the overall director was J. Robert Oppenheimer, a man of rare genius who, with his narrow head, lean features and pointed ears, had the appearance of an elongated pixie. Born in New York in 1904, the son of German Jewish immigrants, Oppenheimer was a child prodigy, who began collecting geological specimens at the age of five. He studied classics as well as physics and chemistry at Harvard, worked under Rutherford in Cambridge, and, in 1927, he went to Goettingen at the invitation of Max Born, a colleague and friend of Einstein's. He had no time for newspapers or radio, but taught himself Sanskrit as a diversion. He became director of Los Alamos in 1943.

James Franck, who had been Professor of Physics at Goettingen until Hitler came to power, moved to Johns Hopkins University in 1933. He had helped to develop Bohr's atomic theories and he too became an adviser to Tube Alloys. Enrico Fermi and Leo Szilard devised the uranium/graphite chain reaction which made the atomic bomb feasible. G. B. Kistiakowsky headed the explosives division at Los Alamos, while R. Bacher, Professor of Physics at Cornell, was charged with the assembly of the explosive core. Another senior physicist on the project, Rudolf Peierls, now Professor of Physics at Oxford, had worked with Otto Frisch on a paper which outlined the thermal diffusion method for the separation of uranium 235 and suggested how the bomb could be detonated. Their paper induced the British government to launch an atomic energy programme.

All saw the need for the bomb, in case the Germans should have it, but many objected to its use once it was made. Franck brought together a distinguished body of scientists who prepared a special document which became known as the 'Franck report', advising strongly against dropping the bomb. Oppenheimer himself, however, whose opinion was crucial, raised no objections.

Oppenheimer resigned from Los Alamos in 1945 and in 1947 became director of the Institute of Advanced Studies, Princeton, but he remained chairman of the General Advisory Committee of the Atomic Energy Commission and when the Commission sought to embark on the development of an H-bomb he used his influence against it. This involved him in a fierce conflict with a former colleague also of Jewish extraction, the Hungarian-born Edward Teller, who had worked with both him and Fermi to demonstrate the feasibility of such a bomb and who perfected the technical devices necessary to explode it. During the war Teller had urged that the H-bomb should be given priority over the A-bomb and he continued to press for it after the war, especially as there were indications that the Russians were working on a similar device. That these fears were not unfounded became clear in 1952, when the detonation of America's first H-bomb was followed shortly afterwards by a Russian one.

The conflicts which had gone on behind the scenes now came out into the open, and Oppenheimer, who had had a passing association with Communists in the 'thirties, was accused of disloyalty. In 1954 his security clearance was cancelled. This was during the height of the Cold War; but in 1963, after international tensions had eased a little, he was granted the Fermi Award by the Atomic Energy Commission for his work on nuclear research.

'Should another Moses arise and preach a Semitic exodus from Germany, and should he prevail, they would leave the land impoverished,' said Sir William Osler, an eminent English physician. 'There is not a profession which would not suffer the loss of many of its brilliant ornaments ...' These prophetic words may have been an exaggeration when they were uttered in 1884. They were hardly that by the time Hitler came to power some fifty years later.

Jews exerted themselves more feverishly, they were more ambitious and determined, and everything in their circumstances and traditions induced them to greater effort. There was nothing more exalted to a Jewish family than a doctor in its midst, preferably a doctor of medicine, for he carried the aura both of healer and scholar and as such was regarded with an almost sacred awe; but a doctor of science sufficed, or even of letters. All this may explain why so many sons from impoverished Jewish families managed to rise so fast in the professional middle classes, so that by 1925 about fifteen per cent of all Prussia's dentists, eighteen per cent of its doctors and twenty-five per cent of its lawyers were Jews. In Hungary at this time about half of the doctors, veterinary surgeons and engineers were Jewish. In Romania, where Jews formed only 4.5 per cent of the population, over a third of the doctors, dentists and vets were Jews. It does not entirely explain why so many Jews should have risen to the very pinnacles of their profession, and why they should have made so massive an impact on so broad a front. One does not become an Einstein or an Ehrlich because one tries harder and it does suggest an inordinate capacity for genius, or it would if all the figures we have mentioned were Jewish. Some were only half-Jewish or, according to Rabbinic law, were not Jewish at all, for only their father was Jewish. Some, though of purely Jewish descent, had not thought of themselves as Jews.

Some had converted to Christianity. Some had been converted by their parents and had not thought of themselves as anything other than Christians, but where they survived to the middle years of the present century they became Jews almost in spite of themselves, Hitler saw to that. Yet there was very rarely a re-examination of self as a result of their experience.

When the idea of a Jewish state, or at least a homeland for the Jews, began to crystallize, numerous people came forward with ideas for research centres and institutions of higher learning: a technical college in Haifa, a hygiene institute in Jerusalem, an agricultural research centre at Athlit and, Weizmann's particular dream, a Hebrew University in Jerusalem. There was little within Palestine itself to support a sizeable Jewish population. Jews would have to live by their wits (which, as we shall see, was not quite Herzl's idea). But apart from the distant aim there was the immediate fact of unemployed or underemployed Jewish talent. It was difficult for a Jew to get into university and difficult to find work when he qualified. Even in America, which to European eyes represented all that was open and free, several medical schools operated a tacit *numerus clausus* and until after World War II it was rare to find a Jewish faculty member in an Ivy League University.

Weizmann was able to recruit the help of people far removed from Zionism: scientists like Ehrlich, Wassermann, and Flexner (a Professor of Bacteriology at Johns Hopkins who was to become head of the Rockefeller Institute), and businessmen like Jacob Schiff, Nathan Straus, Julius Rosenwald, Ludwig Mond of ICI, and the French and English Rothschilds. By the mid-'thirties all his schemes came to fruition, and beyond them something that even he had not envisaged: a centre for advanced scientific studies at Rehovoth, now known as the Weizmann Institute.

When Hitler came to power, some of the foremost names in European science found themselves out of work, including giants like Willstaetter and Haber. Willstaetter, as we have seen, had resigned his chair at Munich University because of anti-semitism but he had continued to work at the Munich Academy of Science. Weizmann pleaded with him to come to Palestine, and he replied:

I know that Germany has gone mad, but if a mother falls ill it is no reason for her children to leave her. My home is in Germany, my University, in spite of what has happened, is in Munich, I must return.

And return he did, only to be expelled, and die in exile.

Weizmann snatched at other famous if lesser names, but with little success. In most cases science was their homeland, and when their work was disturbed by the intrusion of a madman they transferred, hardly raising their eyes from their microscopes, to another shore.

The most tragic case of all was perhaps that of Haber, who with his erect bearing, bald head and bristly moustache looked like the Prussian Junkers he admired and on whom, to some extent, he modelled himself.

A fiery patriot, he lent the full weight of his genius to the German armed forces during World War I, and, among other things, was instrumental in the development of both chlorine and mustard gas. After the war he sought to extract gold from sea-water to help pay for the indemnity imposed by the allies. Germany was everything to him, and there were times when he was made to feel everything to Germany. Every major honour was conferred upon him. He was one of the glories of German science, and he had converted himself and his family to Christianity to be more completely a part of the *Deutschesvolk*; but even he was not spared molestation, and when Hitler came to power everything crumbled about him.

Towards the end of his life he told Weizmann:

I was one of the mightiest men in Germany. I was more than a great army commander, more than a captain of industry. I was the founder of industries; my work was essential for the economic and military expansion of Germany. All doors were open to me. But the position I occupied then, glamorous as it may have seemed, is as nothing compared with yours. You are not creating out of plenty – you are creating out of nothing in a land which lacks everything; you are trying to restore a derelict people to a sense of dignity. And you are, I think, succeeding. At the end of my life I find myself bankrupt.

CHAPTER SEVEN

Alien Seed

Orthodox Jews – and until the nineteenth century few Jews were anything else – have tended to regard the artist and arts as, at best, frivolous, at worst, pagan. There was, of course, the Mosaic injunction against making a graven image, but this attitude extended beyond the plastic arts to the entire spectrum of creative effort, as if the very attempt to make the world a more beautiful or more wondrous place suggested that the Creator had done an imperfect job. If art was indeed 'man added to nature', then art was something Judaism could do without. And it is, on the whole, something that Judaism has done without.

The Mosaic injunction is quite emphatic:

Thou shalt not make thee any graven image, or any likeness of anything that is in heaven above, or that is in the earth beneath, or that is in the waters beneath the earth.

Although it has been more widely observed at some times than others it affected both attitudes and craftsmanship. When Solomon came to build his Temple, for example, the necessary skills were not available in Judea and craftsmen were brought in from Phoenicia. Ahab, likewise, had to resort to Phoenicians to build his 'House of Ivory'.

The situation improved (or, as Jewish writers of the period would have said, deteriorated) with the spread of Hellenic influence to the eastern Mediterranean. From the second century BC Greek cities began to rise in Palestine, complete with temples, gymnasia, baths and exquisite statuary, most of which was the work of imported architects and artists, but which reflected the more developed tastes of the ruling Jewish families. The figures, however, were anathema to many Jews because they represented both a breach of the law and the intrusion of an alien culture. In the short-run, at least, the traditionalists triumphed and as Hellenism was seen to be inimical to the very existence of Judaism, almost all representational art came to be regarded as alien and un-Jewish. Something of this belief has persisted throughout the ages and persists to this very day. It must, however, be added that the conflict of Judaism versus Hellenism was not so much a conflict between Jew and Greek as between one class of Jews and another. It was in the nature of a drawn-out cultural civil war which assumed different forms at different times and which spread far beyond Judea to the diaspora. In those areas where Hellenists were dominant – which tended to be areas where Jews were most prosperous and cultivated – one finds supreme examples of representational art.

Thus, for example, at Dura-Europos on the Euphrates, near what is now the Syrian-Iraqi border, a building was unearthed in 1932 which had all the hallmarks of a pagan temple including masks and figures generally associated with Dionysus, Cybele, Aphrodite and other Greek cults, but which had the ark and other appointments of a synagogue, and which most scholars are convinced was a synagogue. Yet the entire wall area from floor to ceiling is covered with paintings depicting Jacob and his sons, Joseph in Egypt, the childhood of Moses, Samuel anointing David, all attesting to considerable artistry and not inconsiderable wealth. The synagogue was built in the third century and the figures are arrayed in the dress of the day, some in Greek robes, others in Persian, and one can trace the work of at least two painters, one working within the Hellenic tradition, the other strongly influenced by eastern art.

Figurative drawings have been found in several Galilee synagogues, and a sixth-century synagogue at Beth Alfa in the Beth Shahn valley has a mosaic floor with the signs of the Zodiac at the centre, flanked by several Biblical scenes. But nothing has yet been discovered to match the quality and scale of the Dura-Europos murals and it is suggested that the synagogue may have housed a Jewish sect which, while adhering to tradition, did not feel bound by the injunctions of Rabbinic Judaism. It is even possible that they may have been early Christians and there is a picture which is said to depict Moses reading the Torah but which could equally have been a portrait of Christ. The murals are also important to the history of art as a confluence of eastern and western styles which emerged as Byzantine.

One finds mythological figures sculptured in relief on Jewish sarcophagi in the Rome catacombs, and they, almost symbolically, contain some of the last examples of Jewish figurative art between Roman times and our own.

The collapse of the Roman empire led to the gradual extinction of the Hellenistic strain in Jewish culture and the rise of Islam tended to reinforce Rabbinic hostility to figurative art. Jewish artistry found its main outlet in calligraphy and Arabesques (though scribes working on holy writ had to follow closely-defined forms and could not, like their Moslem counterparts, let their imagination run away with them).

The superb decorations in the surviving medieval synagogues in Cordoba and Toledo in Spain suggest that even with its self-imposed limitations, Jewish art forms could achieve striking results, except that the forms were not intrinsically Jewish, but Moorish designs adapted to Jewish use.

In northern Europe one found the occasional synagogue decorated with stained glass, though the best-known example of such work, the stained glass windows in the twelfth-century Mainz synagogue, were removed on the orders of the Rabbi Eliakim ben Joseph. Murals of animals and birds were tolerated in some synagogues, but as a rule even they were discouraged.

One finds human forms in Hebrew illuminated manuscripts, but only up to the neck. The heads are usually of birds or wolves or lions, and one could be forgiven for believing that medieval Jewry was involved in a form of animal worship. Many surviving examples of such work are to be found in *Hagadoth*, the liturgy read at the Passover table, and in the scroll of Esther read on the festival of Purim.

Illustrations among Christians had a practical purpose, for, whether they took the form of murals or illuminations, they helped to tell the Bible story to the illiterate worshipper or, to use an expression of the period, they served as sort of *Biblia pauperum*, the Bible of the poor. Among Jews, however, there was, even in the Middle Ages, a tradition of near universal literacy.

Moreover, a powerful and wealthy church could afford to be, and of course was, a major patron of the arts. The recurring massacres in Europe, the frequent expulsions, the constant wandering, gave a sense of impermanence to Jewish life which hardly encouraged the emergence of an artistic tradition. Synagogues were often rudimentary, and if they kept out the cold and the rain it was as much as their congregation demanded, or, at least, were in a position to pay for.

Where they had money, they preferred to expend it on ceremonial ware associated with the synagogue and the festivals, which had the supreme advantage of being portable. There developed a tradition of *hiddur mitzvah* (which was frowned on by the more puritanical Rabbis), of gilding ritual with one's most treasured possessions. Thus most households, no matter how impoverished, somehow acquired silver candle-

sticks for the Sabbath, and chalices for *kiddush,* to which the more prosperous added herb holders for the *havdalah* ceremony (at the close of the
Sabbath), citrus holders for the feast of Tabernacles, *seder* trays for Passover,
and candelabra for the feast of Chanukah, which, in the main, appear to
have been the work of Christian silversmiths. Attempts were made to
employ Jewish craftsmen for the manufacture of plates, pointers and silver
bells adorning the scrolls of the law. The designs were often crude and
excessively elaborate, with filigree here and stones there, and what they
lacked in delicacy they tended to make up for in bulk. The rich brocades
which formed the immediate covering of the scrolls as well as the curtains
of the ark did, however, give rise to a tradition of exquisite needlework
and embroidery, which perhaps had its finest flowering in the Pale of
Settlement and south Arabia and which is still not extinct.

The inhibitions against graven images began to break down in the
seventeenth century and by the eighteenth we find even the portraits of
revered Rabbis appearing on engravings and in miniatures (an area,
incidentally, in which Jews were fairly prominent until the coming of
photography).

Rabbi Solomon Hirschel (1762–1842), Britain's first Chief Rabbi,
allowed his portrait to be painted, engraved, published (and sold), printed
in the frontispiece to a prayer book, struck as a medal and even distributed
as a plaster bust (it was a flattering portrait). The easing of the prohibition
did not, however, lead to any sudden effulgence of Jewish art. The few
Jewish painters one hears of at this time, like Francesco Ruschi, whose
work anticipated the eighteenth-century Venetian Renaissance, were
converts to Catholicism. They would hardly have been heard of otherwise. And even in comparatively modern times, when it was not impossible for an avowed Jew to gain recognition as an artist, being a Jew was no
advantage, and not a few became Christians. Johannes and Philip Veit, for
example, the sons of a Berlin Jewish banker, and the grandsons of the
eighteenth-century Jewish philosopher Moses Mendelssohn, were not
only baptized but became leading members of the Nazarene school of
painting which concentrated on devotional subjects and introduced a
new style into European art.

Possibly the first professing Jew to enjoy more than local fame as an
artist was Moritz Oppenheim (1799–1882), whose richly wrought scenes
from Jewish life have become almost the standard illustrations for any
work on the subject. He depicted the golden years of German Jewry, that
is the years between emancipation in the early decades of the nineteenth

century and the resurgence of anti-semitism in the later ones, and produced what might be called a Jewish version of the Dutch interior, though without its austerity. The colour is rich to the point of being gaudy, the detail is intricate and he approached his subject with a sentimentality and romanticism which, to the modern eye, is a little cloying. But they went down well with the Victorians and he enjoyed an immense success with the Jewish bourgeoisie. The Rothschilds were among his patrons, and if he was known as the painter of the Rothschilds in his early years, he was dubbed the Rothschild of the painters in his later ones. Yet there was a time when he nearly went the way of the brothers Veit. He was deeply influenced by the Nazarene school and in fact first made his name with Old and New Testament paintings in the Nazarene style. Something of its influence persists in his Jewish drawings, and in the affection and reverence he brought to his subject. Goethe praised his work, the Duke of Weimar made him an honorary professor and he was commissioned to paint a series of portraits of past emperors for Frankfurt's medieval town hall. He was a supreme draughtsman with an extraordinary eye for detail, but if he is remembered at all today it is probably because of his figures and scenes from Jewish life, an area which had remained neglected since Rembrandt.

Another artist who was to touch on the same area was Josef Israels (1824–1911), the son of a Dutch money-changer. But his Jewish paintings such as *Saul and David* and *The Jewish Wedding*, which he treated in the style of Rembrandt (so much so, indeed, that they were almost pastiche), formed the less memorable part of his work. His reputation rests mainly on his landscapes with their pastel shades of green and grey, and his portraits of fishermen and peasants, which are rich with insights rarely found in the work of his contemporaries. It happens sometimes that the Jewish observer, though an outsider both as an artist and a Jew, is better equipped to capture the spirit of a locality than the native artist.

Max Liebermann (1847–1935), the son of a Berlin industrialist, was equally fascinated by Dutch landscapes, their coolness, their calmness, their austerity and pallor, and captured their mood and tone with equal skill. (He returned to Berlin at the end of the century and became President of the Berlin Academy, a post from which he was ousted by the Nazis.)

The John Constable of the Russian landscape was a Lithuanian Jew called Isaac Ilitch Levitan (1861–1906), who enjoyed the friendship and admiration of Chekov. In a sense, he was to the eye what Chekov was to the mind, and paintings like *After the Rain* and *Hay Harvest* convey the haunted quality of the Russian plains, their vastness, their openness, their melancholy. 'This full-blooded Jew', wrote the journal *Nvovoya Vremya* with chagrin, 'knew better than anyone else how to teach us to understand and love our soil and our country.' He influenced a whole school of Russian painting and echoes of his work persist to this day.

Levitan himself was influenced by the Impressionists (as, indeed, was Liebermann, a fact which he did not care to acknowledge), and one of the greatest artists to be born and remain a Jew, Camille Pissarro (1831–1903), was a leading Impressionist who held the group together long after its founders, Cézanne, Renoir and Monet, had dropped out. He was born into an old Sephardi family which had made its home in the West Indies, but he spent most of his life in Paris. His wife was of Catholic peasant stock. A self-portrait in the Basle museum shows a black-hatted, elderly figure, with a white flowing beard, who might have been the head of a Hassidic sect. His appearance belied his temperament, for he was something of a revolutionary, both in his work and his convictions, and he was constantly experimenting with new styles, new colours, new techniques. But though he came in for more than his share of abuse, he lived long enough to acquire esteem, if not prosperity. He had eight children and domestic need forced him to flood the market with canvasses, some of which – such as his cityscapes and landscapes – are amongst the best-loved examples of their genre. But he might have been more highly regarded had he been less fecund. He thought of himself as a citizen of the world, without national, racial or religious ties. He would have been appalled to be thought of as a Jewish artist and there is nothing in his work, his style or his subject matter which could in any way be ascribed to his background.

In the nineteenth century, Jewish artists, though no longer unheard of, were still uncommon, and it was only in the early years of this century that they began to appear in sufficient numbers to form an identifiable group, though what established their identity was not so much their background as the vivaciousness of their work.

The best known among them began to be spoken of as 'The Jewish School of Paris', and their influence was such that murmurings were heard about French art and taste being corrupted by foreigners and Jews. Zadkine, Orloff and Lipchitz were amongst the masters of the Cubist School, and a number of minor Jewish painters enjoyed a passing fame as Dadaists and Surrealists, but the lasting names, though they worked together, starved together and eventually – if in some cases only posthumously – triumphed together, were really too disparate and individualistic to be spoken of as a School. There is little in the work of, say, Chagall, Modigliani, Soutine and Pascin to suggest a common source of inspiration, a common style or even a common subject matter.

They occupied something of a ghetto in Montparnasse, and showed a zest for living which was not always depicted in their work. The mild, delicate forms and the subdued tints of Modigliani did not quite go with the raging fire of his own existence, though the work of Soutine and Chagall was rather more full-blooded.

Modigliani was born in Leghorn, the son of a small businessman. After studying in Florence and Venice, he came to Paris at the age of twenty-two. He learned much from the work of Cézanne, Gauguin and Toulouse-Lautrec, but he also admired African sculpture, which had a considerable effect on his style. His paintings were mainly portraits. His sitters look a little lifeless and spent, but it is difficult to say whether this reflected his own weariness, or that of his sitter. Yet one also finds a glowing serenity about them which immediately establishes their distinct character. They suggest a pensiveness and composure which were completely absent from his own life. Modigliani came almost to symbolize the excesses and dissipation of Left-Bank Bohemianism and when his friend, the sculptor Jacques Lipchitz, remonstrated with him, he retorted that he wanted *'une vie brève mais intense'*, a short life, but a full one, and so it was to be. Frail and neglected, he died of tuberculosis at the age of thirty-six.

An Italian critic, Paulo d'Ancona, has suggested that had he lived longer, he might have emerged as the greatest Italian painter of the century 'and amongst the most significant of all times', which perhaps overlooks the decadence which can come with years. It is, however, undoubtedly true that his legend has as much to do with his posthumous success as with the quality of his work. Many critics would today argue that he was over-sold, but it is worth recalling the opinion of Cocteau that he was 'the simplest and noblest' of an heroic age.

Chaim Soutine was born in Lithuania, the tenth of eleven children of an impoverished tailor. At the age of thirteen he ran away from home and managed to enrol at the Vilna School of Fine Art (his first teacher, a man called Kruger, advertised himself as 'teaching painting in three months'). There he was befriended by a local doctor who admired his work and who sent him to Paris, where he shared a garret with Modigliani. For a time they even shared a bed, in which they slept in turn. Their work could not have been more different.

If Modigliani meant serenity, Soutine meant turbulence, a turbulence which makes even his still-life paintings seem animated. He was a bleak, unhappy figure, deriving little from friendship, from life, or even from his art. There was something rather austere about his subject matter, the herrings, the dead turkeys, the bleeding carcasses, but there was nothing austere about his colours, which were rich, sensuous, and, in a strange way, almost luminous. The forms, however, are vaguely contorted, so that even his still-life paintings seem to experience some inner torment; one can almost hear them crying out. When he was exiled near Tours during the war, he complained of the flat land and the straight trees. 'I need twisted trees,' he protested, and so they emerged, as did his figures. He quarrelled with his patrons, with his neighbours, with those who sought to befriend him. No professional model would sit for him for any length of time and he turned eventually to peasants and children. Yet the former do not reflect the freshness one might have expected of them, nor the latter the innocence.

He had no life beyond his work and was so far removed from reality that when the Germans marched into Paris in 1940 he had little inkling of the danger he faced. He was soon awakened to it, and he had to scurry from place to place, bent double with an intestinal disorder which was becoming increasingly acute. By the spring of 1943 he was desperately ill, and he was smuggled into Paris in a hearse to undergo an operation. It was too late, and he died in hospital. He was forty-nine.

There was nothing in his subject matter, and nothing in his utterances or writing (and he was a man of few words) to suggest anything Jewish in his work, unless one should consider the herrings in his *Still Life with Herrings* as falling into that category. But this has not prevented critics from sensing Jewishness everywhere and the American painter Morris Davidson has described his work as 'saturated with the childish, savage mysticism of his Hebrew heritage'. 'Soutine', he believed, 'was more poet than painter, and most of all, high priest of the synagogue.'

Soutine had left home as a young boy, and had had sufficient opportunity to jettison any part of his Jewish heritage with which he may have been encumbered. Withdrawn from all contact with Jewish life, it is unlikely that he would have remembered what the inside of a synagogue looked like. He rarely spoke Yiddish, though it was his mother tongue, and he disapproved of foreigners in Paris speaking in any language other than French. Maurice Sachs described him as a 'mournful Jew'. Mournful he may have been, but with his round face and thick muscular hands he looked more like a Russian peasant. Nor was there any touch of buoyancy or hope in his work which might have suggested an innate Jewish optimism. If, as Davidson said, he was more poet than painter, then he was the poet of despair, which is certainly un-Jewish. Perhaps the most telling fact of all is that he was not even Jew enough to feel a tremor in his soul when Hitler entered Paris, and it may safely be said that any Jewishness evident in his work lies mainly in the eye of the beholder.

In this respect one is on safer ground with Marc Chagall, for here is an artist whose Jewishness is central to his very spirit, or, as he himself has written:

... had I not been a Jew I would have never been a painter, or an entirely different one ... The only thing that I wanted in life was – not to get near the great masters of the world such as Rembrandt, Greco, Tintoretto and others – but to get close to the spirit of our own fathers and grandfathers, to be of their essence, to mingle myself among their folds as if lying hidden in their garments with their souls and sorrows, with their worries and their rare joys.

Chagall, who, after Picasso, is widely regarded as the greatest artist of this century, was born in Vitebsk in 1887, the son of a herring-packer. He took to painting as a small child and his mother – or so the story goes – was sufficiently moved by his efforts to declare: 'Marc, you have talent. Maybe you will become a photographer one day.' No Jewish mother in a place like nineteenth-century Vitebsk could have thought of her son as a prospective artist. The term hardly featured in the Jewish imagination. But the child was given a place in the local art school, where he won a scholarship from the Imperial Society for the Furtherance of the Arts to study at St Petersburg. Few such scholarships were given and fewer still were given to Jews. In St Petersburg he found a patron who gave him a monthly allowance to study in Paris, where he remained for about four years. He returned to Vitebsk in 1914 for what was to have been a brief visit, and was stranded by the war. When the Bolsheviks came to power he was made Commissar for Fine Arts in Vitebsk, but it was not the sort of role to which he was attuned, nor did his Cubist style – which had been deeply influenced by Picasso – excite the admiration of the party, and in 1923 he moved to France.

Chagall's Cubist period was brief. His lines became freer, his colours lighter and his style assumed an exuberance which was uniquely his own and which can wholly be called Chagallian. But at first he excited rather greater acclaim in Germany than France. When the Nazis came to power however they removed the fifty or sixty Chagalls which were to be found in public collections and in 1937 some of his work was shown in an exhibition of 'degenerate art' mounted in Munich, which, if anything, enhanced his reputation.

Though his style is instantly recognizable, he is extremely versatile. His work assumes many forms, oils, watercolour, gouache, lithographs, etchings, sculpture, ceramics and stained glass. He has designed the stained glass for Metz Cathedral, the glass panels for the United Nations Secretariat building and the Vatican audience hall. He has also painted the new ceiling at the Paris Opera and the murals of the Metropolitan Opera, New York.

Where in other Jewish painters one looks for Jewish influences which, not infrequently, are not there, in Chagall they are inescapable and colour almost everything he does. They may be seen not only in the figures from the *shtettlech* who crowd his canvasses, but in their very mood, their dreamlike quality, their touches of whimsy, as if to suggest that life isn't that serious, and perhaps shouldn't be. The animals are vaguely human, the humans vaguely ethereal, suspended somewhere between heaven and earth, and together they seem to people a Russo-Jewish Arcadia.

He is the most Jewish of the great Jewish painters, with a reputation that has reverberated far beyond the cognoscenti to become a household name even in Jewish households, further than which fame does not travel. He has always retained a close affinity with Jews and Judaism, also unusual among artists, and he has, so to speak, become court painter to the Jewish people. Some of his finest work may be seen in the Jewish state, like the windows of the Hadassah Medical Centre Synagogue, near Jerusalem, and the tapestry and mosaics in the Knesset (Israel's Parliament).

The great commercial success enjoyed by Chagall's pictures on Jewish themes led other Jewish artists of the Paris school to return to the same territory, though not with the same results. In many cases the Pale of Settlement was not merely a world which they had to leave because of persecution or social constriction, but because its very Jewishness was inimical to their temperament. If one wanted to escape everything that the *shtettle* stood for, bohemian Paris was about as far as one could go: but it didn't mean that one could then recover it at will. Chagall was able to recover the body and soul of the *shtettle*, its aspirations and its fears, because in a sense he never left it, or, at least, it never left him.

The sculptor, Jacques (or, as he was known in his early years, Chaim Yankel) Lipchitz, was born four years after Chagall, in the Lithuanian town of Druskieniki, where his father was a prosperous building contractor who hoped to make his son an engineer. Lipchitz had other plans. At the age of eighteen he went to Paris, where, like Chagall, he came under the influence of Picasso, becoming, in time, a major influence in the Cubist movement. He was to sculpture what Picasso was to painting, but, again like Chagall, he wearied of the restraints of Cubism and from about the 1930s his work assumed a more exuberant form, so that even when he worked in stone he seemed to give his material a plasticity it had not earlier possessed, while his bronzes positively threatened to leap from their pedestals. It would not be too much to call him the Chagall of sculpture. His bronzes, in particular, have a spontaneity about them, as if cast in the heat of the moment.

Lipchitz was obsessed with the story of Prometheus. In 1933 he cast a forty-six foot statue on the Prometheus theme for the Palace of Discovery at the Paris World Fair. The vast writhing figure caused a sensation. There were protests both from conservatives, who called it modernism run riot, and from nationalists, who thought it was too gross and alien a work, and it was eventually dismantled. He retained a model of the cast and resurrected the figure for the facade of the Ministry of Health and Education in Rio de Janeiro. He made yet another version for the Philadelphia Museum of Modern Art. He viewed Prometheus as a life force struggling with encroaching evil, and it would not be reading too much into his work to see in the embattled figure something of the Jewish people. *The Miracle*, which he cast in 1949 to celebrate the emergence of Israel, is designed almost on the same lines, like an effulgence of hope.

In his early years his work is full of light, blithe, dancing figures, but it assumes a more sombre mood as he grows older, and after the rise of Hitler he turned increasingly to Jewish themes such as *Jacob Wrestling with the Angel, David and Goliath*, and the rococo tangle he wrought to represent *Prayer*.

He had strong Zionist feelings which grew more intense as he grew older. He left all his casts to the Israel Museum and when he died in 1973, aged eighty-two, he was buried in the Hill of Quietudes, Jerusalem.

It is interesting to compare the career of Lipchitz and another Russian-Jewish sculptor, Mark Antokolski, who was born in Vilna, Lithuania, in 1843. Antokolski stemmed from an impoverished household and after working as a wood-carver was sent, at the age of nineteen, to the St Petersburg Academy of Art, probably the first overt Jew to study there. His early work was nearly all on Jewish themes, usually in the form of bas-reliefs, like his *Jewish Tailor* and *The Talmudic Debate*. By 1870 he was successful enough to embark on a European tour. When he returned a year later the Jewish elements vanished from his work, and he turned increasingly to Russian subjects. He produced a large marble statue of Peter the Great which was widely acclaimed and he was commissioned to do busts of the Russian royal family. He was flattered by the royal patronage; he wore a large gold medal he had received from the Tsar round his neck as a sort of talisman, even while at work. He also executed bronzes of Ivan the Terrible, Jaroslav the Wise, Jesus on the Cross and John the Baptist. Although his international reputation grew, there were murmurs within Russia that a Jew could not be expected to produce true portraits of heroes from either Christian or Russian history. He was shaken by such criticism and he left Russia to make his home in Paris. But Russia and Russians continued to obsess him, and in 1891 he executed a monumental figure of the eleventh-century monk, Nestor.

The Jewish philosopher Ahad Ha-am had followed his career with a mixture of pride and grief, and wrote on his death in 1902:

It was for Russia that Antokolski worked while he lived, and it is Russia that gets the glory now he is dead; while we can only reflect sadly how much he might have given to his own people, and how low we have sunk when men like him have to go elsewhere to find scope for their genius.

He was at a loss to understand why, if Antokolski 'wanted to make a statue of a blood-thirsty tyrant, a dreadful monster of violence and cruelty', he had to alight on Ivan the Terrible. Could he not have chosen Herod? And if he had to portray the mystic, why choose the almost unknown Nestor? Wasn't there a far more probable figure to hand in Antokolski's own birthplace, Elijah, the *Gaon* of Vilna? To which one can answer that had he cut a statue of Elijah of Vilna, he might have been stoned for his efforts.

Antokolski remained loyal to many Jewish observances and would never have resorted to the sort of language adopted by Liebermann, who once explained *Nur durch meine Religion bin ich ein Jude, durch meine Kultur bin ich ein Deutscher* (I am a Jew only by religion, by culture I'm a German). Jewishness was central to his being and he sought to spread an understanding of art among Jews and to help young Jewish artists, but the Russian in him was no less important. The Jews of the Pale of Settlement may have lived a life apart, but they were not entirely insulated from their external environment, either cultural or physical. The very expanse of Russia, its wind-swept skies, its dark mood, impressed themselves upon Antokolski as they had impressed themselves upon Levitan, and with the same effect. But Levitan could give immediate expression to his feelings. Antokolski, working in stone, was more oblique, but like Levitan he caught the spirit of Russia and Russians more completely than his gentile contemporaries.

He was a member of the *Peredvizhniki* school of artists who rebelled against the formal classicism of Russian art, and who felt that art should embody not only beauty and grace, but aspirations and ideals. The effect, certainly in the case of Antokolski, was a mellowing one, and he showed that even the starkest stone could be given an inner life. This 'insistent search for spiritual beauty behind the beauty of external form', said Ahad Ha-am, was 'surely a Jewish trait if ever there was one', and he seemed to feel that by expressing it in a purely Russian context Antokolski had, in a sense, turned his back on the Jewish people.

It is possible that had Antokolski been born half a century later he would have left the Vilna ghetto to join the Parisian ghetto established by his fellow Lithuanians in Montparnasse. But as a nineteenth-century Jewish artist, he was an isolated figure. The cosmopolitan congeries of Paris had not yet been formed and the sculptor, especially where his work assumed massive monumental forms, could only survive within a national and, indeed, nationalistic *ambience*, which in Antokolski's case meant, and could only mean, Russia. He enjoyed the patronage of the Russian Jewish banker, Baron Horace de Guenzberg, but the sort of Jews who had the cultivation and means to patronize art were not the sort who cared to fill their homes with Rabbinical figures, and those who might draw inspiration from the figure of a Rabbi were not the sort who went in for patronage.

Antokolski was a member of the Russian academy. He enjoyed the favour of the Tsar, his sculptures were to be found in the main national galleries. Such honours were rarely bestowed on a Jew and he was sufficiently flattered by them to feel that he had become part of mother Russia. Moreover, he did draw inspiration from the Russian past and anyone who had spent much of his life in Russia, no matter how ingrained his Jewishness, would find it easier to penetrate the dark soul of an Ivan the Terrible than of a Herod. In this sense most Jewish artists (Chagall is an obvious exception), even where they occasionally turned to Jewish subjects, were Nordic. Antokolski was shattered by the anti-semitism he encountered. It is bad enough to be hated, it is infinitely worse to be hated by a people one loves. In fact, after he left Russia, his output declined, and he died as an artist some years before he died as a man.

Sir Jacob Epstein (1880–1959) enjoyed the place in English sculpture that was accorded to Antokolski in Russia, though he was in fact born in New York, the son of a Polish-Jewish immigrant. A non-Jewish writer, Hutchins Hapgood, helped him to study in Paris and in 1905 he moved to London, which became his home. He went through a brief and somewhat sterile abstract phase and made his name with a series of monumental figures, in which one could find traces of Classical, African, Pre-Columbian and even Polynesian influences, but which contained a sort of restless energy which became his particular hallmark. His sculptures were the subject of frequent controversy, which did not, however, impede the flow of commissions, and one can find his work on and in public buildings (a series of eighteen figures adorn what used to be Rhodesia House in the Strand), churches, cathedrals, schools, colleges and convents. Understandably, one does not find them in a synagogue or any other Jewish institution.

He was knighted in 1954 and became a revered establishment figure. But he did not mellow with age and the work executed towards the end of his life, like the *Christ in Majesty* (1957) at Llandaff Cathedral, occasioned as much controversy as anything he had done in his youth. It must be added that one of the reasons why he was such a source of controversy is that many of his figures were exhibited where they could be seen – it was, indeed, difficult to avoid them – and not hidden away in private collections and obscure galleries.

He was helped during his early years in London by a fund set up by the older Anglo-Jewish families to assist struggling young Jewish artists. When he was invited during his prosperous years – and he became a fairly wealthy man – to contribute to the fund he retorted that he had done enough for the fund by accepting its money.

Epstein turned occasionally to Old Testament themes, but perhaps the most important Jewish influence in his work was, he believed, a mellowing one, which, as he said, gave 'human rather than abstract implications' to his work. But one senses also a subconscious adherence to the Jewish belief in a God of wrath, for there is an almighty anger in several of his figures which sometimes threatens to burst out. One would not care to be left alone in the same room with an Epstein figure.

If, as Epstein believed, Jewishness tends to save one from abstraction, Anthony Caro, who was born in 1924, and stems from an old Sephardi family, is amongst the exceptions to the rule, for he is one of the pioneers of what has come to be called minimal sculpture, and whose work is as stark and as removed from human experience as any assembly of metals and girders can be. He represented Britain at the Venice Biennale in 1966 and is today recognized as one of the foremost artists in the country.

The so-called Paris Jewish school did not survive World War II, even if some of its members survived as individuals. If any one place came to harbour artistic talent numerous enough to be called a school, it was New York, with Rothko, Adolph Gottlieb, Arnold Friedman, Ben Shahn, Max Weber and William Zorach, some of whom were born abroad, but all of whom spent their most formative and productive years in America. And here, at last, we come to an area where Jews are not only producing Jewish work, but are enriching the Jewish scene with examples of their work. Ben Shahn, for example, not only drew the set designs for a play on the work of Sholem Aleichem and designed his own Haggadah (for which he also wrote the text – he was fascinated by Hebrew calligraphy) but he also designed the windows and murals for several synagogues. Similarly Adolph Gottlieb designed the *parochet* (ark screen) for the B'nai Israel Synagogue, Millburn, New Jersey, the Beth El Synagogue, Springfield, Mass., and the 1,300 square-feet stained glass facade for the Milton Steinberg Centre at the Park Avenue Synagogue, New York.

In England, three young painters, all of them immigrants or of immigrant stock, caused a considerable stir in the early years of the century: they were Alfred Wolmark, David Bomberg and Mark Gertler. All three were brought up in the slums of London's East End, but they were only vaguely aware of one another. Each had his own distinct style, though all displayed an almost crude exuberance of colour. Wolmark, whose early work drew richly on the East End, became a successful portrait painter. He was fascinated by Talmudic faces, a fascination which sometimes invaded his other work, so that, by an odd irony, even his portrait of G. K. Chesterton (who, together with Hilaire Belloc, had given British anti-semitism respectability) had a vaguely semitic look about it.

Bomberg was rather more interested in landscapes, especially the sun-baked valleys of the Mediterranean lands. He worked in Palestine for a time, but here too he was rather more aware of the landscape than of the people who worked on it (to the annoyance of the Zionists who had brought him out), and he made his home in Spain.

Bomberg had a passing flirtation with Cubism in his early years. His more austere work has the richness and density of Soutine, with whom he had more than a little in common, including grinding poverty and recurring disappointment. He turned to Jewish themes from time to time, and to East End scenes, and although this did not perhaps represent his best work, they had the widest appeal.

He was an exact contemporary of Gertler's, but never enjoyed his success. But then he never had his talent. Gertler was perhaps the most gifted Jewish painter to have lived and worked in Britain, though part of his success was possibly due to striking good looks. 'A lovely little Jew, like a Lippo Lippi Cherub' was how one of his patrons, an elderly paederast, described him. He was born in 1890, was at first apprenticed as a painter with a firm of glass merchants, but with the help of the Jewish Educational Aid Society, formed to help gifted children, he went to study at the Slade School of Art, the most stimulating art school of its time. Within a few years he was exhibiting at major galleries and acquired a following which enabled him to leave the East End home and set up a studio in Hampstead.

He was taken up by the Bloomsbury set, a gifted if somewhat neurotic group of intellectuals, with leftish sympathies, high minds and low habits, which included the economist Maynard Keynes, Lytton Strachey, Virginia Woolf, the painter Duncan Grant, and Lady Ottoline Morrell, whose Oxfordshire home, Garsington Manor, was their principal venue.

Garsington and the East End represented the two extremes of Gertler's existence. He was not so much torn between them as he was a different person to each, and the difference was reflected in his work.

His East End paintings, as represented by the *Jewish Family* or the *Rabbi and Rabbitzin*, both painted in his early twenties, have a caricaturish quality, lacking in his later work. His Jews seemed to inhabit a different universe from his non-Jews, not merely because they were poorer and their circumstances more constricted. His *Coster Woman*, for example, also an East End figure, is given a rural, almost arcadian setting, and she has the richness, roundness and warmth of a Gainsborough; his Jews by comparison were gaunt and stark.

In 1916, during one of the darkest phases of World War 1, when thousands were dying daily in the mud of Flanders, Gertler, who was then twenty-six, and who had managed to avoid military service, exhibited a large canvas, painted in red, white and blue, called *The Merry-go-Round*, with soldiers, sailors and their girlfriends in full cry on a carousel, suggesting that war was but a game. As a painting – it is now in the collection of the Ben Uri Jewish Art Society – it was a masterpiece, but even the art-loving public could, given the mood of the day, be forgiven for not being happy with its message. D. H. Lawrence, on the other hand, was overwhelmed by it, and he was moved to write:

My dear Gertler . . . This is the first picture you have ever painted; it is the best *modern* picture I have seen; I think it is great and true. But it is horrible and terrifying . . . I realize how superficial your human relationships must be, what a violent maelstrom of destruction and horror your inner-soul must be . . . You are all-absorbed in the violent and lurid process of decomposition; the same thing that makes leaves go scarlet and copper green at this time of year. It is a terrifying coloured flame of decomposition, your inner flame. But dear God, it is real flame enough, undeniable in heaven and earth – it would take a Jew to paint this picture. It would need your national history to get you here without disintegrating you first.

There was a dreadful irony in Lawrence's reference to 'a terrifying coloured flame of decomposition, your inner flame' for Gertler was already then beginning to suffer from consumption and he was compelled to spend prolonged periods of his short life in a sanatorium. He was also subject to fits of depression. The critical acclaim and success he enjoyed as a young man began to elude him as he passed into middle age. He married and had a child and his income declined while his needs expanded. He had to take up teaching, which he hated. His health deteriorated further and his depression – especially where external events following the rise of Hitler intruded upon him – became more acute. In June 1939, at the age of forty-eight, he took his own life.

Jews, as individuals, have been among the leading patrons of the arts, but such jews tended to place themselves outside the community and were not inclined to acquire works which might have reminded them of their origins. The outlook of the Jewish patron is changing, which is to say, he is less afraid of Jewish proclivities or reminders. More important, Jewish institutions are also emerging as patrons, but the inhibitions of centuries cannot be removed overnight.

It is often suggested that ghetto life has stunted Jewish sensibilities, but the process began centuries before the ghetto. The Talmud warned that 'he who walks by the way, and breaks off his studies to declare how beautiful is that tree or that fallow field, has forfeited his life'. All of which meant to say that too keen an awareness of the outside world could lead men astray, and that beauty and the appreciation of beauty were but a step from idol worship. Thus, if the Jew was blind to nature, he was doubly blind to the celebration of nature and where he was not he often found himself in conflict with his Jewishness. The Jew who did develop as an artist did so without any body of tradition behind him and if he was to become an artist at all he almost necessarily had to become a rebel.

At the 1905 Zionist Congress, Boris Schatz (1867–1932), a disciple of Antokolski, who had served, in his time, as Court Sculptor to King Ferdinand of Bulgaria, and was founder of the Sofia Royal Academy, tried to impress upon delegates the belief that there could be no effective national revival without an artistic revival and that the Jew would be incomplete as a man and a Jew without an adequately developed aesthetic sense. His ideas were accepted and in the following year he moved to Jerusalem to establish the Bezalel School of Art, which is now the Israel National Museum. Yet in the intervening seventy years, nothing like a Jewish or an Israeli school of art has emerged. The early immigrants brought the influences of the Russian-French schools (with the latter predominating), the later ones, who came after the rise of Hitler, brought the influence of the German schools and particularly the Bauhaus. Here was eclecticism run riot in which students could choose the best from everywhere without evolving a style of their own. One heard of a 'Jerusalem school', which on closer examination proved to be but a version of German Expressionism. There has been a willingness to experiment which is perhaps particularly Jewish, because in this field, as in others, one is less inhibited by precedent or tradition. But the experiments have taken too many directions and although they display a high level of attainment, they have delayed the emergence of a consistent genre.

Art, for all the great names we have listed, is not an area where the Jewish contribution has been outstanding. There is, with the possible exception of Chagall, no painter or sculptor who stands to the arts as Marx stands to politics, or Freud stands to psychiatry, or Einstein to science.

They have been late on the scene in this area, as in others; but if the Jew was prevented from rising in the sciences and the professions by external obstacles, the obstacles he faced in the arts were, as we have seen, largely of his own making, and these are always more difficult to surmount. They lie not merely in the injunctions against the graven images, or the fear of beauty as a diversion from sanctity, but in the very stress on the impalpable and the unseen. In the last resort a nation worshipping an invisible God is unlikely to excel in the visual arts.

When one comes to music two questions immediately pose themselves. Why are there so many supreme Jewish musicians and why is there so little which may be accurately described as Jewish music?

With the exceptions of Francescatti, Szigeti and Thibaud, it is difficult to think of a violinist of the first rank who is not Jewish, usually of Russian origin, frequently from Odessa. Yehudi Menuhin, whose very name has become almost an evocation of all that is noble in the violin, was, indeed, born in America, but his parents were from Russia. Jascha Heifetz is from Lithuania; Mischa Elman is from the Ukraine, as is Isaac Stern; Efrem Zimbalist is from Rostov; Ida Haendel is from Poland; Nathan Milstein and David Oistrakh are from Odessa, as are a host of lesser players. Odessa, indeed, was to music what Bordeaux is to wine, and the traditions of the town are perhaps summed up in the careers of the family Cherniavsky, of whom one brother, Jan, was a pianist, another, Leo, a violinist, and a third, Michael, a cellist. They all began as infant prodigies and were international celebrities before World War I. Another brother, Alexander, also a pianist, formed a trio with his sister Marion and cousin Boris.

When one turns to the piano Jewish dominance is less complete, but many of the supreme virtuosi – Rubinstein, Horowitz, Schnabel, Askenazi and Barenboim – are Jewish.

It has been suggested that the Jew is by nature a soloist and likes to stand out from the herd and that instrumental skills offered the child from a penniless family the chance of an escape from the ghetto. But the sort of skills displayed by a Menuhin or an Oistrakh are not the sort which can be readily acquired with mere application, and they do suggest an inherent streak of musicality kept dormant by other factors in Jewish life. A closer look at the phenomenon of Odessa may perhaps explain what these factors were.

Odessa, the largest industrial and commercial city of southern Russia, had a Jewish population of 165,000 (out of half a million) before World War I, and although part of the Pale, it was not quite of it, for its population was largely Western in outlook, with a sizeable industrial proletariat, many prosperous merchants and bankers, and a large Jewish professional class. About ninety per cent of the doctors in Odessa, and more than half of the lawyers, were Jews. It was looked at askance by other parts of the Pale as a *goyishe stot* (a gentile city). 'The fires of hell burn round Odessa for a distance of ten parasangs,' went a popular Jewish saying. In some ways it was a forerunner of New York (to which many Odessans later found their way). It was dominated, unlike the communities elsewhere in the Pale, not by Rabbis, but by *maskilim*, assimilated Jews who were as much at home in secular culture as in Jewish culture (perhaps more so), and who maintained an aura of enlightenment, absent elsewhere in the Pale, in which music and the arts could flourish.

The Jewish feeling for music is perhaps best seen in the early history of the Jewish people, and, indeed, in its literature. To read the Psalms, or the Song of Songs, or most other parts of the Bible in the original Hebrew is to hear music in one's ears. David, who first moulded Israel into a formidable power, is not recalled in Jewish lore as the Warrior King, but as 'the sweet singer of Israel'. In Temple times, and even before, music was an essential part of the sacred service and the Levites were not only a priestly caste but a musical one:

And David spoke to the chief of the Levites to appoint their brethren to be the singers with instruments of music, psalteries and harps and cymbals, sounding by lifting up the voice with joy.

With the fall of Judea and the destruction of the Temple the tradition not merely lapsed but was wilfully suppressed. What could not be suppressed however was the Jewish love of music, which over the centuries experienced what was virtually an underground existence.

Music was associated in the Jewish mind with joy and elation, and with the fall of Jerusalem any public display of joy was regarded as sinful. To this day there are long periods of the year, associated with past misfortunes, amounting altogether to some eleven weeks, when the devout Jew is prohibited from even listening to music.

Moreover, with the rise of Christianity, music came to play a central role in church ritual and the use of music was therefore banned in the synagogue as *khukas ha'goy* (an alien custom). (In fact Church practice derived in part from Jewish tradition. Not a few of the melodies of the Gregorian chant, for example, are of Jewish origin.) It was, in any case, forbidden to play a musical instrument on the Sabbath or festivals. Nor was vocal music particularly encouraged, for the Talmud regarded the woman as a siren and her voice as a source of temptation so that she could not be heard (and in Orthodox synagogues still cannot be) even as part of a mixed choir. Music could still be played at weddings and on such minor festivals as Purim or Chanukah, but the making of music and listening to it was regarded as at best a frivolous activity in which the highminded and upright did not take part.

Thus if elsewhere religion was the main source of musical inspiration and the Church the main source of patronage, the effect of Judaism was to discourage music as a form of expression.

Here and there, however, one could find voices against the main trend.

'Whoever says his prayer should turn his complete inner self towards God and should never neglect to use the sweet sound of a pleasant voice,' wrote Maimonides in the eleventh century. With the rise of Hassidism in the eighteenth century, music once again became kosher, if not quite sacred. For Hassidism sought to make Judaism a less cerebral experience and urged that, in the words of the Psalmist, one should approach one's maker 'with joy and song'. It gave rise to a new tradition of folk melody, from which, however, it would need a discerning ear to pick out any clear note of joy. The dominant tone was plaintive and, almost invariably, in the minor key, and as there was no consistent body of tradition to draw on, the tunes were largely borrowed from the street, the tavern, the music hall, and sometimes (though never knowingly) even from the church. Anyone anxious to study the folk music of Volhynia, Podolia, Wallachia, Galicia and other east European provinces will find them intact in the melodies of the various Hassidic sects, which is a contribution of sorts, for many of the melodies are exceedingly beautiful and might otherwise have been lost. Better to borrow well than to create badly. The tradition is almost entirely vocal. Musical instruments, having been banned from synagogue on the Sabbath and festivals, were, for good measure, also kept out on weekdays.

At the same time, in the larger, non-Hassidic synagogues the Cantor, or *Hazzan*, who led the congregation in prayer, tended – often to the distress of the Rabbis – to be chosen for his richness of tone and musical knowledge rather than for his personal piety. He became, and to an extent still remains, a hybrid, half-ecclesiastical, and half-performer, a colourful thread in the dark weft of synagogue life. Certain prayers have traditional melodies but each *Hazzan* tends to introduce either his own innovations on familiar themes, or new themes, a tendency berated by eighteenth-century commentators, who complained of rampant individualism, but one which nevertheless continues to this day. Some *Hazzanim* compose their own tunes, others adapt, all borrow, and anyone inclined to wander from synagogue to synagogue on a *Hazzan*-tasting expedition will hear snatches of Verdi here and Rossini there, and even a few bars from a Bach mass. The basic tune will tend to be Slavic, and indeed the *Hatikvah*, Israel's national anthem, whose mood and tune may fairly be said to represent the quintessence of what is regarded as Jewish music, is in fact derived from a Moldavian folk melody.

Outside the synagogue one had the *klezmer* (a corruption of *klay zemer* – musical vessels), usually fiddlers, who played at weddings (there is no music, not even funeral music, at Jewish wakes) and the rare occasions for merrymaking tolerated by the Rabbis. But they were regarded almost as licensed vagrants. In the light of all this it was inevitable that when, in the nineteenth century, composers bearing Jewish names began to emerge, their work should owe nothing to any Jewish idiom. They had to transcend their Jewishness to become composers or even, in the first place, professional musicians.

The intrusion of Jews upon the musical scene was not as sudden or as startling as in the sciences, but it was startling enough to an observer like Wagner, who saw Jews everywhere, as conductors, composers, instrumentalists, impresarios, publishers and musicologists, and who owed no small part of his success to their energy and influence. If Wagner had no love of the Jews, Jews had an almost insuppressible love for Wagner. One of his most devoted disciples was the young Jewish pianist, Joseph Rubinstein, who travelled from the Ukraine on a pilgrimage to Bayreuth. When Wagner died, in 1883, he killed himself over his grave.

Wagner argued that Jews were devoid of any creative faculty and referred to the work of two of his leading contemporaries, Meyerbeer and Mendelssohn, to illustrate his point. He was particularly scathing about Meyerbeer, the reigning composer of his day, whose operas, such as *Robert le Diable* and *Les Huguenots*, were in the repertoires of every major opera house in Europe:

As a Jew, he owned no mother tongue, no speech inextricably entwined among the sinews of his innermost being: he spoke with precisely the same interest in any modern language you chose, and set it to music with no more concern for the idiosyncracies than the mere question of how far it was ready to be a pliant servitor to Absolute Music.

To which Meyerbeer might have pleaded guilty with an easy conscience. The son of a German-Jewish banker, he derived much of his inspiration from the study of Italian opera (which is why he changed his name to Giacomo from Jacob) and found his readiest acceptance in France. Most of his operas were in French.

The same is largely true of Felix Mendelssohn, a grandson of the philosopher and savant, Moses Mendelssohn. There is a sunnyness and warmth, a lyricism to Mendelssohn's music which some have ascribed to his Jewishness, but which is more probably Italianate. For, like Meyerbeer, he too acquired a deep love for the south, yet, like Meyerbeer again, he was open to other influences. His *Scotch Symphony* and *Hebrides Overture* suggest a quality which Wagner condemned, but which is peculiarly Jewish, that is a roving eclecticism, a ready ear for new sounds. An adaptability to change and a readiness to adopt changes added to his sources of inspiration and the richness of his output. Overall, however, his work falls largely within the German romantic tradition. He was converted to Christianity in childhood because, as his father put it, 'Christianity is the religion of the majority of civilized men', but his own Christianity was perfectly sincere. He was a cousin of Johannes and Philip Veit, who were among the leaders of the Nazarene school of painting, and one finds the same degree of religious intensity in his 'Reformation' symphony with its magnificent setting of Luther's *Ein feste Burg is unser Gott* that one finds in their work. Although he was but one generation removed from Judaism, his oratorio *Elijah*, its subject matter notwithstanding, is entirely of the church.

Gustav Mahler was rather more celebrated as a conductor and one of the greatest interpreters of Mozart than as a composer, and he is currently enjoying a vogue which eluded him in his own lifetime. His symphonies call for vast ensembles and make heavy demands on the resources and versatility of an orchestra. An eminent Jewish musicologist, Professor Paul Nettl, has noticed Jewish influences in Mahler 'traceable to his ecstatic personality which reminds one of the Prophets and the Hassidic mysticism. He seems to be conscious in his works of the incompatibility of his existence at once as a Jew and a European.' It is not an impression which other observers might get, for Mahler showed no hesitation in converting to Catholicism to become Director of the Vienna Opera (a post which he was to leave later because of hostile intrigues), and the principal influence in his music is surely the folk song of the German Laender, for which he showed an almost unique love and understanding, though he was born and brought up in Bohemia and thus, one might have thought, doubly removed from Germanic influence.

Jewish adaptability is perhaps seen in its supreme form in the operettas of Jacques Offenbach, for no one more embodied the spirit of *la vie Parisienne*, or rather enhanced it, than this son of a Rhineland *Hazzan* who became to France what Sir Arthur Sullivan was to England.

Such adaptability, though most evident among Jews, is not, of course, confined to them, so that, for example, one finds the most moving setting for the *Kaddish* (the Jewish memorial prayer for the dead) in the work of the Frenchman Maurice Ravel, and the most beloved of all renderings of the *Kol Nidrei* (the opening prayer of the Day of Atonement) in the work of the German, Max Bruch (and were he even a half-Jew would not his Violin Concerto have been thought of as typically Jewish?). Schoenberg, who was a Jew, and who also set the *Kol Nidrei* to music, was critical of what he called the 'cello-sentimentality of the Bruchs, etc', and declared, with no excess of modesty, that his own version was at least free of 'sentimental minor-key stuff'. But it was rarely performed, because of ritual and musical objections, even in Reform synagogues, which, unlike their orthodox counterparts, do go in for musical accompaniment (which was partly what Reform was about).

Schoenberg was born in 1874 and was at first deeply influenced by the music of Wagner and Brahms. But his own work developed to become almost a negation of the German romanticism they represented. By diverting music from what he called 'mere tonality' and enlarging its range, he shifted the source of musical appreciation from the heart to the mind. There was perhaps something inherently Jewish both in the nature of the change and in its direction, though he himself felt that his work was essentially Germanic and that it would 'assure the supremacy of German music for the next hundred years'.

In 1925 he became Director of a master class for musical composition at the Prussian Academy of Arts. Although this gave him a certain amount of economic security, he felt uneasy and out of place. Even in 1923, ten years before the rise of Hitler, he was convinced that the anti-semitism which he felt everywhere about him would result in a policy of extermination. In 1932, while on a trip to Spain, he wrote to Joseph Asch, an American friend:

I am surely the only composer of my standing there has been for at least a hundred years who could not live on what he made from his creative work without having to eke out his living by teaching. And when I think how many things rich people find money for, I simply can't understand that there still isn't some rich Jew, or even several, who together or single-handed could give me an annuity . . . are there not some people, even nowadays some Jews, who could get together and raise, for instance, $200 a month for me?

I am told you have enough influence to achieve something of the sort for me. I was told that some time ago. But it is only today that I can bring myself to approach you about it. Will you try it, will you see if you can get some rich Jews to provide for me so that I don't have to go back to Berlin among the swastika-swaggerers and pogromists?

But already by then there were other demands on rich Jews. Schoenberg returned to Berlin. A year later, with Hitler in power, the government issued a directive to eliminate 'Jewish influence' from the Prussian Academy. He left Berlin and in 1934 he made his home in the United States.

His attitude to his Jewishness was ambivalent. He had estranged himself from the Jewish community and was only to return after the rise of Hitler. Yet he somehow felt that Jews or at least 'rich Jews' (about whose riches and number he had exaggerated ideas) owed him a living. He also felt, possibly with greater justice, that they showed only slight appreciation of his work:

According to my experience, Jews look at me rather from a racial standpoint than from an artistic. They accordingly give me a lower rating than they give their Aryan idols.

In April 1951, shortly before his death, he was invited to become Honorary President of the Israeli Academy of Music. He was deeply moved by the invitation and wrote to say that he would have liked to take personal charge of the academy, but only his frail health prevented him from doing so:

I would have tried to make this Academy one of world-wide significance, so that it would be of a fit kind to serve as a counterblast to this world that is in so many respects giving itself up to amoral, success-ridden materialism . . .

Those who issue from such an institution must be truly priests of art, approaching art in the same spirit of consecration as the priest approached God's altar. For just as God chose Israel to be the people whose task is to maintain the pure, true, Mosaic monotheism despite all persecution, despite all affliction, so too it is the task of Israeli musicians to set the world an example of the old kind that can make our souls function again as they must if mankind is to evolve any higher.

And in fact something like this has been happening, for though a country almost constantly at war might be excused for neglecting the arts, its musical schools have given forth a flow of talent so constant and rich that it may yet atone for all the centuries of suppressed musicality. An Israeli sound, part Russian, part Greek, part Arabic, but with distinct inflexions of its own, has emerged in light music. It has been slower to emerge in classical music, for the weight of European experience is too pronounced. The work of Marc Lavry, for example, still echoes the sounds of Russia, Joseph Kaminski's of Poland, Oedoen Partos's of

Hungary, and Walter Sternberg's of Germany. But new men are coming to the fore and new voices, and one may yet hear in music the unmistakeably Jewish tone one finds in literature.

And it is here that the Jew comes into his own, for if he has been a borrower in music and art, he is a lender in literature, a man not only in love with words, but obsessed with them. There has not been a generation in which Jews have not added something lasting to literature, as if all the creativity which might have gone into art and music was channelled into writing.

The initial impetus was, of course, devotional. In the beginning was the word and so that the word might be made flesh, and given emphasis, word was added to word, and volume to volume. The Mishna was an enlargement of the Torah and the Gemara a commentary on the Mishna (the Talmud incorporates them both), and the Tosafot a commentary on the Talmud. To this day commentary has been piled on commentary, interpretation on interpretation, each telling something of its times – like the different layers of a *tell* – but all drawing their inspiration from the same source, and all devoted to the same end: to make the word of God manifest on earth.

While Rabbis sought to clarify, poets sought to adorn, and wrote to celebrate the glory of God and the grace of heaven. But in time they moved away from the sacred, and in medieval Spain and Provence Hebrew love poems enjoyed a wide circulation.

The *Song of Songs*, one of the most beautiful and erotic love poems in any language, is regarded by the Rabbis as an allegory of the love of Israel for their God. Such themes were not encouraged in writing, and a distinction developed between *kitvei kodesh* (holy writing), and *devarim betailim* (things profane). Some of the greatest medieval poets, like Judah Halevi, Ibn Ezra and Al Harizi, could bestride the two worlds, but as the centuries went on such versatility became uncommon. Secular literature tended to be written in the vernacular, and was mostly directed at women, and indeed the Yiddish expression for such literature was *veibershe-mayses* (wives' tales) (as distinct from tales of the supernatural which were known as *bobe-mayses*, or grandmothers' tales), and in those households where the woman was not illiterate (male literacy was almost universal) she was the main source of secular culture.

There was a hunger in the ghetto for the written word, possibly as an antidote to the spoken word. Jewish literature, or at least that part of it which survived, could hardly be described as escapist. It consisted in large

part of secularized versions of Hassidic tales, or was concerned only with
the dramas of day to day life, except that day to day life in the Pale of
Settlement did not have the repetitiousness that the term implies. One
woke each day to a new challenge and new threats, and if one survived
until the night one went to bed with a mild sense of achievement. The
works of Mendele, Peretz and Sholem Aleichem, in translation, convey
nothing of the moment of chilly despair one finds in the Yiddish. There is
humour, as there was humour amid all the squalor, but it was, to use the
Yiddish phrase, a *bitterer gelechter*, a bitter laugh. Translation robs the
humour of its gall and makes it simply Chaplinesque. The plots, in the
case of Peretz, are slight, and in the case of Mendele, absurd. Their quality
lay in their language, which was the private language of the Pale. Somewhat paradoxically, the English reader, anxious to catch something of the
flavour of Yiddish, can find it in the translations of the works of Agnon.
Agnon wrote mainly in Hebrew, but he seemed to think in Yiddish, and
his Hebrew reads like an immaculate translation. Moreover the setting
for many of his stories was that of the old Yiddish masters, a hapless
universe made habitable by faith.

The Anglo-Jewish, or rather the American-Jewish writers have
addressed themselves to a wider audience, and if they compelled more
universal attention it is only partly because of their very considerable
talents and the fact that they write in a more universal tongue. They are
legatees of unique circumstances.

If six million people are wiped off the face of the earth within a period
of five years there is an inordinate curiosity about the history, the characteristics, the qualities and defects, which can give rise to such a calamity.
The emergence of Israel is another factor. It is one thing to pray for the
restoration of Zion – after all people have prayed for more bizarre things –
but another to see it happen.

Moreover the Jew has made it. One knew of the Rothschilds and the
Montefiores and the Warburgs and the Schiffs; but until fifty years ago
the dominant characteristic of the Jew was poverty. Not all Jews have
since become millionaires, but those who have are happy to celebrate
the fact, with the result that they give a display of opulence which often
arouses interest and sometimes envy (which is but interest with a bite).

Jews have also lost much, if not all, of their secretiveness and Jewish life
is a little like a decaying mansion hidden behind high walls which has
suddenly been thrown open; it is difficult to resist the temptation to look
around. It is, of course, the writers who have thrown it open (some have

not merely thrown it open but have left graffiti on the walls). And finally, the American-Jewish writer is writing in a world where boundaries have been blurred and it is no longer clear where the Jewish world finishes and the outer world begins. Zangwill, writing about *The Children of the Ghetto* at the end of the last century (a novel which, incidentally, was commissioned by the Jewish Publications Society of America), was describing an alien colony on England's shore, but the Levins and Fidelmans of Malamud's novels and the Herzog of Bellow's and, indeed, the Portnoy of Roth's, though displaying obvious Jewish characteristics, are not figures from a foreign enclave but part of the larger America. This larger America is one in which the Jewish and non-Jewish writer can assume interchangeable roles. Norman Mailer, for example, though a writer and a Jew fits entirely within the tradition of articulate thuggery developed by Hemingway, while Damon Runyon, though Irish, reads like an inspired translation from the Yiddish.

America has allowed the Jew, or at least the Jewish writer, to cast off restraints, to let himself go. Mailer is, of course, one example (though he has not so much let himself go as flung himself forward). Another is Roth, who works within an established, though unrecognized, Jewish tradition, that of the *grober yung*, the *paskudnick*, the foul-mouth, whose influence Howe has described in the context of show-business, now invading the sacred realms of literature. (One finds him also in the novels of Mordecai Richler, whom one might describe as a poor man's Roth.) If Columbus was the beginning, Portnoy is the end, the apotheosis of the *paskudnick*, and Roth has been able to get away with it because he can make even pornography amusing.

Bellow's *Humboldt's Gift*, which is in some ways an odyssey of literary America, or at least literary New York (which nowadays has come to mean the same thing), shows how far the process of assimilation has gone, and it is no longer quite certain what has happened to whom: whether the Jew has become Americanized or the Americans Judaized. It is a world in which a writer like Gore Vidal, who can trace his roots back to an older America, must feel like an outsider, or a Court goy.

The suddenness with which Jews appear to have stormed the commanding heights of the American literary establishment is perhaps misleading. The academic keeps were fairly stoutly defended and it was not until after World War II that a visionary and critic like Lionel Trilling could find a chair in a major American university. But the literary heights were there for the taking. The great names of American literature confined themselves to the shires, or moved abroad. The metropolis, the *locus naturalis* of the Jew, was not part of their *medineh*.

But that is only part of the answer. It has often been said that the Jew has a ready nose for those areas where one can make the highest possible profit in the shortest possible time at the lowest possible risk; but the word-trade is assuredly not one of them. No-one anxious to get rich quick, or even to get rich slowly, would dream of going into publishing or any-thing remotely connected with it (except perhaps pornography), but there is something about the written word which still fills even the secular Jew (and Jews don't become more secular than in the word-trade) with an almost religious awe. It is the camp-followers of literature, the reviewers, the soothsayers, critics, editors, publishers and publicists, who dominate the scene rather than the actual writers. And if, as in films, there are among them those who are not, or were not Jews, they become Jewish through the very nature of their craft.

CHAPTER EIGHT

Eternal Radicals

The very survival of the Jews is a proof of their inherent conservatism. No people is so averse to change yet none in recent times has dissipated more of its energy on revolution. To many minds, at the beginning of this century, the very words radical and Jew were almost one and many a left-wing thinker or politician was taken to be Jewish through the very fact of his radicalism.

Von Plehve, the Tsarist Minister of the Interior, who waged an instant war against revolutions and revolutionaries (and was in the end assassinated by them), felt that they were almost a Jewish phenomena, and he told Herzl that although Jews formed less than five per cent of Russia's population, they formed more than fifty per cent of its revolutionaries. This was no revelation to Herzl, for, as he later observed:

By temperament, as well as by the precepts of his religion, he [the Jew] is the most obedient observer of the law that one could wish. But would it be surprising if, in his deep discouragement, in his absolute lack of hope for improving his lot or simply for living he became receptive to radical ideas?

The Jew was law-abiding where the law was just, consistent and even-handed. In Tsarist Russia – a tyranny tempered by corruption, particularly in the Pale – it was none of these things. The very effort to survive involved the Jew in a thousand acts of duplicity and evasion, and he grew up with an instinctive contempt both for law and order. That, added to poverty, gave him an active interest in change, so that even where caution kept him out of the revolutionary movements, he was disposed to see his salvation in revolution.

That having been said, it must be added that most of the leading revolutionaries who convulsed Europe in the final decades of the last century and the first decades of this one, stemmed from prosperous Jewish families which had managed to escape poverty and oppression, and who could enjoy an untroubled existence within the continuing order, but who were yet driven on by distant vision to strive for a new heaven and a new earth. They were perhaps typified by the father of revolution, Karl Marx.

Marx was born in 1818, in the Rhineland city of Trier. His paternal grandfather had been Rabbi of the town. His father, an ambitious lawyer, found his Judaism an obstacle to advancement and converted himself and his family to Lutheranism. Marx was sent to a Jesuit school, where he suffered both as a Protestant and a Jew, and in 1843 he married Jenny von Westphalen, a member of the Prussian aristocracy.

To Marx Jews meant money and as such they were central to the basic problems of the age. 'What is the secular basis of Judaism?' he asked.

Practical need, selfishness. What is the secular cult of the Jew? *Haggling*. What is this secular god? *Money*. Well, then! Emancipation from *haggling* and *money*, from practical, real Judaism would be the self-emancipation of our time.

'Money', he said, 'is the jealous God of Israel, beside which no other God may stand. Money degrades all the gods of mankind and turns them into commodities.'

He was aware that the commercialism of the Jews was in part imposed by circumstances, but argued that they then sought to impose their mores on the western world and that in America, in particular, Judaism had reduced Christianity to an article of commerce:

With the Jew and without him, *money* has become a world-power and the practical spirit of the Jews has become the practical spirit of the Christian peoples. The Jews have emancipated themselves to the extent that the Christians have become Jews.

From there it was but a logical step to conclude:

Thus we recognize in Judaism a universal and contemporary anti-social element which has reached its present peak through a historical development in whose harmful aspects the Jews eagerly collaborated, a peak at which it will inevitably disintegrate. The emancipation of the Jew means ultimately the emancipation from Judaism.

And that, he believed, would come with the extinction of the market economy, for if the market was the expression of Judaism, then there could be no Judaism without the market, and no Jews.

Marx, for all his mental vivacity and range, had an imperfect grasp of Jewish history and based himself mainly on dubious sources and secondary texts. But the venom with which he approached Judaism and Jews cannot be explained merely in terms of intellectual aversion. It was as if he was anxious to distance himself, to establish his *bona fides* as a detached observer. His father had removed him from Judaism by baptism; he removed himself from Jews by anathematization. 'His references to individual Jews', Sir Isaiah Berlin observed in a celebrated essay, 'are virulent to a degree: his origin had become a personal stigma which he was unable to resist pointing out in others . . .'

He rarely spoke of himself or his family life, and never about his origins: the fact that he was a Jew does not appear anywhere in the vast corpus of his writing, and nothing is more indicative of the importance he attached to the fact than his efforts to keep it hidden.

Yet for all his determination to distance himself from the past, it did influence him in one major respect and that was in his search for a system, or rather *the* system. The Hebrew for the code of Jewish laws is *Shulchan Aruch*, which means, literally, the prepared table, and it lays down a system of laws covering one's entire existence, from the time one rises in the morning till one goes to bed, from the torment of birth till the moment of death. It does not deprive the observant Jew of initiative or the need for decisions, but it assures him that he is operating within a divine order and sanctified by divine will. It relieved him, and relieves him still, of doubts and confusions, of wasteful speculation on whys and wherefores.

Marx, too, introduced a system, which was not, of course, divine, but which laid down iron laws, operating irrespective of human will and human effort but which, on the contrary, determined the direction of effort. It suggested an inevitability to the course of human history, it promised certainties. It did not give a ready answer to every question, but it offered sufficient guidance from which an answer might eventually be obtained. It was a *Shulchan Aruch*, and among no one was it embraced more enthusiastically than among young Jews who had discarded the *Shulchan Aruch* of their fathers. It offered a more logical alternative. It cleared the mind for action. It made unhappy events, like the growth of anti-semitism in Germany and Russia, seem like passing irrelevancies within a higher scheme of things, and the very disorder which they threatened, or to which they gave rise, promised to hasten the inevitable. Thus when, after the chaos of World War I, revolutions finally erupted all over Europe, Jews were everywhere at the helm: Trotsky, Sverdlov, Kamenev and Zinoviev in Russia, Bela Kun in Hungary, Kurt Eisner in Bavaria, and, most improbable of all, Rosa Luxemburg in Berlin.

Small, frail, limping, with the frumpish appearance of a maiden-lady who had resigned herself to maidenhood, Rosa Luxemburg did not look like a revolutionary. She was born in 1870, at Zamosc, in Russian Poland. Her father, a prosperous timber merchant, was a member of the assimilated Polish-Jewish bourgeoisie. Her maternal grandfather was a Rabbi and the descendant of a distinguished line of illustrious Talmudists and thinkers. When she was three her family settled in Warsaw. At fifteen she entered an exclusive *Gymnasium* attended mainly by the children of senior Russian officials and army officers. But her radical views made her out of place and at the age of eighteen she moved to Zurich, where she came under the influence of Leon Jogiches, a strange, restless, sinister figure, who moved back and forward across the troubled face of Europe, surfacing, now in Vilna, now in Warsaw, now in Berlin, wherever there was commotion and unrest.

He was born in 1867 into a wealthy Lithuanian Jewish family, and joined the revolutionary Narodnaya Volya, which sought to pull up Russia by its roots through bringing political understanding to the peasants. It in fact found a lesser response among the peasantry than among the rising Russian-Jewish intelligentsia. The Narodnaya Volya denounced Jews as exploiters in the same breath as the Tsar and the nobility, and some of its leaders applauded the 1881 pogroms as a preliminary to a general peasant rising. It published a proclamation which would not have been out of place in a *pogromchik* tract:

People of the Ukraine suffer most of all from the Yids. Who has seized the land, woodlands, the taverns? The Yids. Whom does the peasant beg with tears in his eyes to let him near his land? The Yids. Wherever you look, whatever you touch, everywhere the Yids. The Yid curses the peasant, cheats him, drinks his blood.

Some Jewish revolutionaries, like the writer and philosopher, Chaim Zhitlowsky, were sufficiently repelled by such utterances to reconsider their situation and, eventually, to find their way back into Jewish life, and even into the Zionist movement. But by no means all did so and the proportion of Jewish Narodniks grew as the Narodnaya itself declined.

Jogiches remained with the movement till he was arrested by the Tsarist police. In 1890, when he was twenty-three, he fled to Switzerland, where he busied himself in journalism and edited *The Worker's Cause*, organ of the revolutionary Social Democratic Party. Rosa, who became his mistress, was his most active collaborator. He returned to Warsaw at the outbreak of the 1905 revolution and remained to lead the workers' strike in December of that year. He was arrested and remained in prison for two years before escaping and making his way back to Germany, where he took a leading part in the Spartacist rising of 1918, and where he was murdered in prison a year later.

Rosa was the more revolutionary of the two, the more passionate and the more consistent. She quickly came into conflict with the old Polish Socialist Party which Jogiches had helped to found, but which she found too narrowly nationalistic. Nationalism, she believed, betrayed both the worker's cause and the internationalism which alone could assure universal social justice.

The large centralized capitalist state, she said, was a step in that direction and the creation or perpetuation of petty nationalities was therefore a wasteful and reactionary endeavour. She condemned the Jewish *Bund*, founded in Vilna in 1897 to advance the cause of the Jewish worker, for the same reason. For although it opposed Jewish nationalism and merely sought cultural separatism, she believed that too could impede the struggle for world revolution and socialism. (She did, however, give tactical support to the *Bund* as a means of attracting the Yiddish-speaking, Jewish masses, who would have felt out of place in the Polish Socialist Party, which, for all its protestations about universal brotherhood, was riddled with anti-semitism.) In any case, she was not convinced that the Jews had a culture worth perpetuating. She knew little about it and the little she knew she did not much care for. The distinctiveness of the Jew, as far as she was concerned, lay in his *shtettle* existence, or as she put it, 'in socially backward, petit-bourgeois production, petty-commerce, small town life': the sooner it was brought to an end the better.

Jews, once they had withdrawn from Jewish life, did not always find a ready alternative and many of them found themselves part of a large and growing *déclassé* society, composed of people whose attainments had fallen short of their aspirations: artists, bohemians, failed lawyers, struggling writers, itinerant journalists, intellectual soldiers of fortune, who had cut themselves adrift from their own milieu without arriving upon a more satisfactory shore. They, but especially the Jews among them, were natural citizens of an international commonwealth, if only because they had no secure place within a national one. Being homeless they had no feeling for home, and being de-nationalized they had no feeling for nation, and Rosa was attacked by Polish Socialists for that very reason. They regarded her and her party as both anti-patriotic and 'anti-goy', almost part of an international Jewish conspiracy. 'As all Jews hate non-Jews', wrote one of her Polish critics, 'so Luxemburg's Social Democrats have a passionate hatred for Poles.' Others charged her with trying to Russify Poland.

She was wholly devoid of all Jewish sympathy and although she often spoke out on behalf of oppressed minorities like Poles and Armenians, she never uttered a word on behalf of Jews, even as victims of pogroms. 'Why do you come with your special Jewish sorrows?' she once protested. 'I feel just as sorry for the wretched Indian victims in Putamayo, the negroes in Africa . . . I cannot find a special corner in my heart for the ghetto', and she did not. Her latest biographer, Peter Nettl, sees this as proof of her internationalism; but she was but a further example of those revolutionaries – perhaps it is true of them all – for whom charity begins abroad, which is to say they will crucify their own family and those immediately about them, but be agonized by the afflictions of those they have never known and will never know. Rosa was rather more complicated and she was perhaps a little afraid of compassion. 'To be human is the main thing,' she wrote, 'and that means to be strong and clear, and of good cheer, in spite of and because of everything, for tears are the preoccupation of weakness.'

She came to Germany in 1898 after obtaining German citizenship through a sham marriage. She was principally concerned in building up the German Social Democratic Party (the SPD) as the leading force in the Second International and was joined in her efforts by numerous other East European, Jewish emigrés, like the sinister Parvus, Paul Singer, Arthur Stadhagen, and others, who were sometimes referred to collectively as 'the Great Sanhedrin'. All excited a greater or lesser degree of suspicion because of their rootlessness and their Jewishness, but Rosa, a woman, a Jewess, an ultra-revolutionary and a Pole, at the head of a German party, attracted particular hostility. Gustav Noske, who became military adviser of the SPD, said in his memoirs that the antagonism to Rosa and the others had nothing to do with their Jewishness, but grew out of the fondness of the East European Marxists in the SPD for 'transforming socialism into a dogma, and platitudes into articles of faith'. The Jews, said Noske, had evolved 'a secret science', Marxism, which was 'incomprehensible to the German worker'.

They were not much more comprehensible to the Polish workers with whom Rosa kept in touch through a torrent of articles in the workers' press. The year 1905 found her in Warsaw among the leaders of the Tsarist uprising. She was imprisoned but escaped and made her way back to Germany, where she threw herself into the agitation for improved labour conditions and sought to foment a general strike.

If feared as a revolutionary and polemicist, she was respected as an economist, and many who did not share her revolutionary beliefs accepted her argument that the inadequacy of local markets in a capitalist society must lead to a struggle for overseas markets which in turn must lead to the enlargement of overseas empires. These empires, she believed, would in due course become exhausted. But before that could happen capitalist society would collapse through its own internal conflicts, and the revolutionary proletariat would succeed. She developed these ideas in 1913, and they seemed to be corroborated by the events of the following years.

The First World War was to her one of the stages in the capitalist débâcle. She opposed it as an imperialist venture and spent long periods in jail. When she emerged she joined with Franz Mehring and Karl Liebknecht to establish the revolutionary *Spartakusbund*, which, with the collapse of 1918, made a brief but abortive attempt to seize power in Berlin. She was arrested, and murdered, while in prison, on 15 January 1919.

She continued to address her readers even from jail, and remained defiant to the last. She had been told that with the revolution crushed, order now reigned in Berlin. She retorted with irony:

Order now reigns in Berlin! You stupid lackeys! Your order is built on sand. Tomorrow the revolution will rear its head once more and announce to your horror, amid the brass of trumpets: 'I was, I am, I shall always be.'

At such moments the prophetic fervour of her Rabbinic ancestry glowed through her revolutionary mask.

Rosa was no Marx and she was not troubled by her antecedents. If she showed scant sympathy for Jewish suffering, she showed no hatred for the Jews nor contempt for the Jewish past and she was not afraid to lapse occasionally into Yiddish.

She was under almost continuous attack from anti-semites both from the left and right, derided and lampooned in Russian, Polish and German; but she shrugged it off. The very hostility and derision confirmed her in her beliefs. One cannot change worlds without upsetting men, and she aimed for nothing less.

She was not the only Jewish woman revolutionary. The revolutionary movement teemed with Amazons of Jewish origin like Hessia Mayerovna Helfman, the daughter of a wealthy Minsk family, who left home at sixteen to join the revolutionary movement in the Ukraine. She was arrested, but escaped, and joined the Narodnaya Volya terrorist group in St Petersburg. In 1881 she was implicated in the assassination of Tsar Alexander II and sentenced to death. The execution was, however, delayed, because she was pregnant, and she died in the Peter-and-Paul fortress shortly after the birth of her child. She was twenty-seven.

Anna Kulichev likewise came from a prosperous Jewish home, graduated from university and promptly joined the revolutionary movement. She married first the revolutionary populist Makerewich, then the Italian anarchist, Costa, and finally the Socialist leader, Turati, and became the virtual head of the Italian labour movement.

Rosalie Bograd, who stemmed from a similar background, married Plekhanov, who, with Lenin, stood at the head of the revolutionary movement. Plekhanov was not Jewish and regarded those Jews in the revolutionary movement who harboured Jewish sympathies, or hungered for Jewish culture, as latent Zionists. He defined a Bundist as a Zionist who was afraid of sea-sickness. His wife, however, after a horrifying outbreak of pogroms, confessed:

Deep down in the soul of each of us revolutionaries of Jewish birth, there was a sense of hurt pride and infinite pity for our own, and many of us were strongly tempted to devote ourselves to serving our injured, humiliated and persecuted people.

But not many of them gave in to the temptation. In so far as they gave thought to the plight of Jewry at all, it was to see their salvation in world revolution. Private passions were suppressed for the public good.

When one comes to the enigmatic figure of Lev Davidovich Bronstein, alias Leon Trotsky, one is no longer certain that he had private passions to suppress. He was born in 1879, the son of a fairly well-to-do father, whom he described as 'a wealthy kulak'. Jews had been offered an opportunity to settle in the southern Ukraine in the latter years of the nineteenth century, and his father was among the few who accepted. It removed him and his family from the main centres of Jewish life, which he did not appear to regard as a disadvantage. 'Father did not believe in God from his youth,' said Trotsky. 'Mother preferred to avoid the subject, but when occasion required would raise her eyes in prayer.' They nevertheless attempted to give their son a Jewish education, and attended synagogue during the main festivals.

In 1888 Trotsky was sent to live with an uncle in Odessa and, while still a mathematics student at university, he joined the proscribed Social Democratic Party. He was drawn to Marxism, he said, 'as a universal solution to the problems of mankind as a whole'.

The feeling of the supremacy of the general over the particular experience, of law over fact, of theory over personal experience, took root in my mind at an early age and gained increasing strength as the years advanced.

Loyalty to concepts could mean disloyalty to men and the more he became involved as a theoretician, the less he seemed to feel like a man.

He opposed the Bund and, like Rosa, accused it of endangering the anti-Tsarist front by encouraging Jewish workers along the path to separatism. He dismissed anti-semitism – even in the aftermath of Kishinev – as a passing phenomenon which would cease once the Russian masses had acquired socialist consciousness. He regarded the pogroms as a Tsarist effort to divert the masses from popular discontent. It would, he believed, all end with the revolution.

In 1898 he was arrested for revolutionary activities and sent to Siberia, but he escaped, and, in 1902, fled to England, where he joined Lenin, Martov and Axelrod in editing *Iskra*, the party paper. At first he kept to the Menshevik wing of the party and even attacked Lenin and the Bolsheviks for dictatorial tendencies. It was during this period that he developed his theory of permanent revolution and argued that a bourgeois revolution in Russia would lead through its own momentum to a social revolution even before revolution in the West. The theory was eventually to estrange him from the party leadership and lead to his downfall.

After three years in London he made his way back to Russia to head the St Petersburg soviet in the 1905 uprising. He was again arrested, again escaped and again returned to England. He had the most original and brilliant mind in the party, excelled as a writer, speaker and strategist and possessed what is rarely found with such talents, a unique organizing ability. He became less critical of Lenin as he grew increasingly impatient with the hesitant approach of the Mensheviks. He returned to Russia shortly after the outbreak of the 1917 February revolution and was elected to the Central Committee of the Bolshevik Party. Most Jewish socialist leaders like Martov and Axelrod remained with the Mensheviks, but others, like Kamenev and Zinoviev, joined him in the Bolshevik camp.

If the October revolution could not have taken place without Lenin, it could not have triumphed without Trotsky, who, as Minister of War, created the Red Army out of chaos and found the new men and the new talents (often Jewish) to replace the Tsarist officer corps, a large part of which had joined the White Armies or had fled into exile. Churchill called him the Carnot of the revolution.

To many outside observers, especially those who had imbibed *The Protocols of the Elders of Zion* (which enjoyed a wide circulation in the immediate post-war years), the Russian revolution looked like a Jewish conspiracy, especially when it was followed by Jewish-led revolutionary outbreaks in much of central Europe. The leadership of the Bolshevik Party had a preponderance of Jews and included Litvinov (Wallach), Liadov (Mandelshtam), Shklovsky, Saltz, Gusev (Drabkin), Zemliachka (Salkind), Helena Rozmirovich, Serafima Gopner, Yaroslavsky (Gubelman), Yaklovlev (Epstein), Riaznov (Goldendach), Uritsky and Larin.

Of the seven members of the Politburo, the inner cabinet of the country, four, Trotsky, Zinoviev, Kamenev and Sverdlov, were Jews. The last-named, a gentle-looking figure, with a small pointed beard and pince-nez, became Chairman of the All Russian Central Committee of the Communist Party, and as such was successor to the Tsars as titular head of state. He died suddenly in 1919 at the age of thirty-four. The city of Yekaterinburg was renamed Sverdlovsk in his honour and he has entered the gallery of Communist immortals. It is unlikely that he would have been so honoured had he lived longer. All the other Jews on the Politburo died a violent death.

Zinoviev, who was born Grigori Yevseyevich Radomysiski, the son of a prosperous assimilated family, became principal architect of the Communist International and its first chairman. He joined the Russian Socialist Democratic Party in 1901 and moved over to the Communist wing two years later. Like Trotsky, he played a major role in the 1905 revolution in St Petersburg, and later had to seek refuge in Europe. In April 1917 he rode back with Lenin on the sealed train which was to take them to the Finland station and revolution. He had little of Trotsky's audacity and counselled against launching the October revolution in case it should result in foreign intervention, which it eventually did. But intervention was less effective, while the Red Army proved more effective, than he believed. He remained high in the party ranks and was mainly concerned with the Comintern, the international revolutionary movement. His efforts helped to sustain the belief that Communism was a Jewish conspiracy. The collapse of the German revolutionary movement, which he had done much to forward, weakened his position, but he survived that too and when Lenin died, in 1924, he formed part of the Troika with Kamenev and Stalin.

Leb Borisovich Kamenev (né Rosenfeld) was ten years younger than Zinoviev, but otherwise his career followed a strangely parallel course. Like him he joined the SDP and like him moved over to the Communist wing, and became one of Lenin's close collaborators, and like him again he opposed the October rising, suggesting instead a coalition government of all socialist parties.

The Stalin-Zinoviev-Kamenev triumvirate was formed mainly to keep Trotsky from the succession. They stayed together because they did not trust each other apart. Yet, though Zinoviev and Kamenev feared Trotsky as too militant and extreme, they shared his belief in permanent revolution, which Stalin did not. Russia had been in almost continuous turmoil for twenty years and had suffered revolutions and counter-revolutions, war, invasions and a pitiless and drawn-out civil war. There were limits to which the endurance of a people could be stretched. The Russians wanted to bury their dead and resume what they could of normal life. Stalin understood this. Trotsky, Zinoviev and Kamenev did not. They were, for all their immersion in Russian history and culture, Western in outlook. Trotsky even admitted that nationalist passions were incomprehensible to him, which made him a sort of political eunuch. The very intensity of their internationalist fervour detached them from the aspirations of Russia. All three were consummate intriguers, but they were no match for Stalin. Trotsky was outmanoeuvred. In 1925 he was forced to resign as Minister of War, and two years later he was hounded out of the party. He embarked on a life of wandering which was brought to an abrupt end in August 1940, when a visitor, believed to be acting on Stalin's orders, put an ice-pick through his brain.

Zinoviev and Kamenev were likewise ousted from the party in 1927. Kamenev recanted and was re-admitted, but both remained in comparative obscurity till they emerged as leading witnesses during the Stalinist reign of terror. In the Moscow show trials of the mid-'thirties, together with fifteen other former party colleagues, they were charged with plotting against the state. Both confessed to everything said against them and both were executed.

Churchill, in a book on eminent contemporaries, spoke of Trotsky and his associates as 'cold Semitic internationalists'. He saw 'no trace of compassion' in Trotsky, 'no sense of human kinship, no apprehension of the spiritual' and he had no doubt that his Jewishness was in the end the sole obstacle to his supremacy:

> He was a Jew. He was still a Jew. Nothing could get over that. Hard fortune when you have deserted your family, repudiated your race, spat upon the religion of your fathers, and lapped Jew and Gentile in a common malignity, to be baulked of so great a prize for so narrow-minded a reason!

Trotsky was aware that his Jewishness was no advantage. When Lenin sought to make him Commissar of Home Affairs, he declined because he thought it would play into the hands of the White Russians, but he liked to think that as War Minister he surmounted the handicap, and in his autobiography he recalled with pride that when a Cossack was taunted for taking orders from a Jew, he retorted: 'Trotsky is not a Jew, Trotsky is a fighter, he's ours, he is Russian . . .'

He was certainly not regarded as such in all parts of Russia and as far as the White Armies were concerned he was a *zhid*, the *zhid* who in his viciousness and brutality seemed to confirm all the dark myths about Jews which had been festering in the Russian imagination for centuries. He was a gift to their propagandists. They could represent their struggle as a war, not against their fellow Russians, but against alien intruders, and they explained the pogroms (which they instigated and which led to the death of a hundred thousand Jews in the Ukraine alone) and atrocities reminiscent of Chmielnicki, as a response to the atrocities perpetrated by Trotsky and the Reds.

It is understandable that most Jews, given their suffering under the Tsars, should have welcomed the revolution, and those who had been undecided had their minds made up for them by the pogroms. There was every indication that a White victory could have meant the extermination of Russian Jewry. Moreover, as soon as the Reds were in office they abolished the Pale of Settlement and removed all Jewish disabilities with a stroke of the pen. Jews were soon to suffer other disabilities, but they suffered them in common with the rest of the population: their pariah status was at an end. Indeed, there had been a dramatic reversal of fortunes, and some Jews, who had fled from Russia for their lives, returned to witness the unbelievable.

It was 'a topsy-turvy world', said one. 'The despised had come to sit on the throne and those who had been the least were now the mightiest.' The writer, A. S. Sachs, noted with exaltation:

The Jewish Bolsheviks demonstrate before the entire world that the Jewish people are not yet degenerate, and that this ancient people is still alive and full of vigour. If a people can produce men who can undermine the foundations of the world and strike terror into the hearts of countries and governments, then it is a good omen for itself, a clear sign of its youthfulness, its vitality and stamina.

Trotsky, in particular, was a source both of concern and of pride, concern at the fact that all Jewry would be, and indeed was being, held to blame for his action, yet pride in his achievements. For he excelled in the one area where Jews were thought to be – and had even thought of themselves as being – deficient. As a writer of the period observed:

To the passive heroism of martyrdom was now added the heroism of the sword, the gun, the cannon and the tank, controlled by the Jewish mind; and although I know I am witness to the fact that this Trotsky reneges on his people and turns his back on his brethren, I find it nevertheless difficult not to be proud of him.

All this led to a ready inflow of young Jews, from both bourgeois and working-class homes, into the Communist party, and even the fall of Trotsky and the Moscow trials did not seriously impede the flow. There was a movement which had avenged the pogroms, outlawed anti-semitism, and which, as the spread of Fascism grew more ominous, was alone prepared to battle with the enemies of freedom and progress. And thus, while in Russia one Jew after another was removed from the party hierarchies, Jews had a prominent role in Communist parties elsewhere. In newly independent Poland, which was the main centre of European Jewish life, about a quarter of party members and about a third of delegates to party congresses were Jews. They also formed a considerable, if less conspicuous, proportion of the Communist parties in other parts of Europe, and in left-wing groups, such as the Industrial Workers of the World (the 'Wobblies') in America. The fact that Judaism (in common with other religions) was proscribed was not regarded – by the Jewish left-wingers certainly – as unfortunate. Jews were allowed a certain degree of cultural autonomy (how limited it was was never quite realized in the West until it was suppressed altogether).

When Trotsky wrote that anti-semitism was still fairly rife in the Soviet Union he was answered by the veteran American leftist, B. Z. Goldberg, that Trotsky seemed to have discovered anti-semitism in Russia only after he had fallen from power.

Jewish Communists were troubled by the show trials because they seemed to make a mockery of legality and justice, and because so many of the victims were Jews. But the final betrayal came with the Soviet-Nazi pact of 1939. It seemed to confirm the suspicions about the true nature of Communism which had from time to time impinged upon their consciousness, but which, like true believers, they had refused to entertain. It was only when Hitler invaded Russia in 1941 and was shattered by the Russian armies that they were able to raise their heads again. But then came the renewal of the reign of terror, the 'Doctor's Plot' in Moscow, the Slansky trial in Czechoslovakia, and it was clear that during his last days Stalin was prepared to unleash a personal war against the Jews which would have echoed the Nazi atrocities. Jews did not, as a result, vanish entirely from the Communist parties of Europe and America, but they ceased to be ubiquitous.

Many were to discover in Communism 'the God that failed' and Jewish leftists perhaps found it harder to reconcile themselves to the fact than anyone else. They were not, as Stalin had dubbed them, 'rootless cosmopolitans'. Their roots were in international Communism, which was a new and larger Zion. To a people conscious of centuries of constriction, the ghetto, the Pale, there was a breezy openness to Communism. They were members of a new order, on a par with others, equals, or rather more than equal, for they were charter members, each a minor Moses leading not merely a people, but mankind, into a promised land. Jews have often been accused of stand-offishness, exclusiveness, but, in fact, wherever they have enjoyed free and full access to an open world, they have joined it *en masse*. However, access has never been entirely free and they have had to resort to major or minor subterfuges, changing name, faith, camouflaging antecedents to gain admission. Not that one could dispense with subterfuges under Communism; Bronstein became Trotsky; Sobeisohn, Kamenev, and Wallach, Litvinov, but they were entering a faith partly of their own creation. Here, as in the old faith, there need be no debates on ultimates – that was settled by history, though there was room for active effort to bring the inevitable nearer. And the Jewish Communist who combined his creed with a sense of Jewish history could even tell himself that he was making the vision of the Prophets manifest on earth, for there was hardly a humane sentiment among the slogans of Communism which had not received its first utterance in Scripture.

The desire to improve their own conditions hardly entered their minds. There were various Jewish trade unions with extremely radical inclinations, but short and chaotic histories. The Garment Workers Union of America at one time had a strong Communist element. But Jewish workers, especially in America and Western Europe, where they had opportunities for advancement, did not form a steady class, and in the main did not think of themselves in class terms, but as members of the bourgeoisie, who were, for the time being, in reduced circumstances. For it is not circumstances which form a class, but aspirations, and, in the main, the Jew who turned to Communism was not moved by material ambitions. Many, as we have seen, were from prosperous Jewish homes, and some, like Jogiches, gave over considerable private fortunes to the party. Its appeal was in the promise of a new and better order.

The feeling of disillusion began with Stalin's declaration of 'socialism in one country', for if it ceased to be international, then it would cease to be accommodating to even the de-Judaized Jew. Then came the show trials, the pact with Hitler, and finally, the *coup de grâce* of the Doctor's Plot and the Slansky trial. There was no consolation in the thought that Russia was but a perversion of Communism, for there were by then many other socialist republics, and the more one studied them the more it became clear that Communism was so prone to perversion that it was perhaps inherently perverse.

The young, however, were by then discovering other gods and other company, in circles vaguely referred to as the 'New Left'. It was new in the sense that Russia, instead of featuring in its pantheon, was now in its bestiary. It embraced no consistent doctrines or clear ideology, but it was vehemently against the existing order and was based mainly on the universities. Again Jews were well to the fore, but unlike the old left, there was nothing in the external circumstances of Jewry to explain why Jews should be drawn to it more than others.

The New Left is a general term applied to a chaos of shifting groups, some of them minuscule in size, which have rejected some of the orthodoxies of the old left, but who still find themselves in conflict with existing society and who are struggling for what they think of as a better and more just universe. Most of the leaders who achieved national reputations, like Mark Rudd, Jerry Rubin and Abby Hoffman, were Jewish, though one of the reasons why they achieved national reputations was that they knew how to attract the media, and in some cases the attraction of the media was an end in itself, answering to a need which is almost universal among Jews (and possibly peculiar to them): to rise above anonymity. While the old left scribbled away, unnoticed and unread, for obscure journals and semi-clandestine presses, with one eye over their shoulder for the police, the new only had to spit in the face of authority to become instant celebrities: what was often no more than puerile insolence was raised to the level of a creed. The principal mentor of the movement was the philosopher, Herbert Marcuse, an old Marxist who was born in Berlin in 1898 and took part in the uprisings of 1918–19, moving to America after the rise of Hitler. Marcuse argued that fascism, far from being antithetical to liberalism, was its logical outcrop – that civilized society was necessarily repressive and that capitalist society, through its very need for increasing returns on increasing quantities of capital, will tend to suppress genuine needs and control man as a submissive consumer for the benefit of the *rentier* class. From there it was but a step to show that to tolerate capitalism was to invite repression.

The Vietnam war and the struggle of American Blacks for civil rights seemed to confirm his thesis, and gave his disciples an immediate cause for their zeal. Even if their immediate actions were anti-social and at times outrageous, they could claim, not entirely without justification, to be governed by a higher morality. They were joined in their efforts by a great many people, a large proportion of them Jewish, who could not by any stretch of the imagination be thought of as part of the New or, indeed, old Left, but who had become sceptical of the judgment and good faith of their own government.

All this tended to make the New Left a largely American phenomenon. It had a much smaller following in Europe, where, however, they used their weight at a crucial moment and in May 1968 brought France to the verge of revolution. Here too, the leaders, Alain Krivine, Alain Geismar and Daniel Cohn-Bendit, were all of Jewish origin (a fact which did not pass unnoticed among the French Right).

The upheavals in the American universities in the 'sixties, though damaging and painful, were hardly more lasting than the panty raids of the 'fifties and in the long term they may prove to have been no more significant. Professor Walter Laqueur has dismissed the whole phenomenon out of hand: 'The New Left', he wrote in *Next Year in Jerusalem*, 'lacks seriousness; it seems a repeat performance by hams of a well-known play, bearing out Marx's dictum about great events happening twice, the second time as farce.'

One of the reasons given why Jews were so prominent in the campus upheavals is that they were mainly centred around Berkeley and Columbia, where Jews are particularly numerous. But it could be equally argued that

'one who lives on the interest from govt. bonds

175

the upheavals were centred round Columbia and Berkeley because of their large Jewish intake.

The sociologist, Professor Nathan Glazer, has suggested that because Jewish families were mainly middle class, rationalistic, child-centred and psychologically understanding, they tended to produce children 'intolerant of rules and restrictions and insistent on the achievement of the ideal society'. Here one may see a link between the New Left and the Ultra-Orthodox Jew from what one might describe as the Very Old Right, who also looks for the ideal society, and prays for it daily. Only the latter feels it must come at the end of days, while the former believes that by shaking the world a little it may come in the here and now.

In the nineteenth century, of course, Jews had a vested interest in revolution. Conservatism impeded their progress, and the left, even if it had its anti-semites, was, on the whole, on their side. As Wilhelm Liebknecht, the German socialist leader, observed:

Slavery demoralizes, but it also acts as a purgatory and gives an uplift to those who are strong, it creates rebels and idealists. And so we find precisely as a result of their past experience intense feeling for freedom and justice among Jews and there is more idealism among them, proportionally at any rate, than among non-Jews.

Leon Blum argued that the God of the Jews was justice, but it could also be that Jewish tradition abhorred settled prosperity. There is an almost instinctive feeling among Jews that where there is wealth there must be corruption. Gustav Mayer, the historian of German socialism, compared Marx's analysis of the iniquities of capitalism to the words of Isaiah. Karl Kautsky, on the other hand, argued that while Jews were revolutionary, Judaism was reactionary, and perhaps the latter gave rise to the former. Isaac Deutscher has suggested that the position of Jews as congenital outsiders predisposed them to revolution: 'They were born and brought up on the borderline of various epochs.'

Werner Sombart, the economic historian, saw the restlessness of the Jew in his tendency to think and live in abstractions and in his rootlessness. Rootlessness, he said, made the Jew less deferential to tradition, but it also made him less responsible and more inclined to think in logical principles removed from the realities of everyday life. It did not – as Judaism did not – take sufficient account of individuality. On the other hand, since the existing order was inimical to the Jew, it was understandable that the Jew should have been inimical to the existing order. Today's existing order, however, favours the Jews. Why then are so many Jews still on the other side of the barricades? Is it part of a hereditary habit of mind that one continues to rebel long after the causes for rebellion have been removed?

In the past the Jewish revolutionary had frequent ideological conflicts with other Jewish groups, especially the Bund, and they poured scorn on the *Poalei Zion*, the Zionist Workers Party, who wanted to secure an identifiable Jewish corner in the brave new world. Chaim Weizmann, who, as a student in Switzerland, was a contemporary of numerous revolutionaries in exile, later recalled the conflicts:

Our sympathies were with the revolutionaries; they, however, would not tolerate in the Jewish youth any expression of separate attachment to the Jewish people, or even special awareness of the Jewish problem ... *They* could not understand why a Russian Jew should want to be anything but a Russian. *They* stamped as unworthy, as intellectually backward, as chauvinistic and immoral, the desire of any Jew to occupy himself with the sufferings and destiny of Jewry.

But they, at least, lived before the holocaust, before Stalin, before the purges, before the show trials, before the Nazi-Soviet pact, before the Doctor's Plot, before the idea of Jewish salvation within a socialist universe had repeatedly been shown to be vain and preposterous. Moreover, they lived before the emergence of Israel.

While Israel was small and struggling and seemed impermanent, it was spared leftish anathemas, but after the Six Day War, when it emerged as a power and showed every sign of being here to stay, Jewish members of the New Left joined with others in denouncing it as a nation of imperialists, colonialists and exploiters. The Jewish state was not without faults, but neither was it without virtues, and given the recent history of the Jewish people, one might have thought its achievements would have evoked a spasm of joy in even the most desiccated Jewish soul. But the left too has its Bourbons, who have forgotten nothing and learnt nothing, and who, by struggling for the unattainable, threaten all that has been attained.

The Talmud has a phrase for it: *Tofasto merubo lo tofasto.* He who seeks too much finds nothing.

One consideration, however, has to be kept in mind. The old Jewish revolutionaries, in so far as they were aware of the Jewish problem at all, thought it could be solved in a socialist context. The new think there is no problem, and if there is, it has arisen out of Jewish statehood.

The Jewish revolutionaries have been the Hassidim of the left and have shown the same inability to accept man as he is. Like the Hassidim, they have never let facts stand in the way of their enthusiasms.

The Jew is brought up in a faith which believes that man was born perfect and though he may have gone wrong is still perfectible. It is the sort of belief which lingers long after the other components of the faith have atrophied. Even where a young Jew has turned against Judaism it remains covert as a residual article of faith. The faithful are content in the knowledge that He who promised the good life would in time deliver. The non-believers have no such assurance and are driven into activity by their non-belief.

But perhaps there is something in the Jewish character, or at least in the character of many Jews, which disposes them to upheaval for its own sake: perhaps they have lived so long amidst chaos that they find something unsettling in stability.

CHAPTER NINE

Not Playing the Game

There is but one sport in which Jews have figured prominently, horse-racing, and there, of course, the horses do the running. Jews are not lazy. They are certainly not unambitious or uncompetitive, but there are so many real events to evoke their competitive spirit that they are reluctant to apply it to pseudo-events.

Speed and agility are admirable but they feel no compulsion to out-run the horse or out-leap the hind. There is no Hermes in the Jewish pantheon and no Diana. There is no Jewish pantheon, and all the visions of the One God suggest that He is a sedentary being. One should run to perform a good deed, urges the Talmud, but otherwise there is almost an inference of indelicacy in speed. The Jewish athlete entering upon a race has to contend not only with his fellows, but his own past. Yet in spite of that not a few have risen to the highest pinnacles of achievement.

In 1972 Mark Spitz was the first athlete to win seven gold medals in one Olympics (all in swimming), and this after winning two gold medals, one silver and one bronze at the 1968 games. Another Jewish sporting star, Agnes Keleti, an Hungarian, was already reaching international promi-nence when the war broke out. She had to spend several years in hiding to escape the Nazis. In 1952 she won four medals, including one gold, in gymnastics. Four years later, at the age of thirty-five, she won four gold and two silver medals in the same events. By then the Hungarian revolt had erupted and she did not return to Budapest but made her home in Israel, where she became an athletics coach.

At the first Olympics in 1896 the Flatow brothers from Germany won five medals in gymnastics between them, and Hajor-Guttman, a Hungarian swimmer, won two gold medals. In 1900 Myer Prinstein, an American athlete, won one gold medal and one silver and a further two gold medals four years later in track events. In 1908 Dr Jeno Fuchs, a Hungarian, won two gold medals in fencing, and did the same again in 1912. In that year, in fact, Jewish sportsmen won no less than ten gold and three silver medals in fencing and thereby established something of a tradition. Since then there has rarely been an international tournament where Jews have not come away with at least one gold medal in fencing. The *Encyclopaedia Judaica* shows that between 1896 and 1968, one hundred and thirty-one Jews from seventeen countries won two hundred and thirty-six medals (including one hundred and one gold). Of these, no less than seventy-one were in fencing, which is a curious fact. But those who look for social or historical reasons for particular expertise in a particular field will find none here. Jews were never known for including 'a trusty blade' in their accoutrements and, indeed, in many places, over many years, Jews were not allowed to wear a sword at all. There used to be a popular Polish expression: 'I need it like a Jew needs a sword' (which is roughly equivalent to the Yiddish: 'I need it like a hole in the head'). Is this new-found interest in swords and swordsmanship a subconscious attempt to compensate for the deprived years? One has heard suggestions that the Jewish skill in fencing is a sign of Jewish insecurity or aggressiveness, perhaps even both. But in either case one would have witnessed an even greater Jewish prominence in shooting, or at least javelin-throwing. But although a Jew, Philo Jacoby, representing the American Sharp Shooters Association, won the Berlin shooting championship as long ago as 1868, Jews have won only two medals in shooting in the entire history of the Olympics, neither of them gold. Nor did they get far with the javelin.

In boxing we approach an area where Jews have been rather more successful but then boxing is not only a sport but a livelihood, even if not one which a Jewish mother would care to choose for a Jewish son (one has never heard proud cries of 'my son the boxer').

Possibly the greatest Jewish name in boxing was Daniel Mendoza (1764–1836), who styled himself proudly as 'Mendoza the Jew'. Though a natural middleweight he devised a scientific defence which enabled him to defeat much heavier opponents and brought him the patronage of the Prince of Wales. He had an immense following and toured the entire country to give exhibition bouts. He later formed his own boxing academy and wrote a book on the art of boxing which became something of a classic. When the Boxing Hall of Fame was opened in the United States in 1954 his name was amongst the first to be included.

Mendoza lived at a time when Anglo-Jewry comprised a few hundred families crammed into a small part of east London, and his fame and success encouraged many other young Jews from the same area to take up the sport. They included 'Dutch Sam' Elias, who is credited with inventing the uppercut, Barney Aaron (known also as 'The Star of the East' – presumably the East End), Angel Hyams and Aaron Mendoza (both of them cousins of Daniel), and the four Belasco brothers, Israel, Abraham, Samuel, and John, who between them formed something of a travelling circus. And there were others, lesser known, who appeared in such numbers that for a time boxing seemed to be as much a Jewish calling as the old-clothes trade.

Mendoza, as we have mentioned, was one cause of the phenomenon. Many of the boxers grew to maturity during the Napoleonic War, when trade was widely disrupted, unemployment was widespread, and many a young Jew unable to live on his wits turned to the use of his hands. Moreover, in spite of the personal acclaim enjoyed by Mendoza, Jews were far from popular. They had to learn to defend themselves and where money was short, as it usually was, the more skilful among them turned professional. Thereafter every generation brought forth its own stars, not a few of whom moved to America, where the pickings were richer. One such emigrant, Barney Aaron, a grand-nephew of Mendoza, won the American lightweight championship in 1857.

This was the area in which Jewish skill was most pronounced, with one doubtful exception – one does not find an outstanding Jewish boxer above the welterweight level. Those who made their mark tended to be perky bantams who made up in agility, pluck and perhaps *chutzpah* what they lacked in bulk.

It was possibly the very awareness of their meagre size that led many young Jews to acquire skills in boxing. Moreover most Jewish boxers were from immigrant stock, and most Jewish immigrants were kept small by poverty and hardship. (How then does one explain the great Irish and Black heavyweight bruisers, for they were not less poor? The answer may perhaps lie in the lower level of Jewish infant mortality. A Black or Irish child had to be inherently robust to survive, whereas a Jewish child, if he had any life in him at all, was nursed into survival.)

Benny Leonard (born Benjamin Leiner), who died in the ring in 1947 while refereeing a fight, was widely regarded as the greatest lightweight of all time. Born in New York's Lower East Side in 1896 Leonard entered the prize ring at the age of fifteen. A further four years were to pass before he actually won a fight. In 1921 he won the lightweight championship and retired unbeaten in 1925.

His success in the ring had given him an income which he could not find outside it and in 1931 he returned to professional boxing as a welterweight, but with unhappy results. He retired permanently a year later. During World War II he served as Lt Commander in the Maritime Service. He was among the few Jews to be voted into the Boxing Hall of Fame.

Another was Barney Ross, who was the first boxer in the history of the sport to hold both the lightweight *and* the welterweight championship at one and the same time.

Like Leonard he was born on New York's East Side but moved with his family to Chicago. His father, a baker, was shot dead in a robbery. Barney's younger brothers were sent to an orphanage and his first ambition was to earn enough money to reunite the family. He found it in the ring. He turned professional at nineteen, and five years later won the world lightweight championship at twenty-four, and a year later he knocked out Jimmy McLarin to acquire the welterweight title as well. They had return bouts in which the title passed between them a number of times, but Ross was beaten in 1938 by Henry Armstrong and retired from the ring with a record of seventy-four wins (twenty-four by knockout), three draws, four losses, and one no-decision.

He had changed his name from Rosolsky to Ross but was, according to press handouts, an observant Jew who did not fight or train on Jewish festivals, commemorated the anniversary of his father's death with prayers, wore *tzitzit* under his shirt, and preferred home-cooked Jewish food. His mother, it was said, used to smuggle a *mezuzah* into his trunks for luck (which might have proved to be less than a lucky charm had he been hit below the belt).

Ross served in the Marines during World War II, was injured at Guadalcanal and developed a drug addiction as a result of his treatment. He was, after a prolonged struggle, cured of the habit, and devoted the rest of his life to combating the trade in illegal narcotics. He died in 1967.

Gershon Mendeloff (1893–1970), better known as Kid Lewis, was in substantially the same class as Ross and in 1915 became welterweight champion of the world after a gruelling twelve-round contest in Boston, but lost the title four years later and retired from the ring in 1929 with a record of 155 wins (sixty-five by knockout), six draws, twenty-four defeats, and sixty-five no-decisions. He, too, was voted into America's Boxing Hall of Fame.

Lewis was born in London's East End and began to box professionally at fifteen. In the 'thirties he won a sad notoriety as personal bodyguard to the leader of the British Union of Fascists, Sir Oswald Mosley, till it became increasingly clear to him that as a Jew he was not quite welcome and he left.

Max Baer (1909–59), who was born in Nebraska and raised on a ranch in California, became heavyweight champion of the world after knocking out title-holder Primo Carnera in the eleventh round, in 1934, but he in turn lost his title to James J. Braddock a year later, and was again defeated in 1935 by Joe Louis. He became the darling of the Jewish public when he knocked out Max Schmeling, Germany's reigning champion, and a former world heavyweight, in 1933. It was almost like giving Hitler a poke in the eye.

Baer wore a Star of David on his boxing trunks and claimed that his father was of Jewish extraction, but this appears to have been little more than a publicity stunt. The belief that he was Jewish, however, persisted, especially among Jews, who found it difficult to believe that, at a time when many Jews were trying to hide their origins, someone not Jewish should claim that he was.

Although comparatively few Jews rose to the first rank of boxing champions, a great many have been involved in the sport. To the thrusting, agile youngster from the slums, it promised ready money and possible fame. The fame was perhaps more important than the money, and there can be no doubt that one of the reasons why boxing has appealed to Jews is that it is basically an adjunct of show-business. A man playing as a footballer or competing in track events is part of a crowd. In the ring he has the audience almost to himself. There is drama to the event itself and it offers scope for a certain amount of theatricality. One is less athlete than performer.

Boxing is also an adjunct of the gambling trade, which is largely a Jewish one, and although there are people who would stake money on the outcome of a game of hopscotch, nothing can bring out the sort of stakes which a major boxing match can command.

There are certain parallels between boxing and the art world, for if there are few great Jewish artists, the greatest art-dealers have been Jews. The same is true of boxing promoters. Mike Jacobs (1880–1953), who dominated the sport for nearly half a century, was to boxing what Lord Duveen was to painting.

Jewish boxers of standing are few and getting fewer. The golden days of the Jewish boxer were the golden days of the urban ghetto. It was an immigrant's calling. There are now easier ways of making a living.

Two Jews, Hank Greenberg and Sandy Koufax, have been elected to the Baseball Hall of Fame, and a third, Lipman E. Pike, was among the pioneers of the game.

Pike, who was generally known as Lip, a brawny figure with an exuberant moustache, was born in New York in 1845, becoming baseball's first professional in 1866, when he signed on with Philadelphia Athletics. He moved on to Brooklyn Athletics and, in 1870, participated in one of the most famous games in baseball history, when his team beat the Cincinnati Red Stockings (America's first all-professional team), ending a run of victories which had extended to 130 games and seemed likely to go on for ever.

Pike was a powerful, all-round player, who got off his mark like a rocket. He established the first home-run record in 1866, when he hit six in one game.

He died in 1893 and some forty years passed before American Jewry produced another player of his rank in the improbable person of Henry Greenberg.

Henry, or Hank as he was generally known, stemmed from a prosperous New York family, and it was his intention, initially, to be a lawyer. He was tall, gangling, six feet four inches in height, awkward in movement, slow of pace and flat-footed. If his class had voted on the pupil least likely to become player of the year he would have been the natural choice. But he liked baseball and during his holidays would knock about with bat and ball for some eight hours a day. 'Hank never played games,' said his school coach, 'he worked on them.' He hated losing to boys smaller than himself – which most boys were – and he gained through application an agility which was denied to him by birth. By the time he left school he had developed sufficient skill to interest several talent scouts, and when he enrolled for a law course at the New York University School of Commerce he already had a contract with the Detroit Tigers up his sleeve. The contract had an unsettling effect on his schooling. He left after the first term, joined the Tigers as first baseman and in 1934 helped them to win their first American League pennant in twenty-five years. The Tigers were the champions again in 1935 and Greenberg won the American League's Most Valuable Player award as a first baseman. In 1939 he won the award as left fielder and was the first player to receive the award for two different positions. By 1941 he was earning the highest salary in baseball. After Pearl Harbor, however, he volunteered for active service, and rose to the rank of Captain in the army airforce. He returned in 1945, after a break of four years, when he was already in his mid-thirties, as if nothing had happened, and won the pennant for the Tigers on the last day of the season with a grand slam home run in the ninth inning. By 1946 his age was beginning to tell on him and early in 1947 he heard on the radio, by chance, that he had been 'waived out' of the American League and sold to the National League Pittsburgh Pirates. He continued to draw a high salary and large crowds, but his batting average dropped, his playing was uninspired, an old arm injury began to reassert itself and in 1948 he retired from the game. He later went into management and became general manager and vice president of the Cleveland Indians and the Chicago White Sox.

Sandy Koufax, a dazzling 'south-paw', nicknamed 'The Man with the Golden Arm', belongs to the post-World War II generation. Born in 1935, the son of a Brooklyn lawyer, he was awarded an athletic scholarship to the University of Cincinnati on his record as a basketball player. But he played for the University's baseball team with such effect that by the end of his first term he was being importuned at every turn by talent scouts and in 1954, two weeks before his nineteenth birthday, he signed on with Brooklyn Dodgers.

At university he had shown phenomenal skill as a pitcher, but his performance as a professional, both as pitcher and as batter, was at first erratic. 'Koufax has a bad competitive spirit,' complained a colleague. 'He never had to ride the bus leagues. He doesn't realize what it means to pitch and win in the majors.' It was not until 1961 that he at last vindicated the hopes which had been vested in him. One of his faults, as he himself admitted, was that he was less concerned with precision than force and he projected each ball like a ballistic missile. He changed tactics and in the 1961 season he won eighteen games, lost thirteen and struck out a total of 269 batters, breaking the league record held previously by Christy Mathewson. The 1962 season promised to be equally triumphant until he was forced to withdraw with a finger ailment arising from a blood clot in his palm. For a time it was feared that his finger might have to be amputated. The ailment was, however, cured and in the 1963 season he set a one-game mark of fifteen strikeouts in the World Series against the New York Yankees and he more than any other player was responsible for his team's winning the National League pennant. He was the first pitcher to average more than one strikeout per inning in his career.

In 1965, while still at the height of his career, he developed an arthritic condition in his left elbow, and a year later, when only thirty, he retired from the game.

A tall, lean, somewhat solitary figure, Koufax, like Greenberg, would not play on *Rosh Hashana* and *Yom Kippur*, and one *Yom Kippur*, when his team played without him, it lost. Thereafter it arranged its matches with an eye on the Jewish calendar.

There have been other eminent Jewish players such as Al Rosen, who received the League's Most Valuable Player award in 1953, Lawrence Sherry, one of Koufax's mentors, who was the Dodgers' pitching hero in the 1959 World Series, and Ken Holtzman, who pitched a no-hit game for the Chicago Cubs in 1969. But none have approached the heights of either Koufax or Greenberg.

One game in which Jewish eminence has borne some relation to Jewish numbers is perhaps basketball, possibly because the game was ideally suited to the cramped conditions of the urban ghettos. There have been scores of Jewish All-American players. It is also the one sport in which Israel can field a team of international standing. In April 1977 the Tel Aviv Maccabi players bested the Italian Mobilgirgi team 78–77 to win the European Basketball Cup.

The Jewish interest in horse-racing represents a confluence of two Jewish passions, gambling and snobbery, with the latter predominating. (To run a stable because one enjoys a flutter is a little like burning down one's house to roast a pig.) It is, after all, the sport of kings, and even if one could not be sure of rubbing shoulders with royalty at every race, success did offer one access to areas of society which might otherwise have remained closed. In Victorian England the first mark of the rising family was to acquire a country seat, the second was to acquire a stable. By the end of the century one could rarely attend a major race without seeing the colours of one or another of the Rothschilds, Baron Hirsch, Sir Felix Cassel or one of the Sassoons. In 1871 a horse owned by Baron Mayer Rothschild (who was known as the 'racing Baron', though most of the family had stables) won the Derby. Leopold de Rothschild enjoyed a similar triumph in 1879. His *annus mirabilis*, however, was 1895, when his two-year-old, St Frusquin, won the Royal Plate at Kempton Park, the Sandringham Gold Cup, the Chesterfield Stakes at Newmarket, and the Middle Park Plate and the Dewhurst Plate at Kempton Park. In the following year it won the Two Thousand Guineas. It was also entered for the Derby, but was beaten into second place by Persimmon, owned by the Prince of Wales; it was suggested that St Frusquin was held back to let the Prince win. (When the two horses met a few months later, St Frusquin won by half a length.) Leo, as he was popularly known, was to be compensated by winning the Derby in 1904. Sir Ellise V. Sassoon won the Derby four times.

In 1902 Baron Hirsch's filly, La Flèche, won the Cambridgeshire, the One Thousand Guineas, the Oaks, the St Leger and came close to winning the Derby. Most of the money won by the Rothschilds and all of the money won by Hirsch went to charity, but even if they had kept it, it would hardly have paid for the cost of the stables.

In 1881 Jacob Pincus, who had been a jockey and became a trainer, entered the first American-bred horse to win the Derby. Pincus worked for many leading American owners, including August Belmont (né Schoenberg), Rothschild's agent in America, who was the first President of the American Jockey Club. Julius Cahn, who was both owner and trainer, won the 1897 Kentucky Derby with his horse Typhoon II. The owner-trainer Hirsch Jacobs had more winners – three thousand five hundred and ninety-six – than any other trainer in history. A little improbably, an American Jewish jockey, Walter Miller, has entered the Hall of Fame, and Frenchman George Stern became known as 'the King of Jockeys' after winning every major European event, including the 1911 Derby.

Apart from horse-racing (which could be more aptly described as an industry), the Jewish achievement in sport has been less than monumental and, compared to its achievements elsewhere, derisory. If the arts, as we have suggested, have always been thought of as vaguely un-Jewish, sport has been considered as blatantly so, or as downright 'goyisch'. Even chess, which one might think is a fairly innocent pastime and which is said to have been enjoyed by King Solomon, has been regarded with disapproval, precisely because it is a pastime. If the pious Jew has free time (or even if he hasn't) he is expected to apply it to some pious occupation, like study. The eighteenth-century philosopher, Moses Mendelssohn, summed up the Jewish attitude to chess: 'For a game it is too earnest, for something earnest it is too much of a game.' In spite of that, there have been numerous Jewish chess-masters, and even if one excludes the legendary Bobby Fischer (who has lately become a Unitarian), there are other names to conjure with (most of them Russian), including Mikhail Botvinnik, David Bronstein, Moshe Czerniak, Reuben Fine, George Kiltanowski, Emanuel Lasker, Samuel Reshevsky, Boris Spassky, Mikhail Tal and Savielly Tartakover.

To an extent sport has been a casualty of Judaism's conflict with Hellenism. When the conquests of Alexander the Great placed Palestine under

Greek rule, gymnasia were established in Jerusalem and other cities which attracted many young Jews away from their own cultures. Wrestling, for example, was in the nude and some of the Jewish participants had themselves de-circumcised to remove what they regarded as a blemish. The games, too, were connected with numerous idolatrous cults. But for traditionalists, the most insidious thing about them was that they glorified the body, whereas every Jewish tradition laid stress on the mind. Esau was being elevated at the expense of Jacob.

Under Roman rule the gymnasium was widened into the arena and the athlete was put on display with other animals, sometimes to contend with them. The entire nature of the displays, the violent brutality, the gore, were so repellent that the revulsion which Jews felt for such spectacles came to affect the Jewish attitudes to games as a whole.

Games also require leisure and the one day on which the Jew was free, namely the Sabbath, was too sacred for anything as profane as sport. It was even said that the Temple was destroyed because Jews played ball games on the Sabbath.

The wrestling matches, the tourneys, the games which brightened the life of their neighbours thus remained outside Jewish experience. Israel Abrahams, in his study of Jewish life in the Middle Ages, showed that where Jews did indulge in what was called sport, it was generally in strolling, dancing, chess and children's games (and even these tended to take the form of riddles and other mental exercises). Some Jews did learn to swim, but that was enjoined by the Talmud as a life-saving precaution; they did not join swimming tournaments.

Games called for a physical spaciousness and a relaxed spirit and these were rarely to be found in the ghetto. If the Jewish mind and soul somehow remained healthy, the effect on the Jewish physique was deleterious, and wherever Jewish immigrants arrived in a Western country, observers were appalled at the sight of the stunted, shambling, white-faced figures. When attempts were made to establish Jewish self-defence units after the Russian pogroms, it was found that the number of young Jews able to defend themselves, or anyone else, was sadly limited. At the 1898 Zionist Congress, Max Nordau, an eminent Paris physician, appealed for what he called 'muscular Judaism':

. . . gymnastics and physical training are exceedingly important for us Jews, whose greatest defect has been and is, lack of discipline . . . nature has endowed us with the spiritual qualities required for athletic achievements of an extraordinary quality. All we lack is muscle and that can be developed with the aid of physical exercise . . . The more Jews achieve in the various branches of sport the greater will be their self-confidence and self-respect.

Partly as a result of his efforts, the World Maccabi Union came into being in 1921, and, within a few years claimed a membership of over one hundred thousand. Yet the name of the organization was something of a misnomer, for Judas Maccabeus was the soldier who led the very uprising against Hellenistic rule which established the continuity of Jewish tradition over foreign cults. But the Maccabeans, as his followers were known, did show the martial qualities of hardihood and daring which, it was felt, Jewry lacked, and the name Maccabeans was chosen to symbolize the new Jew they hoped to create. In 1932, a sort of Jewish Olympics, called the Maccabiah, were held in Tel Aviv. It was approved and recognized by the International Olympics Committee and was attended by five hundred Jewish athletes from twenty-three countries. The second Maccabiah was held in 1935, a more elaborate affair which was attended by some one thousand seven hundred sportsmen from twenty-seven countries. Many of the participants were from German-speaking countries and most of them remained in Palestine. When the next Maccabiah was held in 1950, the centre of gravity of the movement had changed. The European contingents, with the heavy participation from Poland, Germany and Austria, had virtually been eliminated and, apart from Israel itself, the main participants were from America, South Africa and Britain. The fourth Maccabiah was in 1953 and since then they have been held regularly every four years.

As athletic events, the Maccabiahs have not been of world-shaking importance and they witnessed no wholesale shattering of records. But they attracted large audiences and they have helped to stimulate an interest in sport, even if they have not entirely altered entrenched attitudes.

Politics intrude into everything in Israel, including games, and so there are Bethar football teams on the right, Hapoel on the left and Maccabi hovering about the centre, to say nothing of Elitzur, which was founded in 1939 to spread an interest in sport amongst religious youths. Apart from the obvious drawbacks of basing athletic associations on political or religious affiliations, Israel is further hampered by the fact that it still works a six-day week (five and a half in fact, but as the half is on the eve of the Sabbath it is not particularly useful for athletic tourneys). Religious youngsters can hardly take part in competitive games at all and those of them who might have wished to attend games as spectators are unable to do so, for they are generally played on the Sabbath. The Ultra Orthodox, who include a not inconsiderable section of the community, are against organized games in their entirety and denounce them as godless and corrupt. When the Jerusalem municipality built a much-needed open-air swimming pool some twenty years ago, black-clad demonstrators took to the streets in an attempt to have it closed down. Yet interest in sport has spread. Soccer, which was introduced almost by accident through matches between the British army and Maccabi teams during the Mandatory years, attracts large crowds (where there are grounds to contain them – and even where there aren't) and excites almost Glaswegian frenzy. The level of play, however, is not high. One of the factors which limits the pool of talents from which players can be drawn is that there are few open spaces on which children can play. Playgrounds are cramped and playing fields are few, and the game most commonly played between schools is basketball.

There is possibly some symbolism in the fact that what is perhaps the most popular of all participatory sports is walking. There is an annual three-day march which attracts tens of thousands of participants from all walks of life. It is a game without winners or, if you prefer, without losers, to be enjoyed for its own sake. An annual cross-country run, usually held about the time of Chanukah (which celebrates the triumph of the Maccabis over the Hellenists), attracts somewhat less eager participation.

The Israeli Government has established a national sports authority which has opened new physical training centres. Pupils in state schools are encouraged to compete for a sports badge. Commercial companies have also given support to athletic organizations and football clubs. But all this has not as yet made Israel a nation of athletes.

A photograph on the front page of the *Jerusalem Post* during the 1976 Montreal Olympics showed an Israeli weightlifter jumping for joy, his arms raised in triumph. At last, one thought, a gold medal, but the young man, competing in the featherweight section, came fifth and, said the paper, 'thus achieved Israel's best ever placing in the Olympics'.

A nation which has had to fight four wars in under thirty years, and is still not at peace, can, perhaps, be forgiven for not having much enthusiasm or energy left to spare for international tournaments. But it is doubtful if Israel's Olympic record would have been very much better even if she had been a normal nation leading a normal life. Olympics, tournaments, gymnastics, athletics, sport, are after all, all part of what is a purely European tradition. There are games, like polo, which may have originated in the East, but the ritualization of games, their elevation to quasi-religious status, is purely Western. Although Jews have lived in Europe for over two thousand years they have only become an integral part of it for less than a century and a half; and for the Jewish masses in Eastern Europe, not even that. At the 1970 Asian games in Bangkok, Israel's small team won six gold medals, six silver and five bronze, finishing in sixth place overall, but in competing with Europeans she is, like other Asian countries, at a disadvantage.

The 'ghetto bend' from which the Jew was said to suffer has been straightened out. The Jew looks healthier (even though he is still more inclined to worry about health), is more erect, more robust. The 'muscular Judaism' which Nordau called for, as the Israeli army has demonstrated time and again, has been achieved. But it has not yet been pushed to the point where it has become muscle-bound Judaism. The sort of dedication necessary to climb new pinnacles, break new records, attain new feats, does not appeal easily to the Jew if, indeed, it appeals at all. There is always a residue of practical, perhaps too practical, common sense, which will ask if the brief moment of glory is worth the sustained years of effort. Few Jews feel induced to climb Everest simply 'because it's there', though if it was on the way to somewhere, it would be another matter. To that extent, it could be argued Jews are unromantic. They may enjoy a game, even though their tradition shuns it, because it is pleasurable in itself, but to push it beyond pleasure to the point of solemn effort is alien.

Thus the Jew will enjoy a game of golf, but that is because it's a semi-social and, indeed, a semi-business occasion. In many a Jewish golf-club, one will find more people in the card-room than on the course. It is also the sort of venue where one can meet a better class, or at least a more prosperous one, and it is a means of making a long walk seem less arduous.

If he is driven to strenuous exercise it will be less in the spirit of gamesmanship than at the behest of his doctor and even then he will be inclined to do so, not through running, skipping or jumping, but by starving himself in a prolonged Lent at an expensive health farm, an example of what might be called conspicuous abstention.

Mens sana in corpore sano is not part of popular Jewish wisdom, for there is an old belief that if one looks after the soul the body will look after itself. The belief is, of course, totally unconfirmed by experience, and most Jews who accept it are physical wrecks. But it has a residual effect even among non-believers. The opposite, however, is also true, and complete dedication to physical achievement leads to a diminution in those qualities which make humans human, to a desiccation of the soul. For example, when most of Israel's Olympic team was massacred at the 1972 Munich Olympics, the other participants were aghast at the suggestion that the games should be cancelled. They had spent the past four years of their lives to prepare for the event; they had dreamed of it; they had built themselves up to the pitch of bodily perfection, but in doing so had also exorcized something of their human spirit, and they raced on over the dead bodies of their slaughtered colleagues.

Such events have led many a Jew to ask himself, if such is the effect of sports and gamesmanship, whether there is not something to be said for bodily neglect. 'The race', said Ecclesiastes, 'is not to the swift.'

· CHAPTER TEN ·

Better to Give . . .

The Jew, it is often said, 'looks after his own', which he does, but people who don't, rarely look after anyone else. The practice of charity is basic to his creed. So are other observances, but of all the injunctions handed down by the Rabbis, the one to give has become second nature. It persists where other observances have lapsed. Yet there is no Hebrew word for charity as such. The term most often used is *tzedaka*, which means justice, and the Jewish poor have therefore always had a tacit claim upon the rich. This may explain the unique position of the *schnorrer* in Jewish lore, for, given the *tzedaka* tradition, he is no mere beggar pleading for alms but a preferential shareholder calling for his dividend.

The Jewish state as initially conceived was to have been an egalitarian commonwealth. To that end the land was divided equally among the twelve tribes, except for the Levites who, as the hereditary priesthood, were to receive a tithe from their landed brethren. Ancestral land thus acquired, in theory at least, could not be permanently alienated, and during the Jubilee any land sold in the intervening forty-nine years reverted to its original owners. However it is not clear that this principle was ever applied in practice and the words of the Pentateuch that 'the poor shall never cease out of the land' were fully confirmed by events and the numerous provisions made to protect them. Thus, for example, during the Sabbatical years, when the land had to be left fallow and untended, the produce was left to the poor:

And six years thou shalt sow thy land, and shalt gather in the fruits thereof: But the seventh year thou shalt let it rest and lie still, that the poor of the people may eat; and what they leave the beasts of the field shall eat. In like manner thou shalt deal with thy vineyard, and with thy oliveyard.

A tithe of all produce was left to the poor, as well as windfalls, gleanings, and anything left growing on the margins of a field. Nor could one join in any festive occasion, especially a religious festival, without providing for the poor: To give to the poor, said *Proverbs*, is to lend to the Lord. 'Go your way, eat the fat, and drink the sweet,' said Ezra and Nehemiah on the eve of the New Year, 'and send portions unto him for whom nothing is prepared.' It was the Rabbis who first enunciated the principle that it was better to give than to receive: 'The pauper does more for the householder [in receiving] than the latter does in giving.'

At the source of the tradition is the belief, in the words of the Psalms: 'that the world and all therein are His'. A pauper once told his Rabbi that he lived on 'fatted chicken and old wine'. 'Are you not worried that you're a burden on the public?' asked the Rabbi. The man looked pained: 'Do I eat what is theirs? I eat what is God's.' The story, which comes from the Talmud, may or may not be apocryphal, but it has given rise to a whole genre of what might be called *schnorrer's* humour.

There is the story of the *schnorrer* who came to Kugelman for his monthly dole. He knocked, there was no reply. He knocked again and finally a distraught-looking Kugelman came to the door.

'Something wrong?' asked the *schnorrer*.

'Haven't you heard? I've gone bankrupt. I've got liabilities of a hundred thousand dollars and assets of ten thousand.'

'Sure I heard.'

'So what do you want from me?'

'Ten cents on the dollar.'

The world, according to the Jewish creed, is based on three pillars, study, prayer and charity, and of the three the last is the most important. All are obliged to give, even those who receive, so that the poor too must pay their tithe for the poor. Charity should begin at home, but must not end there. Kin should receive priority over strangers and the near over the far, and one should give almost furtively. When Rabbi Yannai saw a man giving a beggar a coin in public, he reproached him: 'Better not to give,' he said, 'than to give and shame.' Charity at its most charitable, said the Rabbis, is that in which giver and receiver are unknown to one another, but the highest form of all is to help the poor to help themselves. Thus wherever there was a Jewish community sufficiently established to have its own synagogue, there was an overseer of the poor – or *gabbai*, as he was known. The *gabbai* himself had to be a man of substance, lest he be tempted to rifle the poor box. (A wise precaution. In later years when synagogue-going became less universal and Jewish working men came together to form their own 'friendly societies', or mutual aid clubs, the treasurers, who were not men of substance, not infrequently absconded with the funds.) The *gabbai* dealt with only general needs, and a host of supplementary societies with particular needs. During the centuries when the Mediterranean was infested with pirates, funds were set up for the redemption of captives. In Eastern Europe, until recent times, impoverished students were accustomed 'to eat days', which is to say they were guests of different households for the different days of the week. Some communities had as many as a score of different charity associations for different needs. Today, London Jewry, for example, which is a fairly prosperous community, still has the following:

The Annie Arbib Trust, founded in 1932, to make 'annual grants to indigent Jewish gentlewomen and for training talented Jewish girls'; The Bearstead Memorial Hospital, founded in 1895, as 'The Sick Room Helps' Society'; The Birchland Jewish Hospital; The Children's Country Holiday Fund (established in 1889); The Food for the Jewish Poor (established in 1854); The Friends of the Sick; The Grocery Relief Fund (established in 1891); The Hospital Kosher Meal Service; The Hagadolim Charity Organization; The Society for Relieving the Aged Needy of the Jewish Faith (founded in 1829); Jewish Association of the Physically Handicapped Society; The Jewish Bread, Meat and Coal Society (founded in 1779); The Jews' Temporary Shelter (established in 1885); The London Jewish Hospital; The Nightingale Home for Aged Jews (established in 1840); The Norwood Homes for Jewish Children (established in 1795) and the Beth Holim Home for the Aged (established in 1747); The Jewish Welfare Board (formerly the Jewish Board of Guardians, founded in 1859), which incorporates a host of major and minor charities, serves as a type of supplement to the welfare state. And these are all local charities. There are scores of others concerned with Israel and foreign Jewry. Every provincial community, large or small, will have its own welfare board or benevolent society, without always being sure of having someone to be benevolent to, so that even where the poor are not always with us, societies for the help of the poor always are.

Jewish philanthropic tradition has sometimes been ascribed to the fact that the Jewish rich have never had to hark far back for memories of their own poverty. It is not a convincing argument if only because people who have known hardship may feel entitled to enjoy their plenty without sharing it, and they sometimes do. Not every Jew is a philanthropist and some have become rich and have remained rich through the fairly commonplace process of keeping everything they have to themselves. But the typical Jew is generous by nature – it is one of his most pronounced and certainly his most redeeming feature.

What then of the mean Jews of lore, and of the Shylocks? When Shakespeare wrote *The Merchant of Venice*, no Jew had set foot in England for over three hundred years and the portrait of Shylock could therefore not have been drawn from common experience. Yet the very fact that the myth of the mean Jew could persist for centuries after the Jew had ceased to be a visible presence shows how well established the myth must have been. It may also suggest that the hardiest myths can take root in the shallowest soil. In any case Shylock is less of a study in meanness than vindictiveness. One can be at once generous and vindictive, which many Jews are, for if generosity is their most pronounced quality, then vindictiveness is perhaps their greatest defect, to which one must add that they have a lot to be vindictive about.

A book on *The Present State of the Jews* published in the seventeenth century declared that it was generally accepted that the 'Jews have no beggars', and 'no poor'. They had, the writer went on to say, plenty of both, but the regular distribution of charity 'much concealed the level of poverty'. In London, in the early part of the nineteenth century, about half the Jewish community lived on the generosity of the other half, and when, towards the end of the century, mass immigration threatened to overwhelm the established charity boards, emergency appeals were launched which enabled the tradition to continue. The immigration aroused loud opposition and innumerable charges were made against the newcomers, but nobody could complain – at least not with any justice – that they were a charge on public funds. They were looked after by the community. Some were helped on to America; some were helped back to Russia; almost no one was left to subsist 'on the parish'.

In America, where the influx of immigrants was, of course, much larger, there were similar murmurings against 'immigrant hordes'; but there too they were met and helped by their own welfare committees organized through the Hebrew Emigrants Aid Society (HEAS), which was formed in the aftermath of the 1881 pogroms. HEAS was soon overwhelmed by the scale of the influx and in 1890 was re-established on a much stronger basis as the Hebrew Immigrants Aid Society, which quickly grew into an effective pressure group and which is still active.

Once ashore the newcomers could turn for help to a bewildering variety of institutions, including the Sheltering House and the United Hebrew Charities, the Baron de Hirsch Fund and the Workmen's Circle, the Provident Loan Society and the Hebrew Free Loan Association. But perhaps the most immediate help came from the *landsmannschaften*, informal freemasonries composed of families stemming from the same East European neighbourhoods. Minsk Jews had one and Pinsk Jews another and Tchernowitz Jews a third. There was hardly a Jewish community in Russia, Poland or Galicia not represented by a *landsmannschaft* in America. By 1914 there were no less than five hundred and thirty-four *landsmannschaften*, each with fifty to five hundred members, in New York City alone. All Jews are brothers, went the words of a popular Yiddish song, but *landsmannschaften* were more brotherly still. If a newcomer from, say, Bialystock, could expect the help of other Jews it would come forth more readily from other Bialystock Jews.

The *landsmannschaften* were sustained first by the immigrant's need to protect himself against an alien and sometimes hostile environment, but also by nostalgia; every newcomer brought a fresh whiff of *der heim*. Once immigration stopped the *landsmannschaften* gradually petered out, but as it is always easier to start a Jewish organization than to stop one, there are three or four dozen *landsmannschaften* in being in New York even now.

Some of the *landsmannschaften* were mere social groups. Others were formally constituted as Friendly Societies with rule books as elaborate as the American constitution.

Irving Howe, in *World of Our Fathers*, quotes the rule of the First Kalisher Benevolent Society:

When a member gets married he must propose his wife to the society, the society will then appoint a committee, which will go to the doctor with her to obtain a statement about her health. In case the doctor declares her health to be unsatisfactory, the concerned member will remain single, or if he marries he will not get any death benefit for his wife.

These groups helped to ease the transition from Russian to American life. In the short term they could also save a man from starvation, but such charities and societies could also have the pernicious effect of the Speenhamland system, for if they assured that no Jew starved, they also meant that sweat-shop proprietors could sometimes get away with paying starvation wages.

All charities are troubled by the fear that in helping too readily they could encourage helplessness. For many centuries, for example, it was thought that to have an unmarried daughter was one of the greatest calamities which a Jewish family could experience (it is no joke even now) and many communities had *hachnasat kallah* funds to provide dowries for poor brides. At the same time people wanted to be sure that such brides had made an effort to help themselves, and there was but one acceptable way for a girl from a poor home to raise money, and that was by going into service. Thus in 1638 the Council of the Lithuanian Jewry (which enjoyed a measure of autonomy large enough to make such rules) declared:

Poor virgins from the vicinity ... are not to be given anything until they have in hand some visible proof from the leaders of the community that they have served in the homes of householders dwelling within the community for a period of three years from the time that they were twelve years old, since this age is fitting for domestic service.

The older and more established charities were always on guard against what Victorians called 'undiscriminating charity' and anyone turning to them for help was subjected to the most searching inquiries. The general Jewish tendency, however, was to give first and ask questions afterwards, if at all. The very fact that a man had to ask was in itself accepted as proof of need, for if the *schnorrer* was an accepted figure in society, and *schnorrerai* an accepted calling, it was understood that no man would resort to it if he had the prospect of anything better. It did mean that the audacious *schnorrer* did better than the diffident one, but undiscriminating charity did not give rise to a dynasty or dynasties of *schnorrers* or a race of mendicants. Applicants in the main tended to be the last people off the boat, and if the practice meant that help was sometimes given to the undeserving, it at least assured that no needy person went hungry. If there were errors, they were on the side of charity. In any case there was no fear, as there was among non-Jewish charitable organizations, that money given to an unworthy applicant would go on drink (though there was sometimes the danger that it might go on gambling). This did not mean that the remedial principle in charity was ignored. Attempts were made to find paupers jobs and even to equip them, or at least their children, with trades. The London Jewish Board of Guardians, for example, ran apprentice schemes for Jewish youngsters.

Some *schnorrers* faced with the prospect of having to work no doubt felt that they were being exploited, as one can see from *Fishke the Lame*, a novel written about a century ago by Mendele Mosher Seforim, which is a sort of *schnorrer's* odyssey:

A revolution had just taken place. The rich young men of the town had just started something new. They decided it wouldn't hurt the *schnorrers* to work for their daily bread – except for the old, the sick and the crippled. There was no reason for healthy young men and women to live on alms and charity. The foolish Jewish spirit of charity causes only trouble, they claimed. That's why, they said, there are so many lazy loafers among the Jews – who suck other people's blood like bed-bugs. The rich young men set up a sort of factory where the beggars were put to work making ropes and sewing sacks and – in return – were given goods . . .

The field beggars that we met there were up in arms against this new custom. 'G'vald!' they cried. 'What's happened to the world? Where is Jewish charity? Jewishness is dead . . .'

The veteran *schnorrer* knew how to avoid such snares, for with all its venerable charitable institutions and their trained almoners, Jewish charity has tended to be spontaneous rather than considered.

One important principle of charity which has failed to take root among Jews, though volumes have been written to commend it, is anonymity. 'He who gives alms in secret,' said the Talmud, 'is greater than Moses.' It is not, by and large, the sort of greatness to which Jews aspire, for if they are inclined to do good, they also like to be seen to be doing good and to receive due recognition both from contemporaries and, if possible, from posterity. Some Jewish institutions are lined with plaques as a study is lined with books. One will find plaques on buildings, plaques on doors, plaques on walls, and where the institution is an old age home or a hospital, there will be plaques on beds. One half expects to find plaques round the necks of the patients. In the Hebrew University, buildings, parks, gardens, all carry the names of benefactors. Synagogues cannot be so named, but synagogue halls can and are, as are ecclesiastical appurtenances, furnishings and prayer books. There was a synagogue in the East End of London whose entire gallery was covered with the names of benefactors, complete with the sums given – all in letters of gold. Sir Isaac Wolfson, one of the most generous philanthropists of our age, has colleges named after him in both Oxford and Cambridge, a distinction enjoyed hitherto only by Jesus Christ.

There is a fairly common, and on the whole forgiveable, desire among Jews that the good that they do should live after them, that there should be some small mark left somewhere in the universe to indicate the fact that they passed through it. It represents a subconscious yearning for immortality which may be due to the fact that the hereafter has no firm place in Jewish belief. If there are Jews who believe they will rise again, perhaps they would like some memento of their previous stay.

It must, however, be added that the main cause for the plaque-mania is filial piety, for the names usually perpetuated are those of departed parents. But it does mean that it is easier to raise money for palpable causes like synagogues and community centres than for impalpable ones like education.

It would be wrong to give the impression that there is no such thing as the anonymous Jewish benefactor, but the anonymous remain unknown, except where a benefactor takes pains to be known for giving unobtrusively, or, as a Yiddish obituarist once wrote: 'The late Mr — was celebrated throughout Europe for his benefactions, all of which he gave anonymously.'

To an extent there is a conflict between the ideal of anonymity and the belief that one should not only help the needy but show personal concern for their needs, and the Jewish concept of charity is perhaps best summed up in the epitaph to a Jewess who died in the Thirty Years War:

She supplied scholars with Bibles, and the plundered with prayer books.
She ran like a bird to weddings, and often asked the poor to dine with her in her home.
She clothed the naked herself, preparing hundreds of shirts for distribution among the poor.

To give only money was hardly more than paying taxes; one had to give oneself. Charity offered from a distance was less than charitable, as can be seen in a refrain from a popular Yiddish song:

Orm is nit gut
Orm is nit gut
Min tor zich nit shemen
Mit eigene blut.

('It's not good to be poor, it's not good to be poor, yet one must not be ashamed of one's own blood.') Yet in so far as one was ashamed that shame could be benign, for a poor relative was a reproach to a rich one, and as a rule, he did not remain poor for long. The number of partners to a Jewish enterprise was less dependent on the needs of the company than on the size of the family. The Jewish family, indeed, may be the origin of the chain store. It was un-Jewish to disinherit an obstreperous grandson or nephew. Better to open a new branch, if necessary overseas, which is perhaps why almost every major Jewish family in the old world has a cadet branch in the new. A relationship, a claim to kinship, has always been a recommendation, and what is regarded as nepotism elsewhere is accepted as an elementary obligation among Jews. In Israel the process has been carried further so that Jews without money – but with position – have tended to fill jobs with relatives as if it was their own private business. There are Rabbis who bequeath their pulpits to their sons or their sons-in-law as if they were hereditary (which among Hassidim they are).

Older Jewish families have always been supremely conscious of the generations to follow. Among the Rothschilds, the Cohens, the Waley-Cohens, the Montagues and the Franklins, who formed part of the late-nineteenth-century Anglo-Jewish ruling class, every father felt obliged to leave each of his children as much as he was left himself, and if he left more it was better still. Capital was sacrosanct; one tampered only with the interest. Punitive death duties put an end to that tradition, but in any case only the old, established families thought in terms of wills and posthumous handouts. Most Jews were anxious to see the benefits of their generosity with their own eyes and – save where death caught them by surprise – they have tended to pass on what they had in their own lifetime. The effect of all this was to generate a continuing redistribution of income so that it was uncommon – as it still is – to come upon an indigent branch of a wealthy family.

If Jewish generosity begins at home, it does not end there and one can rarely find a city with a sizeable Jewish community which has not benefited from Jewish philanthropy in one form or another, as one can see from the innumerable hospitals, clinics, libraries, concert halls, and other welfare and cultural institutions which bear Jewish names. Indeed one not infrequently hears complaints among Jews that this or that millionaire will give money to anything, provided it is free of Jewish connections.

Zionism has given a new dimension to Jewish charity, except that money given to Israel is not spoken of as charity. The organizations to be found in every Jewish community to raise funds on behalf of Israel function as voluntary, or, as we shall see, not-so-voluntary, tax agencies. Since 1948 American Jewry alone has given over three billion dollars to Israel.

Jews, generous as they are, do not part with such sums out of mere kindness of heart. Guilt and thanksgiving also come into play. Every Jew who lived through the Hitler era has a sense of guilt about the holocaust, as if he – though he may only have been a child when it happened – could have done something to avert it, or to save this or that individual from the ovens, if only he had been more alert to what was happening, or more generous, or had felt a greater sense of urgency. Wherever a Jew is threatened, he reacts now as he feels he should have reacted then; and the response of his children is even more emphatic. One gives money partly as anodyne and partly in thanksgiving.

Moreover, Israel, in psychological terms, offers a place of refuge, though not a secure one. For if matters should move to the point where even American Jewry should no longer feel safe on their own soil, then they would not feel particularly safe in Israel either. The safety of Israel is bound up inexorably with the strength and self-assurance of American Jewry. Yet in psychological terms, the fact that it is there, welcoming and open, has done something to ease old Jewish anxieties, even if it has given rise to new ones. The heroism of the Israeli soldier has also given the Jew a new source of reassurance and pride. Israelis pay for such reassurance with their lives and limbs, the diaspora only pays with money. Therefore those who have money but do not part with it can face social and commercial ostracism. Appeals committees are based on trades and professions. One might be composed of leading figures in the jewellery trade, another in textiles, a third in furs: all have a fair idea of what their co-religionists in the trade are in a position to contribute (the Jew is, in any case, a natural assessor) and if they don't give as much as they should their business could suffer. Here certainly is an instance where it is better to give, but in fact such pressure is rarely applied. What is frequently evoked is the competitive spirit. Donors in any particular trade are brought together at an annual dinner or reception and each makes a public pledge of his sum, so that those who might have been inclined to give less feel shamed into giving more and there is almost an annual race to be amongst the biggest, or at least the bigger donors. At times of acute emergency such ploys are hardly necessary and rich and poor make spontaneous offerings which involve them in genuine sacrifices. On the eve of the Six Day War, for example, a London housewife donated the money she had been saving for eight years to install a new kitchen; a young couple donated the deposit they were about to lay down for a house. Others sold wedding rings, engagement rings, family heirlooms. The pupils of a Jewish public school in Berkshire fasted for a day, and gave the money saved to Israel.

Jewish mutual concern arises, in part, out of the knowledge that if they did not look after each other no one else would. There was nothing, of course, for the Jew to expect during the centuries when the churches were the sole source of charity. In later years, when the state began to concern itself with human welfare (in England the process began as early as the sixteenth century with the Elizabethan Poor Law), it was not too hospitable to the stranger. The least that the host society expected of its Jews was that they should be solvent, and that they should not be a charge upon its coffers, which they were not. It was only with the advent of the all-embracing welfare state in our own time that Jews began to claim any benefits to which they were entitled, and many of the homes run by the Jewish Welfare authorities are in good part financed out of public money. Donations from the community provide extra comforts which would not otherwise be available. This does not mean that Jewish charity has become redundant, for if everyone within a modern state is assured the basic necessities of life, the observances and ceremonies of Jewish life call for something more. The education of children, the festive Sabbath board, the *matzot* on Passover, the wine for *kiddush* and *havdalah*, the demand of the dietary laws (which mean in effect that every Jewish home needs at least two sets of cutlery and crockery), to say nothing of such happy occasions as a *brit*, *Bar Mitzvah* or wedding, all cost money, and those who do not have it are given it. No Jew is free to celebrate a festival while he is conscious of a neighbour in need. The *seder*, the Passover meal, which is part banquet, part holy-communion, opens with the invocation:

This is the bread of poverty which our ancestors ate in the land of Egypt. Let him who is hungry enter and eat, and he who is needy enter and celebrate the Passover.

'All Israel is responsible for one another,' said the Talmud. Am I my brother's keeper? To the Jew it is a rhetorical question. He is, and his cousins. It may, in part, explain why the Jew will strive a little harder; his responsibilities are a little greater. Which brings one finally to what may be the main source of Jewish generosity – it is part of the immigrant's instinct. Every immigrant established in the West was a lifeline to relatives in the East. No one thus burdened could regard his income as his own and in the last decades of the nineteenth century and the first decades of this one, whole townships in Eastern Europe (the same was, of course, true of Italy, Ireland and Greece) subsisted on remittances from America.

'If I am only for myself,' asks the Talmud, 'what am I?' This question becomes a little less pressing the further a Jew is removed from his immigrant origins and, with exceptions, the generosity of a family tends to be in inverse ratio to its antiquity, though, of course, old families are sometimes old enough to have lost not only their instinctive Jewish generosity, but their money. In New York, as in London, those who came most readily to the help of the immigrant were immigrants themselves.

The dispersal of the Jewish community has also had a limiting effect on generosity. Until not much more than a century ago, Jews, whether rich or poor, were herded into the same ghetto, so that the prosperous could never be blind to the wants of the needy.

It is difficult – difficult certainly for the Jew – to sit down to a laden table while there are hungry faces pressed against his windows. And the Jew, for all the Rabbinical injunctions against over-indulgence, enjoys his food. If enough is as good as a feast, too much is even better. He will also spend lavishly on holidays, travel and entertainment and enjoy this world as if there were no other (which he suspects may probably be the case). Where he is troubled by his conscience a donation to the poor is a form of absolution. If Jewish generosity was born out of Jewish piety, it is sustained by Jewish hedonism. Not every Jew is open-handed, but it is rare to find a Jew who is both self-indulgent and tightfisted.

CHAPTER ELEVEN

New Jews

When Theodor Herzl, the founder of political Zionism, published his blueprint for a Jewish state in 1902, he sought to create not merely a new Judea but a new Jew, and he believed that the one would be the making of the other.

Jews, he wrote in his diary, 'must be made strong for war, taught the joy of work and the exercise of virtue'. He meant the martial virtues. Life in the ghettos, he felt, had demoralized and demeaned them, made them more ready for flight than battle. To the same end, he argued that Jewish education would lay stress on 'patriotic songs, the Maccabean tradition, religion, heroic stage-plays, honour, etc.' and he would 'incline the *jeunesse dorée* towards English sports, and in this way prepare them for the army'. Above all, he was concerned to give the Jews a sense of dignity:

One of the major battles I shall have to wage will be against the Jewish spirit of scoffing. This spirit represents at bottom the impotent attempts of prisoners to give themselves the air of being free men ...

He would breed self-reliance. The Prussian Junker represented his ideal. 'Our character has been corrupted by oppression,' he complained, and the qualities most obviously corrupted were those of manliness, self-respect, honour. He had, as a student, fought several duels to redress real or imagined slights. When an Austrian duelling fraternity refused to accept challenges from Jews because they were a people 'devoid of honour', he was mortified, and what pained him in particular was his belief that it was true. Those qualities of knightliness, chivalry, daring, which he so admired in the Prussian, had, he believed, died in the Jew.

It was a view shared by many of his contemporaries, both in the emancipated West and among the oppressed masses in the East, and one of the reasons, perhaps the main reason, why he had such an electrifying effect on world Jewry was that in his very appearance and bearing he represented those qualities of knightliness and chivalry which Jews felt they lacked. The historian, Joseph Klausner, who attended the Basle Congress at which the Zionist movement was born, recalled:

Herzl created something that can hardly be expressed in words. A different atmosphere prevailed, something altogether new had come into being . . . One Hebrew writer was so bold as to apply to him the Biblical verse: 'And he was King in Jeshurun' . . . It can be said that the whole of Zionism acquired something regal.

When a number of successful Anglo-Jewish professional and business men came together to form a sort of Jewish Rotary club in 1891, they gave themselves the name of the Maccabeans. The Maccabis were not the last heroes in Jewish history, but they were the last to have triumphed in battle. Thereafter Jewish heroism usually took the form of martyrdom and it was perhaps natural that with the revival of Jewish nationalism the Maccabis should have figured so hugely in the Jewish imagination. They were to the nineteenth-century Jew what the Arthurian legends were to the Victorian Englishman. The national revival was also a romantic revival. Romance called for men of valour and any instance of Jewish heroism, agility or strength was a particular source of pride.

Sir Moses Montefiore, the Jewish philanthropist (he died in 1885 at the age of a hundred and one), was greeted on his last visit to Palestine by a party of horsemen whom he took to be Bedouin. When they turned out to be Jews, his joy was boundless.

If there be many such horsemen in the Holy Land like these two supposed Bedouins, they certainly ought not in justice to be regarded as the descendants from sickly parents, as some persons supposed.

Herzl, on a visit to Palestine with a group of Zionist leaders a few years later, responded in much the same way when some young Jewish settlers staged a *fantasia* in their honour:

Wolffsohn, Schnirer, Bodenhelmer and I had tears in our eyes when we saw those fleet, daring horsemen and the proof that our young clothes-peddlers could thus be transformed.

Here was the ultimate in manliness, Jews on horseback.

In 1880 there were about seven and a half million Jews in the world of whom about five and a half were crammed into the Russian Pale of

Settlement. Although there had been a resurgence of anti-semitism in central and western Europe since the 1870s, it was generally believed that the social, cultural and material progress made by Jews outside Russia would be maintained and that with the spread of enlightenment Russian Jewry too would find its place in the sun.

These hopes were shattered by the pogroms which followed the assassination of Alexander II in 1881, and a Jewish trek towards the West began which was mainly directed towards America. A trickle also moved towards the Holy Land. Persecution in Poland and Germany quickened the flow and by the outbreak of World War II some two hundred and sixty-five thousand Jews had made their homes in Palestine. Their number more than doubled in the next decade, and when Israel became independent in 1948 there were over six hundred thousand Jews in the land.

They never became a nation of horsemen – the advent of the car, apart from other reasons, saw to that – but the transformation Herzl had envisaged in other respects was largely fulfilled. As fighting men they showed that the traditions of Gideon, of David and Abner and of the Maccabis were still intact. But it did not happen overnight.

When David Ben-Gurion arrived in Palestine in the early years of the century, he found that the Jewish settlers hired Circassians to defend their lives and property:

Jews did not readily take to bearing arms. As a people we have an ingrained abhorrence to violence. In the centuries of exile we were often martyred. Yet we submitted in abnegation, rarely fighting back. Our weapons were intellectual, based upon reason and persuasion. Our brains were finely attuned to dialectical argument through long study of the myriad complexities of the Talmud, that great edifice erected during our dispersion to comment and elucidate the far greater edifice of the Bible. To take up arms seemed abnormal. It was all very well to buy land with the contributions of the mass of Jewry in the diaspora. To cultivate that land in accordance with the pioneering ideal seemed the best way of spending one's life. But for Jews to take rifles and defend that which they had sown seemed at first as going too far.

But there could be no hope of a Jewish state without a Jewish army. They soon took up rifles and out of their efforts there grew the *Hashomer*.

The *Hashomer* was established to cope with Arab marauders whose main purpose was theft, but when Arab attacks grew in frequency and scale and when it became clear that their aims were political, the *Hashomer* was reorganized into the *Haganah* ('Defence'). The basis of the entire corps was voluntary. Training was undertaken after work in the evenings, or at week-ends, though officers were sometimes given leave to undergo more extended training. Its stance was initially defensive and it was engaged in repulsing or averting Arab attacks. Although both officers and men displayed great ingenuity and courage, they lacked professionalism and this was eventually provided by a British army officer, Captain Orde Wingate, a mystic who regarded Zionism as the fulfilment of a divine promise. Captain Wingate established a base at Kibbutz Ein Harod for the training of the Special Night Squads, which, in spite of the misgivings of Chaim Weizmann and other Zionist leaders, quickly went over to the offensive. The SNS came to form the nursery of Israel's general staff.

In 1941 crack units from the *Haganah* were organized into a small full-time army which came to be known as the *Palmach*. Its formation was entirely illegal, but illegal or not some of its members were given commando training by the British army for missions behind the enemy lines. The skills thus acquired were later employed against British troops in Palestine when, at the end of the war, it became clear that Britain had no intention of implementing the Balfour Declaration. Attacks were launched against bridges, railway lines and radar installations, and when an Anglo-American Commission visited Palestine to consider the future of the territory they were satisfied that in the event of a British withdrawal the Jews would be able to look after themselves.

The Jews themselves were not so sanguine. When the British withdrew in May 1948, there were some forty-five thousand men in the *Haganah*, of whom three thousand were in the *Palmach*, with about a further ten thousand equipped and ready for action. But more worrying than the paucity of men was the paucity of arms. There were large forces of Arab irregulars in action in Galilee and in the Judean and Hebron Hills even before Britain withdrew. Then on 15 May, the moment the British mandate came to an end, four regular Arab armies crossed the frontier in the south, the east and the west. The Egyptians, who formed the largest group, had a sizeable airforce (which opened the campaign with a raid on Tel Aviv), tanks, armoured cars, heavy artillery. Syria and Iraq were also well armed, and Jordan's Arab Legion, headed by General Glubb Pasha, was widely regarded as the most efficient and best equipped fighting force in the Middle East. Israel, at the outset, had no planes or tanks and its artillery consisted of a handful of French field pieces, forged in 1887 and known affectionately as Napoleonchiks; even small arms and ammunition were scarce. There were initial set-backs. Jerusalem was under siege; the Old City was abandoned; a number of isolated settlements in the Hebron Hills had to be evacuated, and there were moments when Jewry, only three years after the holocaust, seemed to be on the brink of yet another catastrophe. But gradually Israel went over to the offensive. The Jordanians were held, the other Arab armies were thrown back, and after thirteen months of bloody fighting an armistice was finally signed. Four thousand Jewish troops and two thousand civilians were killed, tens of thousands were injured and whole towns lay in ruins, but Israel had survived, and in a form much larger than had been envisaged. When Jews gathered for thanksgiving, they were able to declare, in the words of the prayer written to celebrate the victory of the Maccabis:

We thank thee O Lord for the miracles, for the redemption, for the mighty deeds and saving acts wrought by thee . . . thou deliverest the strong into the hands of the weak, the many into the hands of the few . . .

Some indeed regarded the events as a miracle from heaven, but many were satisfied that the Jew had at last vindicated himself as a man. Jewish leaders explained that they had a secret weapon – *ein breira*, 'no alternative'. This was not a war in which one side won and another lost, in which the latter made some concession to the former and everybody went back to their homes again. The Jews were fighting for their state and their lives and if they lost once there would be no return engagement. The prospect of death not only concentrates the mind, it gives a desperate courage, and the Jews fought with a determination and fury which astounded the world and perhaps even themselves.

If the War of Independence established the Jew as a man, the whirlwind Sinai campaign of 1956 established him almost as a superman. Yet when war threatened again in June 1967, the triumphs were momentarily forgotten, and old fears returned – one almost heard the Auschwitz waggons roll again. Israelis were rather less apprehensive than diaspora Jewry but they were apprehensive enough. Every new round of fighting brought the old threat of extirpation, but when the fighting did come they acquitted themselves with even greater ingenuity and valour than in the previous wars. It was all so swift, so dramatic, so dazzling that the Jews seemed to be invincible. Thus when war erupted yet again in 1973, it took everyone by surprise. Surprise, is, of course, everything in modern warfare and as a result the Israelis suffered initial setbacks, but they soon recovered their posture and within a week were advancing on both fronts. By the end of another week they had thrust far into Syria and were threatening Damascus, had encircled an Egyptian army, captured Suez and were astride the main road and rail links to Cairo. In any place but Israel the Yom Kippur War would have been regarded as a triumph, in Israel it is still spoken of as a calamity. They had been taught to expect the impossible, and when Israeli generals proved themselves to be capable of errors of judgment a mood of despondency set in which was partially lifted after the Entebbe raid, but which has not entirely vanished.

Israel has made spectacular advances in many fields, some of which we shall examine later, but none of them have meant as much as her feats of arms, not only in the obvious sense that they have assured her physical existence, but in the assurance and pride they have given to Jews at large. The fact that she was raising cattle where only jackals roamed before, that she was reaping golden harvests from what was thought of as desert, that she developed new avenues of scientific research, were important, but not astounding. Such advances were almost taken for granted. Jews were known, and knew themselves, to be clever and resourceful, and indeed they were almost afraid of their own cleverness, but they had serious doubts about their ability as fighters. These doubts, even with the set-backs of 1973, have now been finally laid to rest.

Yet it cannot be argued that the mere experience of living on his own soil restored the Jew to manhood. Many of the troops who fought so valiantly in the War of Independence had come straight from displaced persons camps in Germany with concentration camp numbers still fresh on their arms. A new mood of resolve had gripped the Jewish people in the aftermath of the holocaust; there would be an end to torment. Jewish poets, historians, preachers had dwelt at length on 'the glorious tradition of martyrdom'. It was now felt that there was perhaps less glory than shame in such a tradition, and that if there was glory in death it must be in a soldier's death.

What added to their resolve was the fact they were now, after centuries of wandering, finally fighting on their own soil. If they were astounded by their own victory and prowess it was partly because they had underestimated their own strength. That the Jews had at one time been men of valour was well-known; now it was equally well-known that they had not quite degenerated into the meek lambs of lore; the last Jewish hero had not died with the Maccabis.

The fighting skills of Jews were widely acknowledged both by the Persians and the Romans and they served in considerable numbers as mercenaries in the armies of both. They also fought in the Arab armies which swept across the North African littoral and into Spain in the seventh and eighth centuries. It was only with the spread of Christendom that they were subjected to a process of degradation as a result of which, in the words of St Jerome, 'they lost their manly bearing'. They were not allowed to serve in the army, they were in many cases not allowed to bear arms, and were thus continually at the mercy of the ruling power. Their very situation as protégés was, in itself, enfeebling. They were in many instances the king's property, which had its compensations where the king was sure of his authority, but where chaos prevailed – a not infrequent occurrence – they were almost defenceless. Yet even then they did not always take flight or submit themselves meekly to slaughter. Thus, for example, when, in 1452, John of Capistrano sought to apply to the Jews of Fuerth the oppressive decrees he had imposed elsewhere, the Jews, who could not have numbered more than a few hundred, rose and drove him out of town.

Such risings were not infrequent, but it is remarkable that they happened at all, for the Jews lived in scattered handfuls in central and western Europe and in countering one attack they almost invariably invited others, and no feats of bravery could have saved them from annihilation.

In eastern Europe, where they did form large and established communities, they often fought pitched battles involving thousands of men before being finally overwhelmed. In 1648, during the Cossack rising against the Poles, Jews were actively engaged in the defence of Lvov, Przemysl, Jazlowiec, Buczacz, Niemirow and Kamenetz Podolsk.

After the 1881 pogroms Jews began to organize self-defence units. In the late 'eighties, for example, a large gang which set upon the Jews of Odessa found themselves confronted by Jewish bands, armed with clubs and iron-bars (and according to the police, fire-arms), and quickly drew back. The same happened in Berdichev and several other centres. Jews often gave as good as they got, even better on occasion, but their efforts were restricted by the police and the army, nominally there to keep the peace, but usually siding with the attackers. In August, 1903, there was a pitched battle in the streets of Gomel between Jews, peasants and railway workers in which twelve Jews and eight Christians were killed and many hundreds were injured: much property was looted and destroyed.

In a pogrom at Zhitomir which extended over three days in April 1905, ten Christians and sixteen Jews were killed – mainly through police action. On the third day of the fighting a crowd of about a thousand Jews made their way to the governor and warned that if their attackers were not called off they would embark upon a general slaughter. 'Rivers of blood will flow. We will kill all Christians irrespective of their age, sex, class . . .'

Troops were immediately given orders to separate the warring sides and the fighting stopped within minutes.

Thus even within the cramped conditions of the Pale the humbled Jewish masses were not quite as meek or helpless as they were made to appear. If little of this was known in the outside world it was partly because the self-defence groups were entirely illegal, and also possibly because Jewish leaders may have feared that reports that they were fighting back could reduce the sympathy they were enjoying in the West. If so they seriously misunderstood the West, for if there is sympathy for the underdog, there is infinitely more sympathy for the underdog who fights back (provided, of course, that he does not fight back so well as to become top-dog).

The experience of the Jew within the Pale of Settlement was not such as to endow him with any love of country, and when there was general mobilization, as at the time of the Russo-Japanese war, he understandably did his best to avoid military service. One of the few exceptions was Joseph Trumpeldor (1880–1920), himself the son of a soldier, who volunteered for service with a Siberian regiment, lost an arm at the siege of Port Arthur in the Russo-Japanese war, and, although his injuries were such as to qualify him for demobilization, continued in active service. He was decorated for valour and raised to the rank of Captain and was probably the first Jew to hold commissioned rank in the Russian army. He later moved to Palestine, where he sought to establish a Jewish army and was killed in 1920 during an attack by Arab marauders near the Syrian frontier.

In Austro-Hungary, where they had enjoyed full civic rights since 1782, Jews formed about eight per cent of the Hapsburg officer corps by the end of the nineteenth century, several of them rising to the rank of general, including Eduard von Schweitzer, Adolph Kornhaber, Hazai Samu, Simon Vogel, Johann Mestitz, Leopold Austerlitz, Emil von Sommer and Marton Zold. About two hundred and seventy-five thousand Jews served in the Hapsburg armies in World War I and nearly thirty thousand died in action. About two hundred and fifty thousand American Jews served in the forces during the eighteen months that America was involved in World War I. About ten thousand were commissioned, including three generals, Milton J. Foreman, Charles Laucheimer and Abel Davis. In World War II about half a million Jews fought in the allied armies, including Major General Maurice Rose, who negotiated the unconditional surrender of German forces in Tunisia, and who led the Third US Armoured Corps through France and Belgium. He died in action a few days before the cease-fire.

In Britain the highest ranking officer to wear the King's uniform in
World War I was Lt General Sir John Monash. He was an Australian, and
even without the Australian army it is unlikely that he would have risen
so far and so fast had he not enjoyed considerable renown as a civil
engineer. He commanded the Australian and New Zealand Army Corps
(the 'Anzacs') on the Western Front and was widely regarded as the outstanding allied commander of World War I.

The first Jew to reach the rank of Colonel in the British Army proper,
A. E. W. Goldsmid (1846–1904), was not known as a Jew, and did not
know himself to be Jewish, until after he was commissioned. In this
century only two Jews in the British army were advanced beyond the
rank of Brigadier, and not many rose beyond the rank of Major even
where they had devoted a lifetime of service to the army. Most Jewish
officers in the British army appear to have been specialists – doctors,
dentists, engineers.

In the Soviet Union, where after the October revolution a large part
of the Tsarist officer corps went over to the White Russians, or fled into
exile, the army was suddenly thrown open to new talents. Four of Trotsky's
divisional commanders were Jews, and Jews were particularly active in
building up Soviet air power. J. B. Goldberg became deputy commander
of the Air Force, and Grigori Stern commanded the Soviet forces in the
Far East and routed a Japanese army which tried to invade Mongolia. He
died in 1940 during the Russo-Finnish war.

During the Mongolian campaign Stern was assisted by a young officer
called Yaakov Shmushkevitch. In 1936 Shmushkevitch was sent to Spain
to reorganize the Republican Air Force and did so with such notable
success that he was made a Hero of the Soviet Union. He then succeeded
Stern in the Far East command and was made a Hero of the Soviet Union
a second time – one of the very few officers to be thus honoured – for his
work in establishing an effective air defence system. Later he became
commander of the Soviet Air Force but was dismissed from his post in
one of Stalin's purges, shortly before the Nazi invasion, tried for treason
and executed. He was given a posthumous rehabilitation.

About half a million Jews fought in the Soviet forces in World War II,
of whom (according to Soviet sources – Jewish sources put the figure
higher) one hundred and seven were made Heroes of the Soviet Union.
Over seventy became generals, of whom about half were engineers or
doctors.

While all this does not prove that Jews were a warrior race, it does not suggest that they were congenital cowards. Yet their reputation as limp and feeble creatures persisted and among Arabs, indeed, Jews were referred to as *Wallad al Mitha* (Children of the Dead).

The triumphs of Israel changed all that. Jews were not only shown to be winners, but winners in circumstances which raised them to the level of heroes.

After the Six Day War awe-struck commentators vied with one another to find some adjectives to express their wonder at the speed and the scale of the victory and one described the Israelis as 'the Prussians of the Middle-East'. Herzl would have been delighted at the description; Israelis were incensed. Yet their feat of arms had not shown them to be new Jews; their new circumstances had encouraged the emergence of old qualities.

When Herzl speculated on his proposed Jewish state he was aware that its citizens would not be drawn from the bankers and brokers, textile merchants and diamond merchants of London, Paris, New York and Amsterdam, but from the Jewish masses of eastern Europe. It was their predicament which had given urgency to the Zionist debate. But although they were impoverished, they did not quite constitute a working class, for there was little industry in the Pale of Settlement and people snatched at whatever opportunity to make a few roubles that might come their way. Many were petty traders of the pettiest sort. Others were *luftmenschen* living from day to day, sometimes from meal to meal, sustained by faith, hope and charity, but above all hope. Of the two thousand Jewish immigrants who passed through the Poor Jews Temporary Shelter, London, during 1895-6, no fewer than four hundred and sixty described themselves as 'merchants', a somewhat grandiose title for men who were self-confessed paupers, and who would not have been given room in the Shelter had they been anything else. The term merchant was an expression of hope rather than fact. Numerous Jewish thinkers and philanthropists attempted to combat this tendency and to make the Jews a more productive element in society. Many saw in a return to the land a solution to the problems of both the land and the Jew. There was almost a mystical belief that in becoming farmers Jews would recover their souls.

They had, after all, begun in their own land as farmers and freemen, each settled on his own soil, a nation of peasants and priests, and the ideal was reiterated, even while Jewish fortunes were at their lowest, by the thirteenth-century German Jewish sage, Eliezar ben Yehuda ben Kalonymus, who declared that God 'created the world so that all shall live in pleasantness, that all shall be equal, that none shall lord it over the other, that all shall cultivate the land . . .'

And when Jews were wrenched from their land – or so the popular belief went – they lost something of their true selves. Yet they had, in fact, begun to leave the land long before they were wrenched from it. In Roman times, and possibly before, there was a discernible drift from the country to the towns, where farmers became artisans and traders; others emigrated to various parts of the Roman empire. As an occupation farming stood in the way of study. 'If one ploughs in the ploughing season and reaps in the reaping season,' asked Rabbi Simeon Bar Yochai, 'what is to become of the Torah?' Urban occupations left one with more time for such callings. Penal taxation also made farming unprofitable and by the third century AD what was left of the Jewish peasantry had largely deserted the land. On the other hand the large Jewish colony in Babylon, which had been settled on fertile soil watered by the Tigris and Euphrates since the sixth century BC, was largely engaged in agriculture, with such success that one Rabbi observed: 'the reason God exiled Jews to Babylonia was that having plentiful dates for food they could devote themselves to the study of the Torah.' But even here the agricultural economy gave way to a more urbanized economy and by the time of the Moslem conquest there were few Jews on the land.

In Spain, France and Italy there is evidence of considerable Jewish agricultural activity in the Middle Ages, though Jewish farmers were the exception rather than the rule. In eastern Europe, prior to the breakup of Poland, Jews became leaseholders of the large agricultural estates of the Polish nobility; but they were managers and entrepreneurs rather than farmers. In the Pale as a whole, most Jews found themselves in a semi-rural environment and even where they were craftsmen or petty traders they tended to have a small vegetable garden, a few goats and perhaps even a cow or two. This did not, however, quite make them farmers, and even if their setting was rural their proclivities were urban.

In the early nineteenth century the Tsarist authorities sought to colonize southern lands by attracting new settlers, including Jews, to the area, through generous land grants. A total of thirty-eight Jewish agricultural villages were formed as a result of these efforts and by the end of the century they had a total population of about forty-two thousand, with each farmer settled on a holding of about thirty-two acres. There were similar settlements in White Russia, but in smaller holdings on less fertile land and they were less successful. By the end of the century they comprised about six thousand farms with a total population of about thirty-six thousand. After the revolution, though enlarged partly with the help of Jewish money from abroad, they gradually lost their Jewish identity. There were also about thirty thousand Jews actively engaged in farming (as distinct from trading in farm produce) in Poland, and perhaps as many in Austrian Galicia, and by 1930 it was estimated that there were as many as half a million Jewish cultivators in eastern Europe. But that was partly because Jews had been virtually forced back onto the land by hunger in the Soviet Union.

In the late 'eighties a young disciple of Tolstoy, called Aharon David Gordon, set himself to combat this powerful entrepreneurial instinct in Jewish life and he saw the remedy in what he called 'the dignity of labour'. In 1901, at the age of forty-eight, he left Russia to work as a farm labourer in Palestine. He was old for his age, a frail, bearded figure who had never done any physical work in his life. He was a socialist, but opposed Marxism because it sought to change society rather than man. The only effective revolution, he believed, was within us, and such revolutions were attainable only through plain physical endeavour: '. . . the first thing that opens my heart to a life I have not known before is labour,' he wrote, 'not labour to make a living, not work as a deed of charity, but work for life itself.' The very smell of the soil awakened him to new sensations. Agricultural toil, he believed, was an act of creation: here was man truly acting in the image of God. He, more than anyone else, was instrumental in the evolution of the kibbutz movement (though it has eschewed some of his more fantastic flights of romanticism). He also believed that a return to the land would lead man to rediscover religion, and the Jew to rejuvenate his Judaism. This has happened to a limited extent among a handful of religious kibbutzim who, on the other hand, have rejected much of Gordon's socialism.

The kibbutzim, however, were not amongst the first pioneers. In 1882, in the wake of the pogroms, a group of young Jews from southern Russia made their home in Palestine. 'The recent pogroms', wrote one of them, 'have violently awakened the complacent Jews from their sweet slumbers.' He continued:

Until now, I was uninterested in my origin. I saw myself as a faithful son of Russia, which was to me my *raison d'être* and the very air I breathed. Each new discovery by a Russian scientist, every classical literary work, every victory of the Russian kingdom would fill my heart with pride. I wanted to devote my whole strength to the good of my homeland, and happily to do my duty, and suddenly they came to show us the door . . .

They found work in Mikveh Israel, an agricultural school near Jaffa which had been founded by the *Alliance Israelite* in 1870.

Some of them later moved on to Rishon Le Zion. Other colonies were formed in Petach Tikvah and Gedera. But in spite of the determination, tenacity and grit of the colonists, all would have foundered but for the help of Baron Edmond de Rothschild.

Baron Edmond, or *Hanadiv* – the benefactor, as he was known among Zionists – was head of the French branch of the family. He was not interested in banking but devoted himself mainly to philanthropy and art. He was not, he was at pains to declare, a Zionist, and when Herzl tried to press upon him his plans for a Jewish state he recoiled with dismay. But he was one of those non-Zionists without whose efforts Zionism could never have been rebuilt. In all, he spent about ten million pounds on his settlements, which in today's terms would be worth about twenty times that much. But in spite of his generosity, the settlers were inclined to look his gift-horse in the teeth, and perhaps even to prod it in the tonsils, for he was determined that the settlements should run efficiently, as if they were some sub-branch of the Rothschild empire, which in a sense they were. To this end he sent out managers, experts in agriculture and soil culture, doctors and teachers, and the settlers, shorn of all initiative, received a monthly allowance for their efforts. They were understandably restive under the régime and there was a good deal of conflict between managers and colonists until the Baron finally handed over the settlements to the Jewish Colonial Association in 1900 and the settlers eventually became masters of their own lands.

Herzl had been critical of the Baron's efforts and felt he was breeding a generation of *schnorrers*. A more serious criticism was that the Jewish immigrants who began to arrive in considerable numbers towards the end of the century found it difficult to get jobs in the new settlements. Arab labour was cheap and abundant and Jewish workmen could not compete. Rishon Le Zion, which, by 1890, had a mere forty Jewish settlers, had attracted some three hundred families of Arab labourers, and Zichron Yaakov, with a population of about two hundred, employed over a thousand Arabs. This was hardly the new social order which Zionist thinkers envisaged.

In 1901 the Zionist movement established the Jewish National Fund to acquire land on behalf of the Jewish people in Palestine and many new-comers were employed on stone-clearing and other such tasks by the Fund. Here too conflicts developed. Perhaps the Jew is not an ideal employee, or employer, perhaps he is neither. But where the one works for the other the first tends to suspect that he is being given too little, and the other that he is being asked too much. Many of the newcomers, while prepared for every hardship, had not fled from Russian task-masters to be confronted with Jewish ones, and if many were imbued with Gordon's belief in the dignity of labour, they were not happy in the role of hired labourer, even where, perhaps especially where, the employer was Jewish. In 1909, after prolonged friction, a handful of men working on the southern shore of the sea of Galilee undertook the cultivation of an extensive area of land without the benefit of managers or overseers. They did so briskly and efficiently and out of their efforts grew the first kibbutz, Deganiah. They had started without set plans or fixed ideology, beyond that of self-labour. The form of the kibbutz was determined by circum-stances. If any group hoped to become economically viable, function without external interference, and defend themselves against Arab marauders, they could only do so on a communal basis. The most distinctive, the most venerated and possibly the most productive element in Israeli society came into being almost by accident.

There are today some two hundred and thirty-five kibbutzim in Israel, with a total population of about ninety-four thousand, and they comprise the nearest thing Israel has to the landed gentry. They form less than three per cent of the population but, like the landed gentry elsewhere, they have an influence out of all proportion to their numbers. Of Israel's six Prime Ministers, three – Ben-Gurion, Levi Eshkol and Golda Meir – were, at one time or another, kibbutzniks. Deganiah, the burial place of Levi Eshkol, is the birthplace of Moshe Dayan. Kibbutzim are heavily represented in the upper ranks of the Histadruth, which is both Israel's TUC and its greatest commercial holding company, and they also form a large, perhaps the largest part, of Israel's officer corps. This means that in war they also suffer the highest proportion of casualties.

The kibbutz has moved far from its spartan origins. The older settle-ments especially are garden suburbs with spacious lawns, tree-lined walks, hissing sprinklers, red-roofed, air-conditioned homes, eaves deep in oleander, ornate dining rooms and beach umbrellas beside Olympic-sized swimming pools. But the hours are still long and the work is still hard and the principle of equality, with 'From each according to his ability and to each according to his needs', remains, so that the *merakesh hameshek*, who might be described as the managing director of the entire settlement, will receive no more than the lowliest member doing the lowliest job, and if he is a comparative newcomer, he will probably receive less. Seniority is all.

Many kibbutznicks, especially as they grew older, found the socialistic principles too rigorously applied, the communal existence too communal, especially where the care of children was concerned, and in 1921 some broke away to establish what was known as a *moshav*.

The *moshav* is a co-operative settlement in which each farmer works his own plot of land and pockets any profit it may yield. Produce is marketed on a co-operative basis through the *moshav*, which also helps its members to buy seed, fertilizer and fodder and to obtain credit. It also maintains machinery and vehicles (sometimes in association with neighbouring *moshavim*), workshops and stores, and erects and maintains all public installations, including pumping stations, central irrigation plants, supplies, stores, dairies, cold stores, canning and packing plants, and social facilities such as schools, clinics and sports clubs. There are about three hundred and fifty *moshavim* in Israel, with a total population of about a hundred and twenty-five thousand.

What the *moshav* has theoretically in common with the kibbutz is that neither of them employ outside labour. But both have, in fact, departed from this principle, the latter with a rather greater show of reluctance than the former.

Hired workers contravene one of the most fundamental kibbutz principles. In the early years of the state when there was a shortage of work, Ben-Gurion almost had to compel the kibbutzim to take on outside labour. Now that there is a shortage of labour, kibbutzim can hardly exist without them, and they can no longer be strictly considered as self-employed communities.

Over half of the Jews living on the land are new immigrants who arrived since 1948, and most of them were directed there on arrival. But the numbers have been declining in both absolute and in comparative terms. In 1958 agricultural workers formed 15.7 per cent of the labour force; in 1963, 11.5 per cent; 8.9 per cent in 1969, and under 8 per cent now. The decline in the Jewish farm labour force has been offset partly by an influx of Arab labour and increasing mechanization. At harvest times, giant combine harvesters, cotton pickers and hay balers rumble through the fields like prehistoric monsters. The acreage under cultivation has nearly tripled since 1948 and yields have been quintupled, much of it from areas which have never felt the plough for over a thousand years. The need for Israel – a country in an almost constant state of war – to be agriculturally self-sufficient has meant that water has had to be directed at great and sometimes uneconomic cost to areas which would otherwise have remained barren. But it is an amazing fact that a country which hardly a generation ago was heavily dependent on imports to feed a population of just over a million, has trebled its population, doubled its standard of living and has yet become self-sufficient in vegetables, potatoes, fruit, milk, eggs and poultry, and supplies twenty-five per cent of its wheat and legumes, about forty per cent of its meat, over thirty per cent of its sugar and about seventy per cent of its fish (about half of which are raised in fish ponds).

Israel's achievements in agriculture are of course less dramatic than those in the battlefield, but are no less remarkable, and result from a rare combination of ingenuity and grit. There is no one more conservative than a farmer, but both kibbutz and *moshav* have been ready – sometimes too ready – to apply the latest results of agricultural research – new seeds, fertilizers, pesticides, machinery. Israel's land has been a laboratory. The mere statistics tell only half the story. To visit Israel at frequent intervals is to witness the slow unrolling of a vast green carpet. The desert recedes on every side like hair on a middle-aged head.

And all this has been done with sweat. What miracle the Israelis might have wrought with oil! Zionism has been defended in terms of historic connections, divine rights, and as a haven for an oppressed people. But even if the Israelis had descended from Mars their case for holding on, certainly to her pre-1967 territories, would have been overwhelming, merely in terms of achievement. The right of conquest is not recognized in the modern world (except where the great powers are the conquerors), but there is such a thing as the right of salvage. Palestine was not all a wilderness before the Zionists came, but most of it was, and the rest was salvaged through industry, ingenuity and care.

The Israelis, we may therefore readily agree, have produced a super-farmer, but have they produced a new man? On the face of it, yes.

Many of the *moshavniks* are from North African ghettos; they have hardly handled a spade in their lives, let alone a tractor. But a large corps of agricultural advisers has patiently coached them and they are eager and quick to learn. It is no mean achievement to convert an unskilled, semi-literate artisan into a skilled farmer within a few short years.

The productivity of kibbutzim is less surprising, for they have attracted a higher calibre of member, who represents not only a new type of farmer, but a new type of being who has somehow transcended the pull of money. Yet if the kibbutznick has, the kibbutz hasn't. What has happened is that individual greed has given way to communal cupidity. Private enterprise has few men as enterprising, as hard-headed and as shrewd as the average secretary of the average kibbutz. But this does not gainsay the very real sacrifices made by the abler members for the sake of the commune as a whole. Some kibbutznicks can and even do earn very high salaries, through being seconded to the Histadruth or other organizations, but their salaries are paid into the kibbutz treasury, from which they draw on the same basis as everyone else. The novelist, Amoz Oz, a member of kibbutz Hulda, for example, has in recent years been receiving a torrent of royalty cheques, but they all go straight into the kibbutz. It must, however, be added that kibbutz life, apart from conserving an ideal, has its material compensations.

Most middle-class Israeli families are small, partly because most middle-class incomes are small and the cost of living is high. On a kibbutz families are comparatively large, but then expense is no object, and every child receives a level of education not available elsewhere in Israel. Classes are smaller, facilities are better. The teachers are themselves members of the kibbutz, know the children intimately and where a child has special aptitudes, be it in swimming, basketball or ballet, he is given special attention. And where he falls behind he will get remedial teaching of a quality perhaps not available elsewhere in the world, for the kibbutz is as determined to get the best out of its personnel as to get the best out of its soil, and it usually does. All children remain at school till eighteen and most go on to university. The physical amenities, especially at the older kibbutzim, are also not inconsiderable, and they are taxed on a preferential basis in a country where taxation otherwise verges on the confiscatory. Kibbutznicks work hard, but people in town work harder and there are very few Israelis who enjoy the standard of living available on the kibbutz without having two or three jobs.

Why then are kibbutzim not overwhelmed with applicants? Why do they have a shortage of manpower and why do they constitute less than three per cent of the population? One reason is that they are very selective in whom they admit as members, but the main one is that Jews have remained Jewish, incorrigible individualists who do not wish to have their lives determined by committee – as they are on the kibbutz – and who like to enjoy the fruit, if any, of their own enterprise. The kibbutz also offers a sort of security which few Jews expect, or even desire; they like to have an area of their existence open to chance.

Nor does the kibbutz movement as a whole quite represent the Gordonian ideals of its founders, for if the principles of equality survive, much else has atrophied. Not all of their members can describe themselves as horny-handed sons of toil. Many kibbutzim own factories, workshops, hotels and guest houses and between them control something like ten per cent of the country's industrial output. In their early days kibbutzim used to rotate jobs, partly to vary them, partly to prevent the emergence of an élite holding the more responsible jobs. But with increasing specialization in farming and the advent of factories with their production managers and engineers, rotation has become less practical. Natural economic forces induce a specialization of labour, and labour is becoming specialized even in the kibbutz. Gordon's vision of the *turyah*-wielding labourer subsisting on the sweat of his brow could only have survived in a primitive agrarian society, whereas Israel is becoming, indeed has become, a forcing house of technological advance. For a parched, hilly country it probably derives the highest yield per acre in the world in almost every department of agriculture, but that is partly because it almost certainly has more scientists per acre than any other country in the world, and still hasn't acres enough to employ all its skills. There is no free secondary or university education in Israel, yet with a population hardly larger than the Birmingham conurbation (which is to say about three and a half million, of whom about half a million are Arabs) it has no less than seven major institutions of higher learning – two in Haifa, two in Tel Aviv, and one each in Jerusalem, Rehovoth and Beersheba. And these are not sufficient to accommodate everyone clamouring for a degree so that there are thousands of Israeli students in Europe and North America. Egalitarian traditions in Israel are still strong. A dustman with a large family can earn more than a don with a small one, but notwithstanding that the dustman will try and see his sons through university and, more often than not, he will succeed. None of the ideals of the labour movement which, until recently, has controlled Israel's destinies since its inception, and even before, none of the lay sermons on the dignity of labour or *kibbush ha-avodah*, the conquest of labour, has checked the continuing trend from manual to sedentary occupations. Even the manual worker on the early-morning bus with his brief-case under his arm tends to look like a public official who has seen better days. Ber Borochov, David Ben-Gurion, A. D. Gordon, Berl Katznelson, Joseph

Brenner, all the ideologues of Zionism lamented the fact that diaspora Judaism was removed from the basic sectors of the economy and confined to finance, commerce, teaching, medicine and the law. If the Jewish state was to become a viable reality, they insisted, Jews would have to learn to work in the fields, in the mines, on the roads. In the early years they did, and in the early years of the state, too, with the influx of hundreds of thousands of unskilled immigrants, it was not difficult to direct them to where they were most needed. But once they settled down they began to direct themselves, and if not themselves, their children, to where they most wanted to go. In the 'fifties and 'sixties much of the manual work was done by new immigrants. Now that immigration is declining it is being increasingly undertaken by Arabs, while Jews are drifting back into finance, commerce, teaching, medicine and the law. One hopeful departure is that many of them are now engaged in the applied sciences, and another, less helpful, is that many – far too many – are also engaged in administration.

What is more, Israel, though its population and economy have been continuously growing, has not been able to accommodate its talents and enterprise. During the 'fifties and 'sixties, when Israel enjoyed a prolonged honeymoon with what were then called the developing countries and are now referred to as 'the third world', thousands of Israeli engineers, architects, agronomists, meteorologists and others could be found all over Africa and Asia on public works schemes and as advisers to various governments. Israelis and Israel gloried in their role. It was as if the prophetic ideal of being 'a light unto the nations' was enjoying practical application. Israel had raised herself by her exertions, she could raise others by her example. Since 1973, however, with the growing political isolation of Israel, the aid programme has been drastically curtailed, if not abandoned, and an important outlet for Israeli skills has been dammed. The paucity of such outlets has led to a great deal of frustration and many Israelis – the figure usually quoted is about three hundred thousand, but the actual one may be nearer half a million – have moved abroad, mostly to North America. This is not new. There has been a continuous process of self-selection from the days of the first settlers. The ablest, the hardiest, the most idealistic remained, as did those without the skills or the energies to move. If all the Jews who had moved to Palestine/Israel had remained, Israel might by now have had a population of five or six million. There are, as a result of the continuing efflux, few second-raters in Israel. It is a society of first- and third-raters so that the qualities and defects one finds in

Jewry at large are magnified in the Jewish state. The Israeli is not a new Jew, he is like the old Jew – only more so.

All this arises largely out of the fact that Israel has never been able to relax into its natural setting and, so to speak, go native. It is an European enclave on an Asiatic shore; but it could have acclimatized itself to it. In the 'sixties, when Israel had known almost a decade of peace, and few minds were troubled by the prospect of war, there began to emerge a new movement called The Canaanites, which wanted to end the association with world Jewry and to follow its own course and its own destiny. The Eichmann trial, which had been stage-managed by Ben-Gurion to give Israelis an understanding of recent Jewish history and to link them more closely with the diaspora, had, if anything, the opposite effect. Many young people wanted to shrug off their history and the oppressive weight of Jehova and their dirges and their martyrs, the boom of Zionist rhetoric and the descent of American UJA missions in funny hats and Bermuda shorts, and Hadassah ladies in slant-eyed glasses. They wanted to begin life anew, with the past, if not erased, at least kept firmly in place. The Six Day War, and the events leading up to it, changed all that. The crisis brought a feeling of solidarity among all Jews which had never been experienced before, and if it might have abated since, the Yom Kippur War, and the propaganda war, with the characterization of Zionism as racism, has sustained it. The Canaanites are no more, and instead there has been a growing resort to mysticism. Many a head which has never accommodated a holy thought is now crowned with a skull-cap. At a recent meeting of the Union of Kibbutzim, a secularist organization which used to be anti-religious, one of the principal speakers declared, with the evident approval of the gathering:

No intellectual acrobatics can stop Zionism from withering away once it has been cut off from its mystical messianic dimensions, the very root of its existence. The profound affinity of Eretz Yisroel, this holy madness with which the Jewish people has been sick these twenty odd centuries is something the only logic of which is non-logic. Any attempt to understand the Zionist phenomenon without taking into account the 'holy madness' of it is a sterile one.

All this and more was said on behalf of the efforts of the *Gush Emunim*, religious zealots, who had been attempting to settle in parts of the occupied West Bank which the government had declared closed to Jewish settlement, and whose efforts too were applauded by the meeting.

It is almost as if Israel is doomed to replay the history of the Jewish people, so that failing to be accepted by its neighbours as one of themselves, it is thrown back upon itself. It has been forced to keep its alien, occidental, Jewish identity almost in spite of itself. It had hoped to become the Switzerland of the Middle East; it has remained, inexorably, a ghetto, a show-place for Jewish genius, but also one in which Jewish deficiencies become glaringly evident. Instead of creating a new Jew, Israel has refurbished the old one, and brought forth qualities which had been allowed to wither, without, however, suppressing defects which had been allowed to flourish.

These defects, as we have suggested, arise out of the distortions imposed by external circumstances. A nation continually braced for war cannot – even if one overlooks the abnormal history of the Jewish people – develop along normal lines. There is, for example, a dreadful irony in the fact that one of Israel's principal exports – and indeed one of its growth industries – is arms. In trying to be self-sufficient in arms it has had to develop a productive capacity which is uneconomic if limited to its own needs and, as a result, Israel, of all nations, has been compelled to beat its ploughshares into swords.

There are, however, even graver distortions, which arise not out of external circumstances but out of wilful blindness.

Ahad Ha-am, perhaps the principal ideologue of modern Zionism, envisaged the revived Jewish state not merely as a political entity, but as a 'spiritual centre' which would give rise to a spiritual and cultural awakening among Jews at large (he never thought of Palestine as a home for all or even most Jews). A Hebrew University was to be part of the scheme, and when the foundation stone was laid on the barren slopes of Mount Scopus, even while guns were booming in the distance, it was thought of as a typical piece of Zionist day-dreaming. But seven years later the University was open and today it is in the front rank of academic institutions, a university of world renown. As we have already noticed it is but one of several major institutions of higher learning. Yet although they produce a ready flow of gifted graduates, they have not yet made Israel that spiritual centre which Ahad Ha-am envisaged, and which his disciple and biographer, Leon Simon, defined as 'a national spiritual centre in which the secular and religious aspects of Jewish nationalism are subtly blended'. There has been no such blending, subtle or crude.

When Zionism first emerged as a political force, it was dismissed by most Rabbis as an usurpation of the Messianic ideal. They were also troubled by reports that the young chalutzim who exposed themselves to every hardship to make their homes in Palestine were disregarding the dietary laws, desecrating the Sabbath, and that even, or so the reports went, 'men were seen dancing with maidens'. Certainly among many young people Zionism was a conscious revolt against the fatalism, the resignation, the apparent helplessness of their elders. They intended to be masters of their own fate and such an ambition has no place for traditional Judaism.

They encountered criticism from others as well as the Rabbis. Baron Edmond de Rothschild, whose own way of life was eons removed from Jewish tradition, insisted that Jewish colonists in his settlements observe the Sabbath and festivals and the Jewish dietary laws.

Chaim Weizmann, the most moderate of moderates in other respects, loathed and feared Jewish clericalism. When friends pressed him to establish a 'Jewish Faculty' within his proposed university, he retorted:

... a Jewish Faculty would appeal to many, especially in this country, but you have to face a terrible difficulty, that a Jewish Faculty is not possible without Biblical research and other subjects of this kind, which would create a storm, likely to blow away the whole of the Faculty.

To eliminate all the 'free thinking' and the spirit of 'free research' from a faculty means to reduce it to dust ...

A Jewish faculty was in fact established and it pursued its researches in the full spirit of free inquiry. But as a result, although the University was to have Orthodox Jews among both its students and faculty, it was always regarded as vaguely non-kosher. In 1955, Bar Ilan, a religious university, was founded at Ramat Gan, near Tel Aviv. The plans for Bar Ilan aroused the sort of storm which Weizmann had anticipated the Hebrew University would face and various Rabbis feared that Bar Ilan could become a breeding ground for heretics. Their fears have proved unfounded, for Bar Ilan has evolved a compromise which might be described as controlled schizophrenia, for while studies in, say, science or economics may be pursued with an open mind, those touching upon Judaism must be pursued within the limits of accepted tradition.

But Bar Ilan, with all its self-imposed restraints, is at least part of this world and it feels some sort of responsibility to Jewish society as a whole, whereas a large part of Orthodox Israel is removed from it, and indifferent to it, content in the belief that they need only maintain their own ways for the rest of the world to follow.

In the 1880s there were in Israel some twenty to twenty-five thousand

Jews, settled mainly in the holy cities of Jerusalem, Hebron, Tiberias and Safed, deeply devout, poverty stricken and riven into tiny factions each with their own religious authorities.

Their numbers grew slowly as their circumstances improved, but they were largely oblivious to the efforts of the newcomer to build a new world, and in so far as they were aware of their efforts they were troubled by them. There were Rabbis, like Samuel Mohliwer (1824–98), and Zvi Hirsch Kalischer (1795–1874), who combined with their deep orthodoxy an appreciation of the failings of Orthodox Jewry and an awareness of contemporary problems, which they believed should not be entirely left in the hands of God. They still believed in Messianic redemption, but felt that it would be brought about by human endeavour and to this end advocated Jewish settlement in Palestine, and particularly agricultural settlement. Mohliwer also spoke of Palestine as a spiritual centre, but in less subtle terms than Ahad Ha-am. What he meant was a centre of Torah learning in which Jews would conduct their lives according to the precepts of the Torah. He got scant support and much criticism from other Rabbis, especially as he was prepared to work with assimilated Jews, and *Maskilim*.

The meaning of *Maskilim* (singular *maskil*) is enlightened ones, and it tells one something of the temper of Orthodoxy that it was employed as a term of abuse. Mohliwer proceeded undismayed and went on to establish a religious Zionist movement which was the forerunner of what is now the National Religious Party. But because of Rabbinical opposition, religious Zionism was slow to grow and religious Zionists were comparative latecomers to Palestine. Religious kibbutzim are now amongst the showplaces of the kibbutz movement. But the first of them was not in fact established until the mid-'thirties and the more worldly, religious Jew, as represented in the NRP is, and always has been, a minor partner in the rebuilding of Zion. But even if a minor partner, he has been zealous, energetic and resourceful and his role has been indispensable. A large part of Orthodox Jewry, however, has remained aloof from the entire endeavour, and their opposition to Zionism has been unaffected either by the holocaust or by the achievements of the Jewish state. They castigated the direction which the rebuilding of Zion took; they have, with the exception of brief periods, not taken part in the government of the country; none of their daughters and few of their sons serve in the army; not an inconsiderable portion of them refuse to recognize Israel, and although they are critical of all Zionists, their particular hatred is directed against religious Zionists who have in fact tried, and to a considerable, perhaps excessive, degree succeeded, in giving a traditional character to the Jewish state.

These Ultras are enjoying something of a revival. Before the war they represented a significant part of Polish, Hungarian and Romanian Jewry who, in spite of hardships, hesitated to emigrate because, in the words of the Rabbis, the West, particularly as represented by America, was a snare for the faithful. There is, in any case, something about Jewish orthodoxy – unquenchable optimism, or perhaps resignation – which induces one to remain where one is, and they remained till they were trapped by the advance of Hitler and all but extirpated. But a hundred or two hundred thousand survived and they emerged from hell, strengthened in their belief, declaring in the words of Job: 'Though He slay me yet will I trust in Him, and will I maintain my ways before him.' Some made their way to Israel. Many settled in America, Britain and Western Europe. They prospered, were fruitful and multiplied. One of the biggest, perhaps *the* biggest, threat to the continuity of Jewish life is the falling birth-rate. Among the Ultras, however, who on the matter of contraception would out-Vatican the Vatican (though they take a more lenient view of abortion), families of six or seven are fairly common, and of nine and ten are by no means rare, and they are spreading beyond their self-imposed ghettos in the decaying parts of New York and London into the suburbs.

They are also attracting new recruits, especially in America, which is enjoying something of a religious revival, though it is not yet clear whether the revival has assumed the form of a regeneration of belief, or whether it is a mere search for ethnic roots and folkways. Certainly the Jew who wants to re-trace his origins does not have to search hard, for the Ultras, and especially the Hassidic sects among them, have kept the past intact. They do not necessarily represent authentic Judaism, any more than the Pennsylvania Dutch necessarily represent authentic Christianity, and it is likely that if Moses were to come among them he would wonder what religion and what God they were worshipping. But there is a simple, untrammelled quality to their existence which comes with the reassurance offered by belief; they are colourful and warm; they often lead exemplary lives; and they give a sense of immortality, which comes with an attachment to the past. Whole areas of doubt and concern are sealed off, and the urgent process of decision making is slowed down. Because so many decisions are made for one, stress is diminished and sometimes even eliminated.

It also, possibly, represents a tacit revolt against rationalism. One could, perhaps, argue that unreason, the determination not to see sense, is also part of the American way of life. For there is no cult, however obscure its origins and bizarre its aims, which will not claim its adherents. The last thing which the young Jew expects of his Judaism is intellectualism, which is why the young Reform Rabbi, with his Ivy League degree and his well-thumbed copy of Kierkegaard, has had a comparatively slight impact on his generation.

And the Conservative movement has not done very much better. Conservatism only became a force in American Jewish life in the early years of this century, when, like the United Synagogue in London, it was taken over by the old families for the assimilation of the new. Schiff, its greatest benefactor, himself a Reform Jew, recognized that the immigrant would feel alien in a Reform synagogue and therefore poured fortunes into the Conservative movement, to provide traditionally-minded, decently-dressed (their equivalent in England were required to don dog-collars), English-speaking Rabbis, to offset the influence of the foreign ones, and properly appointed synagogues to replace the chaotic huddle of unsanitary bethels that were springing up in immigrant areas. By the end of World War I Conservatism had become a major trend within American Judaism, catering mainly for the sons of the immigrant rather than the immigrant himself. Today its three hundred and fifty thousand families, representing some one and a half million Jews, probably comprise about half the synagogue-going public of America; but of late its growth has been checked.

Until a decade or so ago it was generally assumed that the son of an Orthodox father would in due course join a Conservative synagogue and that of a Conservative father, a Reform synagogue. (What the son of a Reform father might do was left open to debate.) That trend has, if anything, been reversed, which is not to suggest that there has been a headlong rush into Orthodoxy, but Orthodox institutions are booming in a way which Conservative and Reform are not.

This reversal of trends is due in part to the efforts of Menachem Mendel Schneerson, the Lubavitcher Rebbe, who made his home in Brooklyn in 1940 and who, though now in his seventy-sixth year, inspires his followers with a degree of missionary effort one had previously associated only with the Jesuits. They have established Hassidic enclaves in the most improbable parts of America and beyond. They have been particularly active in the universities and have won over many students, and not a few professors, who had been totally estranged from Jewish life. Their dialectic may be naive but their concern is deep, their affection sincere, and their zeal endless. One may sometimes question their doctrine of Rabbinic infallibility, but they somehow manage to combine extreme fundamentalism with an appearance of rationalism and even modernity, and they enjoy the goodwill and support of very many individuals far removed from everything Hassidism stands for. Something of the charisma of the Rebbe (whose bearded portrait is to be found, like an ikon, in the homes of each of his adherents) permeates through every level of the movement. Many of his followers are prosperous businessmen, industrialists, heads of public companies, professional men and their wives with an elegance and charm we had not hitherto associated with Hassidism. They comprise a sort of chic Orthodoxy.

But what is perhaps more remarkable is the revival in what might be called plain-clothed Orthodoxy. It was believed at one time that Orthodoxy could never take lasting root in America. It went through a lean time in the inter-war and the immediate post-war years, and for a time it looked as if it might become extinct, but it has enjoyed a spectacular growth in recent years in both the size of its membership and the quality of its members. Americans like to rub shoulders with those who have made it, and the Orthodox were, in the main, people who hadn't. They were the less successful, the less educated, the less confident, the less attractive. People who were not drawn to the Conservative or Reform movements by changes in belief were sometimes brought there by social ambition. All that has changed. The Orthodox too have made it or are making it, and the Orthodox seminary at Yeshiva University has brought forth a new type of Rabbi, with feet planted firmly in both the Orthodox world and the secular one. They feel sufficiently secure in the claims of Orthodoxy not to have to turn their backs on the outside world or to insulate themselves from it.

At the same time both the Reform and Conservative movements have been veering towards the right, have become more traditional, and have laid greater stress on ritual, and although each congregation is a rule unto itself, many Reform Temples are not unlike Conservative synagogues, and many a Conservative synagogue has become barely distinguishable from the Orthodox.

The Orthodox have an important advantage over the other synagogual groups which arises out of the rather mundane fact that they do not travel on the Sabbath. This means that habitations must be within walking distance of the synagogue, and thus of one another, and as a result they have a cohesion and compactness missing in others. In resting their cars for a day, the Orthodox have recovered something that has been missing in the American suburbs, the sense of community: they have revived the *kehilla*.

There has also been a considerable scholastic revival, centred both round the seminaries of the three synagogual organizations and round the departments of Jewish studies attached to many universities. There has been a flow of publications which have been more than the mere transmission of received truths but which represent an earnest attempt to grapple with the problems of Jewish, and particularly Jewish religious, life in the twentieth century.

These developments have tended to make America, rather than Israel, the spiritual centre of Jewry. It is not, of course, that Israel is deficient in Jewish scholarship or Jewish scholars. It has a wealth of great minds and original talents, but their influence on the religious life of the nation, and in particular the Rabbinate, has been limited. This is because they draw their wisdom from secular as well as religious sources, and because they are usually university teachers, and a university, even a religious university like Bar Ilan, is in the eyes of most Rabbis not quite kosher; and kosher or not, it is *terra incognita*. The average Rabbi may spend four, five or even ten years poring over the Talmud in a *Yeshiva*, and is in the main trained to accumulate and regurgitate, but not to think. One may find individual Rabbis who have transcended the narrowness of their training, but they are few and as a result the actions of the Israeli Rabbinate have been such as to fill even devout Jews – indeed, especially devout Jews – with distress. The extreme right, which is to say, black-clad Orthodoxy, knows only how to denounce. Plain-clothes Orthodoxy, which is to say the ruling Orthodox establishment as represented by the National Religious Party, the Ministry of Religion and the Chief Rabbinate, do attempt to grapple with problems but only on an ad hoc basis, and even so with the greatest hesitation and much glancing over their shoulders at what the right will say. Both they and the Ultras in theory want a state governed on Torah principles, but neither have worked out, or attempted to work out, what it would mean, though the Establishment is realistic enough to know that it would mean paralysis and that Israel is able to continue as a viable, or semi-viable, entity, because the majority of Jews are not Orthodox and are content to act as *Shabbat goyim* for those who are. 'We prayed two thousand years for a return to Zion,' said Rav

Maimon, Israel's first Minister of Religion, 'and it had to come in my time.'

What happened was that an entire corps of codes and traditions which had been evolved for life in the diaspora, and which was becoming inadequate even for that, was transferred intact to the Jewish state. Within the diaspora, however, the inadequacies, even if blatant, were tolerable, for they affected only the devout, who, if they found them harsh, could comfort themselves with the belief that it was the will of God, while non-believers could ignore it. In Israel, however, large parts of the religious law have been incorporated into the law of the land, where they affect agnostics and atheists as well as the devout. One is not, for example, stoned to death for desecrating the Sabbath (or at least not yet), but there is no public transport on the Sabbath or festivals. Car-owners and those who can afford a taxi can get around, but the poor cannot. Family law, to give a more important example, is entirely in the hands of the Rabbinate, and where a marriage breaks up, but the husband refuses a divorce, or disappears, the wife remains an *agunah*, which means 'chained'; she can never remarry. In the diaspora, if the wife is not Orthodox, she can resort to a civil court for a divorce and re-marry. In Israel she cannot.

According to Jewish law all agricultural work must cease in the Sabbatical year, which is to say, one year in seven. If this were applied, in fact, Israel would grow bankrupt. What happens, however, is that the overwhelming majority of farmers ignore the law; the ultra Orthodox – a mere handful – leave their fields fallow and resort to hydroculture. As for those who like to keep within the law, but appreciate that they cannot, like the religious kibbutzim, the Rabbinate sells the land to the Arabs for that year, so that Jews can still work on it, and eat the produce. It's a solution that satisfies no one. Ultras boycott Jewish produce and buy their fruit and vegetables from the Arabs, and no one is happy about the idea of selling Israel – even symbolically – to the Arabs.

There have also been the personal squabbles between the Ashkenazi Chief Rabbi, Sholomo Goren, and the Sephardi Chief Rabbi, Ovadiah Yosef, and it is difficult to explain, even to the faithful, why a people worshipping one God and supposedly bound by one Torah should need two different Chief Rabbis. The result of it all is that religious life in the diaspora, far from being illuminated and enriched by the existence of Israel, has often been confounded by it, and the religious Jew, whatever his degree of Orthodoxy, will often look to New York for inspiration rather than Jerusalem.

New York is the seat of the larger Hassidic dynasties, such as Lubavitch and Satmar, of Yeshiva University, where Rabbi Joseph Soloveitchik, the foremost Orthodox thinker of his generation, is Professor of Talmud, of Rabbi Moses Feinstein, an authority on Rabbinic law whose decisions are accepted by all shades of Orthodoxy, and of the Jewish Theological Seminary, which probably represents a confluence of the ablest minds to be concerned with the challenge to Judaism in our time.

For a thousand years, long after the Jewish commonwealth had been re-established and the Temple rebuilt, Babylonia, to which Jews had been taken captive in 586 BC, remained the major centre of Jewish life and learning, and although Zion was the seat of the Temple and the source of the law, the actual law-makers, the codifiers, interpreters, commentators, lived mainly in exile. Editions of the Talmud were collated in both Babylonia and Palestine, but it is the former which became more authoritative.

The circumstances of Babylonia were such as to encourage the preservation and enrichment of Judaism, for it was a place of many cultures and groups, each distinct from one another, and all careful to maintain their distinction. Such heterogeneity suited their imperial overlord, whether Achaemenidian, Macedonian, Seleucid, Roman or Parthian. It was not uncommon for conquerors to transplant populations to sustain such diversity and the Jews, already transplanted, alert, intelligent, literate and orderly, formed a particularly useful element. Their loyalty to Zion remained intact and there was a constant flow of tribute to the Temple in Jerusalem, and a constant traffic of pilgrims.

America is not quite the new Babylon. But it might be fair to say that traditional Judaism, which is largely a product of exile, can only thrive in exile, and that once transplanted to Jewish soil it threatens to be overwhelmed by its own anachronisms.

CHAPTER TWELVE

Survivors

The oldest inscription to mention Jews by name is a monument by an Egyptian Pharaoh who claims to have killed off the Hebrews and left none to survive. Later oppressors had similar aspirations and made similar claims: they were equally mistaken.

Of the fourteen million Jews in the world today nearly a third are in the Soviet Union and although no one in Russia is entirely free Jews are somewhat less free than others. They are a troublesome minority and an enigma both to the Russians and, indeed, to their fellow Jews. Given their isolation from the rest of Jewry, the suppression of all Jewish schools and cultural institutions, the rigorous indoctrination of atheism, and the dedication of a large part of Russian Jewry to socialism and the revolution, they should by now have faded out of existence, yet, they are, on the contrary, showing every sign of resurgence.

After the revolution Soviet Jewry was at first allowed to maintain contact with the outside world and even to establish Zionist groups, but it was widely believed that with full emancipation Russian Jewry would gradually dissolve into the Russian people, a process which influential Communist Jews sought to hasten. Jewish sections (Yevsektsiya) were established in the various branches of the Communist party, with Jewish personnel who made strenuous efforts to suppress all traces of Jewish observance – even though freedom of religion was guaranteed by the constitution – and Judaism led an underground existence. Zionism was proscribed in 1928 and the Hebrew presses closed down. At the same time a 'Jewish proletarian culture' was encouraged which, in the words of Stalin, 'would be national in form and socialist in content'. A Yiddish press was set up, Yiddish papers were produced, Yiddish theatres were established, as well as faculties of Jewish culture in the Universities of Kiev and Minsk. It seemed to Yiddishists in the world at large – whose universe was otherwise shrinking – that Russia was giving Yiddish a new lease of life, and several Yiddish writers made their way back to Russia. More important, a network of Yiddish schools was formed, which by 1932 – the peak of the period – had an enrolment of a hundred and sixty thousand (about a third of Jews of primary school age). But though the language of instruction was Yiddish, there was almost nothing Jewish to the content and the Yiddish itself was de-Hebraized. They were a sham and were soon seen as such. Their intake declined and they were closed down. Most Jews were, in any case, attracted to the large cities where these schools did not exist and where assimilation was rapid.

Jews rose in the professions and the administrative hierarchy, but they stayed out, or were kept out of, the senior ranks of the party, and, with the exception of members of the old guard like Zinoviev, they were not seriously affected by the 1930 purges.

In 1939–40 Russia annexed Lithuania, Latvia, Estonia, Eastern Galicia and Western Byelorussia, Bessarabia and part of Bukovina: the size of the Soviet Jewish population was doubled, to over five million. Nearly a million of them perished in the holocaust; and when the war ended the survivors found themselves facing new perils from the Soviet authorities themselves. In 1948 there began the nightmare of the Stalinist terror with attacks on 'rootless cosmopolitans' mainly directed at the Jewish intelligentsia. The Jewish anti-Fascist committee, formed during the war to encourage Jewish support for the Soviet war effort, was dissolved, and its leaders were murdered. It was the darkest period in the history of Soviet Jewry.

Yet the beginning of this same period saw a brief honeymoon in Soviet-Israeli relations. The Soviet Union was the first country to accord Israel *de jure* recognition. It also supplied Israel with arms (via Czechoslovakia) and economic aid (via Poland) which were crucial to Israel's war effort. But Soviet policy seems to have been more concerned with ejecting Britain from the Middle East than with Zionist aspirations.

Israel, for her part, placed the highest value on good relations with the Soviet Union. It was only three years after the war and no Jew could forget the stoicism and bravery of the Russian people in the war, and the feeling of relief and joy as they held and then threw back Hitler's armies. Many Jews were still drawn ideologically to Russia, and an influential section of Israel's labour movement was avowedly Marxist and looked forward to years of fruitful collaboration with the Soviet Bloc. When an Israeli Ambassador had to be appointed the choice fell on one of the most senior and most respected members of the administration, who was herself of Russian birth and whose family had fled from Russia to escape the pogroms, Mrs Golda Meir.

In September 1948, not long after her arrival in Moscow, she attended a New Year service in the main synagogue, and her presence may have been the turning point in Soviet-Israeli, and possibly Soviet-Jewish relations, for she excited emotional scenes which startled the Soviet authorities and, indeed, herself. She was mobbed. Crowds milled round her to touch her. People broke down and wept; some became hysterical. Zionists have always believed that the emergence of a Jewish state would lead to a Jewish awakening, but within a free and open society. Few imagined that Soviet Jewry, cut off for so long from Jewish life, would also be affected. They were, only they dared not display their feelings beyond attendance at synagogue and, sometimes, not even that. The Stalinist terror intensified and in 1953 came the 'Doctor's Plot'.

The plot was almost an updated version of the blood-libel. In January 1953 *Pravda* announced that nine eminent doctors, six of whom were known to be Jews, had been arrested for conspiring to murder several Soviet leaders. 'Most of the participants in the terrorist group', said *Pravda*, 'were connected with the international Jewish bourgeois organisation, the "Joint", established by American intelligence ...' The report caused panic among Soviet Jews and fears of another holocaust. On 5 March, however, Stalin died and a month later *Pravda* announced that the doctors were innocent, but even then the Jews did not feel quite free to breathe.

The antipathies of centuries cannot be removed overnight or, indeed, in fifty years, and although anti-semitism as such was illegal in the Soviet Union, it was no advantage to be a Jew. The emergence of Israel added to his difficulties. 'Soviet Jews', declared Ilya Ehrenburg, 'do not look to the Near East, they look to the future', but to the suspicion they incurred in being Jews was added the suspicion that they might be Zionists. Moreover, about half of Russian Jewry lived in areas which had come under Soviet rule since 1940 or 1945, like Bessarabia, where anti-semitism was endemic, so that even those Jews who were anxious to assimilate received rude reminders of their origins, and their very identity cards marked them out not as Russians, or Ukrainians, or Lithuanians, but as *Ivrei* – Jews.

Once the Jewish state was an established fact, there was a continuing deterioration in Soviet-Israeli relations. During the 1956 Sinai campaign Russia sent threatening notes demanding an immediate Israeli withdrawal, and finally, during the Six Day War, the Russians broke off diplomatic relations altogether, accusing the Jews of precipitating a war of aggression against the Arabs. A virulent campaign was launched in the Soviet press charging Israel with Nazi tactics.

Soviet Jews, however, distressed by the attacks on the Jewish state, but heartened by its triumphs, began to take their future into their own hands. In November 1969, eighteen Jewish families from the Soviet Georgian Republic protested publicly that the Soviet government was denying them their right to settle in their historic homeland, Israel.

Georgia, in the Caucasus, only acceded to the Soviet Union in 1926. The revolution had in many respects passed it by, and its thirty thousand Jews had been allowed to preserve their traditions and way of life almost without molestation. Others, however, followed their example, and took the matter further. They staged demonstrations, organized press conferences, maintained open contact with the West and made their grievances known. The Soviet authorities, by now more sensitive to world opinion, began to relent, and gradually restrictions were eased. In 1970, about a thousand Jews were allowed to leave Russia; in 1971, fourteen thousand five hundred. In 1972, the number rose to thirty thousand, and, in all, something like one hundred and twenty-five thousand have left Russia. It is said that about a further one hundred thousand have applied to go.

All this was greeted as proof of a Jewish revival and certainly a considerable number of people who had been totally removed from all Jewish influences, who had, in their youth at least, been zealous members of the Communist party, and who had been largely or entirely indifferent to their Jewishness, began to feel a stirring of the Jewish consciousness they hadn't thought they possessed. They began to study Hebrew and search out material which might tell them something of their Jewish past. A great many more Jews began to attend synagogues, or crowd around outside them, not because they had been seized with religious belief – though some had – but to establish their association with their fellow Jews, to make an open declaration of their Jewishness. These, however, were individuals. They did not represent a mass awakening. The majority of Jews who applied for emigration to Israel stemmed from the periphery of the Soviet Union, which had come under Soviet rule only after the war; they had thus not been subjected to the same coercive assimilation as that experienced by Jews in Russia proper. They came mainly from cities like Vilna and Kishinev and Czernowitz which had, until World War II, known an intensely Jewish life, and where Jewishness is deeply ingrained. What had happened, therefore, was not so much a revival of Jewish consciousness as a revival – inspired by the example of Israel – of Jewish courage.

And then came the cyclical effect. Russia is an intensely patriotic society, proud of its achievements in war and peace, and the fact that anyone should choose to leave it, and make that choice publicly known, not only within Russia, but trumpeted abroad to the foreign press, was regarded as a type of treason, especially where Jews who had reached exalted positions in the sciences, industry and the arts, who enjoyed the many privileges reserved for the élite, also chose to go. It seemed to confirm the belief, widely asserted in Tsarist times, that Jews were of doubtful loyalty and inherently untrustworthy. Anti-semitism, never far from the surface, became more open and widespread. Jews found it more difficult to enter the better institutions of higher learning; Jewish graduates found it more difficult to get jobs equal to their qualifications, and those in junior grades found it more difficult to advance. As a result, many Jews who might have reconciled themselves to Soviet life found themselves becoming second-class citizens and they too joined the exodus. But they were less interested in going to Israel – if, indeed, they were interested at all – than in getting out of Russia, and today many Soviet Jews regard their application to leave for Israel as a mere exit visa.

If the situation of Soviet Jewry continues to deteriorate there may yet be a third exodus, of people who are at present too established and set in their ways to uproot themselves and move; but there will always be Jews, hardened Communists, who will regard any antipathies and slights they may encounter as a passing aberration to be tolerated – even if they should take a lifetime to pass – for the sake of a higher ideal. However there is no certainty that their children or grandchildren will have the same attitudes, and it would be a mistake to write off even those Russian Jews who would disown or deny their Jewishness as permanantly lost to the Jewish people. There is a movement to revive Jewish culture in Russia itself, not as a prelude to emigration, but as the reflection of deeply-held feelings and beliefs and, indeed, as the affirmation of a right guaranteed by the Soviet constitution. There is no sign that the endeavour will meet with anything but hostility from the authorities, but there is an ineradicable streak of contrariness in the Jewish character and if there is anything guaranteed to keep Jewishness in the Soviet Union alive it is proscription.

But what of toleration? Numbers are themselves a form of reassurance. It would be difficult to envisage circumstances in which the six million Jews of America could fade out of existence; one is rather less sanguine about the two million Jews scattered in small pockets over the rest of the globe.

France, which, with five hundred and fifty thousand Jews, has the largest community in western Europe, has always been quick to assimilate strangers to French culture and French ways. What there is of the organized Jewish community has always consisted of the last wave of immigrants – German Jews at one time, Polish Jews the next and now, mainly North African Jews from Algeria, Tunisia and Morocco, who made their homes in France after the various French territories became independent. There are numerous Jewish institutions, the principal of which, the Consistoire Central Israelite, is headed by Baron Elie de Rothschild, and there are many synagogues and youth groups. But Jewish day schools are few and ill-attended. The Zionist movement is riven by feuds and has hardly more than a nominal existence. The Jewish Agency sends numerous emissaries from Israel and spends thousands of pounds in trying to sustain viable Jewish youth organizations, but with slight effect. Jewish observance is nominal, assimilationist tendencies are strong, as they always have been in France, only this time there is no wave of prospective new immigrants to replace the old as they fade from Jewish life.

Moreover, many of the young people who might have checked the process of erosion have moved to Israel and are encouraging others to do the same. At the other extreme, those families who, though marginally Jewish, might, through their very conservatism, have been inclined to perpetuate their Judaism, have been discouraged from doing so by anti-semitism – never an insignificant factor in French life – and it is quite possible that in another generation or two French Jewry could cease to exist as an identifiable group.

The same could be true of Argentinian Jewry (and indeed other Latin American communities such as the Brazilian community with its one hundred and seventy five thousand Jews, or Chile with its thirty thousand Jews), though for entirely different reasons. Latin American Jewry, apart from the small groups who may have settled there during Spanish and Portuguese colonial rule, is of recent origin, and dates mainly from the final decade of the last century and the inter-war years. They hail mainly from eastern Europe and though not particularly devout, they have a strong Yiddishist tradition and numerous cultural institutions which have helped to maintain their identity in spite of their isolation from major Jewish centres.

They are however, mostly composed of prosperous middle-class families who feel threatened by social and political upheavals. Where, as in the past, they have tended to look apprehensively to the right (as they still do), they now look even more apprehensively to the left. Many of the young Jews (and not a few of the old) have radical sympathies, and the Zionist organizations tend to be left wing; but few Jews feel they would have a future in any country which could go the way of Castro's Cuba or Allende's Chile, and as a result an increasing number of them are emigrating to Israel and North America.

The four hundred and fifty thousand Jews of Great Britain, on the other hand, look as if they are here to stay (that is, if the United Kingdom is here to stay). Apart from anything else, they are sustained by the inherent conservatism of the Englishmen about them. The English are not xenophobes but they have a fairly developed sense of their own identity. It takes a very long time for a foreigner to become an Englishman – 'about three hundred years' in the words of a member of one very old Jewish clan. Most Jews have given up trying and have reconciled themselves to being that little bit different. On the whole they are preferred that way, for there is nothing so distasteful to the Englishman as the Jew who tries to pass as anything else, a distaste which was given classical expression by the most articulate of English anti-semites, Hilaire Belloc, in a book written in the classical period of British anti-semitism, 1922:

Take the particular trick of false names. It seems to us particularly odious. We think when we show our contempt for men who use this subterfuge that we are giving them no more than they deserve. It is a meanness which we associate with criminals and vagabonds; a piece of crawling and sneaking . . .

Men whose race is universally known will unblushingly adopt a false name as a mask, and after a year or two pretend to treat it as an insult. This is particularly the case with the great financial families. Some, indeed, have the pride to maintain the original patronymic and refuse to change it in any of their descendants. But the great mass of them concealed their relations one with another by adopting all manner of fantastic titles, and there can be no object to such a proceeding save the object of deception. I admit it is a form of protection, and especially do I admit that in its origin it may have mainly derived from a necessity for self-protection. But I maintain that today the practice does nothing but harm to the Jew. There are races who have suffered persecution, many of them, up and down the world, and we do not find in them a universal habit of this kind.

There has been less name-changing recently, partly because most of the present generation of Jews have inherited their changed names, and because, unlike France, England has not experienced any sizeable inflow of newcomers.

Anglo-Jewry has been vitally affected by the heavy influx of coloured immigrants, which has heightened racial consciousness, and in becoming more aware of his neighbour, the Jew has become more aware of himself. The newcomers, moreover, have necessarily brought down educational standards in some areas with the result that many Jews who would not otherwise have been interested in a Jewish education for their children have been sending them to Jewish day schools. Eighteen per cent of the Jewish school population now attend Jewish schools, which does not mean that eighteen or even eight per cent of the Jewish population subscribes to the beliefs and observances inculcated in such schools, but they do not mind if their children should pick up some Jewishness in the furtherance of their general education. It does mean that the generation now growing to maturity will have a far better understanding of Jewish tradition and history than was enjoyed by their parents.

Another factor which must help to preserve Anglo-Jewry is the growth of Celtic nationalism, with Scotch, Irish and Welsh striving with different degrees of success to detach themselves from the United Kingdom. Welsh Nationalists, for example, have complained that Welsh Jews show scant sympathy for their aspirations. They bring to mind the complaints of Polish nationalists in Hapsburg Galicia that Galician Jews were rather more interested in being Austrians than Poles, which they were, and who, in the light of their subsequent experience within an independent Poland, could blame them? Jews may not be rootless cosmopolitans but they have generally felt happier within the larger nationalism than the smaller.

Until a decade or two ago the one hundred and twenty thousand Jews of South Africa seemed secure in a golden land which was partly of their creation. Although they formed only about five per cent of the white population they enjoyed an influence and prosperity which was out of all proportion to their number. Their wealth is still intact but they have been immobilized by it. Most South Africans derive from Lithuania, whose Jews have always been famed for their alacrity, astuteness and enterprise. They were a sort of Jew's Jew, cool, rational, level-headed, and for that reason were known among their more mystical brethren as *tseilim kopf* – cross-heads, which is to say they had strong predilections to Christianity, or, at least, were as quick to lose their faith as to make their fortunes. South African Jews have never been noted for their religious zeal. They treat their membership of synagogues as an affirmation of Jewishness rather than Judaism. Zionism is the better part of their religion. No community gives more generously to Israel, and none has sent such a high proportion of its members to live there. It is urbane, cultivated, colourful and contributes richly to the cultural life of the country. Johannesburg Jews in particular are to South Africa what Viennese Jews were to Austro-Hungary, and, indeed, are as much disliked by provincial dwellers. But unlike Viennese Jewry they can hardly be described as an element alien to the indigenous culture, for alien though they may be, they are hardly less so than the English or the Afrikaaners, and the South African whites are not so numerous that they can afford to fall out among themselves.

The South African Jewish Board of Deputies, the representative institution of South African Jewry, has refused to make any pronouncement on the one issue which is, and for the past thirty years has been, uppermost in the minds of every Jew, the question of apartheid, on the grounds that the community is divided on the matter and it is therefore not in a position to offer a representative opinion. But there is hardly a South African Jew, no matter how far removed from Jewish observance, who is unaware that the entire system, with the virtual enslavement of the black races by the white, is anathema to everything Judaism stands for. The old and devout, as has been their custom, have tended to accept the system as it is and to leave it to God to sort it out in His own way and in His own good time. Most of the rest have been too calloused by prosperity to do anything about it, and it has been left mainly to the young, who in their beliefs and way of life are very far removed from Jewish tradition, to assert the spirit of Judaism. What there is of white opposition to white supremacy has derived largely from the Jews. Some of these Jews have been forced into exile, others have gone of their own accord, but now many Jews who might have been disposed to live with the system if it had a future are beginning to leave, and few see South African Jewry as an organized entity beyond the present century.

One finally comes to American Jewry, which, with its six million Jews, contains nearly half of the Jewish population of the world, the half, moreover, on which most of the others are dependent. Israel, certainly, could not have come into existence or continued to exist without the political, financial or moral support of American Jews. The community contains a few Sephardim who can trace their origins back to the Iberian peninsula, some German Jews whose families came over after the 1848 revolution or as refugees from Hitler, but the overwhelming majority of American Jewry is Russian, the sons and grandsons of the two million Jews who left the Russian Pale of Settlement between 1881 and 1914. (About half of Israel's three million Jews can trace their origins to the same area, as can the larger part of British, South African and Latin American Jewry. In fact of the fourteen million Jews in the world, about twelve million may be classed as Russian.)

And this fact must be kept in mind when considering the attitudes of the community, for if the snow on their boots was quick to melt and they abandoned many of the beliefs and observances of their fathers, many of the apprehensions of the old world remain intact in the new. American Jewry is passing through its golden age and there is a widespread feeling that it cannot last, coupled, possibly, with a subconscious belief that it shouldn't last. This may, perhaps, explain some of the extravagances of American Jewish life, its ostentation, the relentless pursuit of pleasure, the search for new experience, to taste any good that is going while the going is good. If one were to sum up the feelings of American Jewry in the present decade one might do so under the heading: 'Waiting for the Backlash'.

The Jews who made their homes in America in the middle years of the last century came mainly from the more emancipated areas of Europe, Germany, Austria, Hungary and Bohemia, and their old beliefs did not survive long in their new environment. Where they set up synagogues and formed communities they generally followed the pattern of worship established by the German Reform movement. But that movement could in some respects claim to have evolved naturally out of Orthodoxy. The American Reform movement however, certainly in its early years, was a conscious effort to blend in with the dominant elements in American society, which is to say the white, English-speaking Protestants, and, in contemporary terms, they attempted not so much to maintain 'a low profile' as to lie so low as to remain unseen. Their Judaism amounted to a sort of Christianity without Christ. They, of course, abandoned their dietary laws; the liturgy was truncated and its Hebrew content reduced to a minimum; Sabbath observance was abandoned, or, rather, moved to Sunday. Many would have abandoned their religion altogether, except that to be irreligious was to be un-American.

It was a me-too Judaism which displayed a rather stronger belief in America than in God. But its leaders were not devoid of sincerity. They saw Judaism as an evolving force whose forms must change with the changing times, and energies which had earlier been largely devoted to ceremonial found new outlets in social action. Rabbi David Einhorn, for example, one of the pioneers of American Reform, had to abandon his Baltimore pulpit in 1861 because of his unswerving opposition to slavery. The changes introduced by Reform were however too many, too sudden and too sweeping, and out of their excesses was born Conservative Judaism, which is now a major force in American life. But it only came into being in 1887. In the meantime Reform swept all before it, and of the 206 established synagogues in America in 1880, 200 were Reform. It is likely that with time they would have carried their congregations into oblivion. In a sense that was their purpose, assimilation with honour.

Then came the Russians. The Germans – if one may so call the earlier immigrants – had lived in comparatively isolated communities in which the inroads of assimilation were already being felt. The Russians had lived in an insulated world of their own, and whenever they sought to escape to the outside world by reaching for a place in the high schools or universities, or to establish themselves in the cities, they were generally whipped back in. They were, moreover, in the main, deeply Orthodox, and Orthodoxy induces a sense of resignation. *Ha'kol be'yedai shomayim,* all is in the hands of Heaven. If they were living through harsh times – and most of them were experiencing a degree of destitution which would have been unimaginable to their grandchildren – then they must suffer it (not, indeed in silence, which is something Jews have never done), till Heaven should bring them upon a happier age. It was only the 1881 pogroms which finally set them moving.

The Russians arrived in sufficient number to bring Russia with them and there was no longer any concerted attempt to adapt themselves entirely to local mores. Nor was there the same compulsion to do so. The two million Russians who descended on America between 1881 and 1914 were but a small stream in a torrent of over thirty million immigrants who arrived at about the same time. They were not, or did not feel themselves to be, like the Jewish immigrant in England, newcomers intruding upon an old and settled society, but foreigners among foreigners, and while the Italians remained ostentatiously Italian, and the Poles Polish, the Jew saw no reason why he should cease to be Jewish. There were, however, other forces to erode his singularity.

The Russians, in the main, arrived without their religious leaders. The giants of Russian and Polish Jewry, the mystics and scholars, the heads of the great academies, remained in the Pale, the hazards and hardships notwithstanding, and they urged their disciples to do the same, for if America was *die goldene medineh* (the golden land), it was also *die goyische medineh,* and the immigrant went in peril of his mortal soul. The precept, 'what shall it profit a man if he shall gain the whole world, and lose his own soul?' was commonplace among Jews long before it was uttered by Christ, and, as a result, in spiritual terms the newcomers were almost leaderless. Moreover, they were no longer, as in the Pale, scattered among villages and townships, but concentrated in large cities, working in sizeable factories and workshops, and it proved much easier than it had been in Russia to organize them into unions. And with unionization came radicalization. There were few among the Orthodox to countervail the influence of the many left-wing Yiddish papers that were appearing in New York, especially the virulently left-wing *Abendblatt* and its offshoot *Forward*, which, at the peak of its influence, had a daily circulation of two hundred thousand. Its building in New York's Lower East Side also housed the United Hebrew Trades, the Workmen's Circle and the Jewish Socialist Federation, which between them sought to replace traditional Judaism with a sort of Yiddish culture. Moreover, in Russia the Jew lived and died in substantially the same world as he was born in, and the very changelessness of his circumstances helped to keep his beliefs unchanged. The transfer to America in itself involved him in a personal revolution, and the revolution did not cease with his arrival. Change continued before his very eyes. It brought new hopes, opened new horizons, so that it required more than ordinary determination to keep one's way of life intact. In Russia high schools and universities had restricted entries. In America, everything (or almost everything) was open. These were the years of the 'melting pot', when America was anxious to reduce its heterogeneous elements into a homogeneous compound through special courses of instruction in the schools for the children, through night-school for the adults and through such occasions as 'I am an American day'. America was sufficiently confident in its own particular credo to feel that all newcomers would and should wish to adopt it. The overwhelming majority of newcomers did, not merely out of gratitude for the freedom and opportunities which they had been denied in Europe, but because it represented a *weltanschauung* (world picture) which particularly recommended itself to the Jewish newcomer, and at this time almost symbolized freedom and opportunity. America believed in itself and they believed in America.

If a Jew in Europe got ahead of his gentile neighbour, he did so almost with a sense of apology. There was always the inference that he was somewhat underhand in his efforts, while in America the very fact that he got ahead was in itself a commendation. If, in doing so, he had to steal a march in the night, then that too was to his credit. England, for example, was also a free and open society, but the Jew who took any opportunities that came his way was regarded as an opportunist. The same term, if used in America at all, would not have the same pejorative meaning, and might, indeed, reek faintly of praise. Chances were there to be taken.

The Russian Jew who settled in Austria, Germany or England had to adapt himself to the mores of an established and conservative society. The Jew who settled in America arrived upon a society which was still in a state of flux, was socially mobile, and if he had to adapt he was also, partly through his very numbers, able to affect attitudes. The world in which he settled was therefore partly of his own making, and that world was New York. Jews also moved to Philadelphia, Chicago, Boston and other major urban centres, but in the Pale, certainly, when a Jew spoke of America, he meant New York. Many of those who came to New York were so vaguely aware of the America beyond that to all intents and purposes New York was America. Many Americans, for their part, began to resent New York as foreign to the 'real' America, and to resent its influence.

To such resentments, which became fairly traditional, were added fears of the new radicalism brought in by the immigrants, many of whom had been members of the Russian socialist revolutionary movements and whose socialism had not been abated by their American experience. Others, who had been far removed from socialism in Russia, were won over to the movement in America. What there was of the American Socialist Party was largely a Jewish phenomenon and between 1910 and 1920 the predominantly Jewish Lower East Side returned a Socialist Congressman, Meyer London, to the House of Representatives for three successive terms. The newcomers were warned by American Jewish leaders that their socialism could have harmful repercussions, but such warnings were rejected with contempt by the Yiddish press, and, it would seem, by the Jewish masses.

The Russian Revolution was greeted ecstatically by the immigrants, not a few of whom felt moved to dispose of their meagre possessions in America to return to Russia and witness the miracle of socialism at first hand. A large part of the socialist movement gravitated naturally towards communism and when the American Communist Party came into being it could have effectively conducted its business in Yiddish. Growing prosperity on the one hand and growing disenchantment on the other led to the continuing exodus of members, but sufficient newcomers were recruited to preserve the Jewish flavour to the party and to leave the impression that there was something inherently Jewish about communism and communist-type conspiracies. That the Communist Party was, in American terms, a minuscule group, was almost beside the point. The Red

Scares to which America was subject were always accompanied by strong undertones of anti-semitism, which sometimes erupted into open Jew-baiting. Thus, in May 1920, motor-car magnate Henry Ford launched his weekly *Dearborn Independent* to defend America against what he called 'Jewish subversion' and produced a torrent of anti-Jewish propaganda. His campaign was taken sufficiently seriously for President Wilson, ex-President Taft and over a hundred other leading Americans to add their names to a public declaration denouncing his calumnies, but it continued for seven years, and helped to create a climate of opinion which led to the passage of the Johnson Immigration Act of 1924, designed to cut down immigration altogether, but so worded as to virtually close America to the East European, i.e., Jewish immigrants.

The Act transformed American Jewry, for without the continuing influx of new blood from eastern Europe, the old *landsmannschaften* began to crumble, the old neighbourhoods to empty. The sounds of Yiddish gave way to English, and sons, not infrequently accompanied, and sometimes even preceded by fathers, climbed out of the proletariat and into the middle class. By 1940 most American Jews were native born.

During the 'thirties, with the world-wide dislocation of trade and industry, there were fears that the Judea-phobia which had gripped Germany might spread to the rest of Europe and the Americas. In London there were street battles between Jews and the Blackshirts of Sir Oswald Mosley's British Union of Fascists. In America the spectre of a large scale anti-semitic movement was represented by Father Charles Coughlin. Mosley had been a Cabinet Minister in the 1929 Labour administration, but was now a political outcast with no influential following. But he was still a demagogue of fearsome power, and his presence at a rally could pack the largest halls in London. Father Coughlin in some ways represented the graver threat, for he was supported by official Catholic publications like the *Boston Pilot* and the *Brooklyn Tablet*, and he had access to a radio audience of millions. There were fears that the hatreds which had riven Europe for centuries might be transplanted in America.

Coughlin (like Mosley) was silenced by the war, but considerable anti-Jewish feeling persisted throughout the war years (a poll taken in 1944 showed that about one in four of the respondents regarded Jews as 'a menace') and there were fears that with the economic dislocation which, it was thought, would follow the war (as it had followed World War 1) America would experience an unprecedented wave of anti-semitism. But there was no serious dislocation, and any open expression of anti-semitism was confined to small and maniacal groups. There was another Red Scare which had its apotheosis in the McCarthy hearings. Jews were fairly prominent in the lists of suspected Communists and Communist sympathizers, but by way of compensation a Jew was one of the leading counsel for the prosecution. Similarly, when Ethel and Julius Rosenberg were tried and found guilty of spying for the Communists in 1951, the Judge who sentenced them to death was likewise Jewish.

The Red Scare of the 'twenties was something of a Jew Scare because the radicalism of the immigrant seemed to be part of a general Jewish conspiracy, emanating from Moscow, to win dominion over mankind, as described in *The Protocols of the Elders of Zion*. By the 'fifties the Jews had been virtually eliminated from the Politburo and the *Protocols* were no longer in general circulation. The Reds, while still taken seriously, were no longer thought of as inherently Jewish. Moreover, it was only five or six years since the end of the war and the smoke of the crematoria had not yet cleared from the skies. The residual decencies of American life made anti-semitism a shameful emotion, and whatever injury McCarthy and McCarthyism may have inflicted on America itself, it left American Jewry unscathed.

It was then feared that the humiliation of America – the most powerful nation in world history – in Vietnam might in turn lead to a backlash, for although numerous factors had led to the débâcle, the opposition which the war had aroused at home was certainly one of them, perhaps even the main one, and Jews, especially young Jews, played more than their part in arousing public feeling. But as the débâcle was reaching its climax, the attention of the general public was seized by Watergate. It is also possible that the Vietnam protestations were expressing the views not only of an articulate minority, but also of a good part – perhaps the greater part – of the silent majority, for the general response to the retreat was relief and thanksgiving rather than recrimination.

Now with Vietnam out of the way, a backlash is feared over the American involvement in the Middle East and the billions in American aid – over and above the millions offered voluntarily by the Jewish community – given on behalf of the American taxpayer to keep Israel militarily secure and economically viable. The nervousness of the Jews arises out of the ambiguities of their position, for to demand an end to American involvement in the Far East in one breath, and to call for greater involvement in the Middle East in the next, was perhaps depending a little too heavily on the understanding, patience and goodwill of one's neighbour.

They can also be embarrassed by the sort of moral compromises they are sometimes expected to make on behalf of Israel.

American Jews have always been in the vanguard of American liberal opinion, so far in the vanguard, indeed, that they have sometimes been out of touch with the rest of America; but on Israel they have, on occasion, seemed to reverse their attitudes. Thus, for example, during the 1956 Suez crisis, when liberal opinion throughout the world unhesitatingly denounced the Anglo-French-Israeli invasion of Sinai and the Canal Zone, American Jewish opinion was overwhelmingly on the side of the invaders. But in 1956, Israel was weak, puny and only eight years old, and the Arabs had not yet reconciled themselves to her existence. Egypt was sending nightly marauding bands deep into Jewish territory, and was bringing together the surrounding Arab states under one military command. Israel was fighting for her life and, whatever might have been said for the Anglo-French role in the affair, it was not difficult for even the most uncompromising liberal to take the side of the Jewish state.

Now, twenty years after Sinai and ten after the Six Day War, American Jewry is being asked to support not merely a safe and secure Israel but, with the election of Mr Begin, an enlarged one. American Jewry is so conditioned to falling in with Israeli wishes that it has not, as yet, recoiled from the idea, or at least, it has kept its misgivings subdued. It has no doubt felt constrained to do so partly by the howl of horror and execration with which the election of Mr Begin was greeted in the American press, and the hope that he may prove to be more amenable in office than he was in opposition.

In her autobiography, *My Life*, Mrs Meir describes a telling little exchange with Mr Begin. She had tried to explain that unless Israel fell in with American wishes, she would not get American arms, which seemed to leave him a trifle confounded. 'What do you mean we won't get arms?' he asked. 'We'll *demand* them from the Americans.' On another occasion he demanded (though he did not get) an emergency debate in the Knesset on a most favoured nation trade pact which America was about to conclude with Russia, as if the former was a Jewish dependency.

Mr Begin is the most formidable Israeli leader since Ben-Gurion, though he has not been cast in the same mould. Ben-Gurion, a towering figure of international stature who excited the awe even of his enemies, had about him the aura of a Biblical prophet. Begin, a slight, wiry individual, looks like a minor official in a minor bank, but he has a presence out of all proportion to his size and a charm which blinds one to his otherwise unprepossessing appearance. And he radiates authority. The left-of-centre alliance, which has ruled Israel since its inception, has an intricate system of checks and controls which hampers the capacity of the party leaders to lead. Ben-Gurion transcended the system, but Eshkol, Mrs Meir and General Rabin all had to accept party guidance and all were prone to dither and hesitate. There is nothing hesitant about Begin, and one of the reasons why so many Israelis who voted against him in the election are disposed to support him now is that they have at last found someone indubitably in charge, who knows what he wants and perhaps even how to get it.

He is also more a man of the people – which is to say, more a man of the Jewish people – than Ben-Gurion ever was. The latter may have graduated as a horny-handed labourer in the barren hills of Galilee and may have ended his days as a member of Kibbutz Beth Ha'emek, but he was by nature an academic and, had not circumstances pushed him into politics, he might have spent his days – as he spent much of his free time – as a student of Greek and oriental philosophy. Moreover, although the movement which he led built the Jewish state and still forms its backbone, it was never – precisely because it was a *labour* movement – part of the mainstream of Jewish life. The *Chalutzim* may have drained the swamps, built the outlying settlements and manned the stockades, but if they transformed the face of Palestine, they failed, as we have seen, to change the character of the Jewish people, which was still urban, petit-bourgeois and overwhelmingly engaged in commerce. The idea of a Jewish state only became probable (and the Arab masses only woke up to its probability) when small businessmen began to pour in from Poland and Galicia in the 'twenties. When they were followed by larger traders from Germany in the 'thirties, the state had virtually become an irreversible fact. Begin represents that spirit in a way that Ben-Gurion never could, never did, and which, if anything, he hoped to suppress. Moreover, Ben-Gurion, for all his immersion in Jewish history and lore, never quite came to terms with Judaism. Like most of the labour movement he had been in revolt against it and, although his attitude mellowed with the years, he had never defined its place in the Jewish state. To Begin, Judaism poses no challenge or difficulty. It is part of his birth-right and, if he is not quite the skull-capped, Wall-clutching, Bible-quoting zealot that he has appeared to be since his election, he has always shared many of the beliefs and conformed to many of the observances of the devout Jew. He was born in Poland in 1913 and trained (though he never practised) as a lawyer and arrived in Palestine as a member of the Free Polish forces in 1943. He later deserted from the Polish army and became commander of the Irgun Tzvei Leumi and for the next four years waged a relentless war against British rule; he came to be seen, and perhaps even to see himself, as the embodiment of Jewish pluck and defiance. His Irgun years were not without their blemishes, but he is not, as much of the world's press seemed to suggest, a cross between Attila and Ghenghis Khan, and compared to some Prime Ministers and Presidents now spoken of with deference as elder statesmen, he is a Galahad. Past Jewish humiliations weigh heavily upon his memory. He tends to presume that all goyim are anti-semites, unless they show definite proof to the contrary, and that what happened in the holocaust could, given half the chance, happen again. He has a tendency to re-write history so that he will not explain past blemishes in terms of the exigencies of war, but will insist that they never happened. He has a Talmudic frame of mind and can make mutually contradictory statements without being aware that they are irreconcilable so that, for example, he will declare everything to be negotiable, yet in the same breath insist that not an inch of the West Bank can be returned. He is so obsessed with Jewish grievances and fears that he has diminished grip on reality and confronts the world with a clenched fist, which is not an impressive gesture when it is accompanied – as on his visit to America – by an open palm.

Like many Zionists, especially of the right, he does not think of diaspora Jews as entities in their own right, with their own character, life and interests, but as temporary phenomena without a future and existing largely to serve the interests of the Jewish state. It is this mainly, which leads him to believe that Israel is in a position to make demands of America, for he has infinite faith in the power of American Jewry and in its readiness to use that power on behalf of Israel. He is also an accomplished speaker and debater and knows how to play upon Jewish fears, and among the reasons why he is anxious to hold on to the West Bank is a belief that there may yet come a time when Jews, perhaps even American Jews, may need the space; but in this he underestimates the staying power of American Jewry even as he overestimates its influence.

There are certain factors in his favour. In withdrawing from Sinai and Gaza, Israel was given assurances (such as the maintenance of free passage through the Straits of Tiran) which proved worthless and which were to lead to the Six Day War. Also, as we have noted, there has been a rapid growth in Jewish Orthodoxy and fundamentalism which regards the acquisition of the West Bank as the fulfilment of God's promise to Abraham and which believes that Jews have no right to return holy soil to unholy hands. And finally, for reasons which we shall note, there has been a growing disenchantment with liberalism in some Jewish quarters, but none of these factors, either singly or together, are sufficient to induce a *volte face* in Jewish attitudes. If Mr Begin should fail to win over the American administration to the wisdom and justice of his case, he is unlikely to have much greater success with the American Jewish community. American Jewry, as it has shown in a thousand ways, is immensely loyal to Israel, but is not devoid of feelings for America. It is imbued with American attitudes and responds, perhaps more readily than any other minority, to the strain of idealism in American foreign policy, a strain from which Israel has reaped, and continues to reap, many benefits. America may be committed to keeping Israel alive, but no one, not even American Jewry, is committed to keeping it King-Size.

There were times when it was difficult for a Jew to get into a private American university (especially the medical schools) and almost impossible for him to find a place on its faculty. All that has passed. Four Jewish youngsters out of every five of university age actually attend universities. Jews form about ten per cent of university faculties, and in the top universities their proportion rises to a fifth.

Large Jewish defence agencies like the Anti-Defamation League of the B'nai Brith, the American Jewish Committee, the American Jewish Congress, have studied and fought, with success, every instance of social or commercial discrimination. They believe that there is still something they call 'executive-suite' discrimination, and point to the fact (if it is a fact) that only one in every two hundred executives of major American companies are Jews, while Jews form more than three per cent of the population. They do not appear to have asked themselves how many Jews want to be executives in major American companies. And if Jews did form three per cent of the executives in major American companies, could they continue to form fifty per cent (or whatever the proportion might be) of the creative staff in advertising and the media, or twenty per cent of the teaching staff of the top universities? That there is some discrimination in major companies is well established, but one of the reasons why they have such a paucity of Jews is that the sort of Jew with the skills necessary to hold executive office prefers to own the works, which is rather difficult in General Motors, or even Chrysler.

They also fought, with rather greater effort than the cause deserved, discrimination in health resorts, so that it not only became improper to suggest that Jews were unwelcome in a particular hotel, but even to say that it was near a church. There are Jews who are never satisfied until they have got into a place in which they are thoroughly unwanted. For them exclusiveness is all, and the more exclusive a place, the more determined their efforts to get in. The defence agencies were, of course, concerned with the principle. But not every principle is worth even a war of words. Most Jews are in fact happier in exclusively Jewish company. Other groups, no doubt, have the same instinct, and as a rule the imposition of fraternity by fiat impedes the evolution of healthy relationships. In 1940 a nation-wide poll suggested that about sixty-three per cent of the public attributed 'objectionable traits' to Jews; by 1962 the proportion had fallen to twenty-two per cent. No doubt as many Jews, if caught off-guard, would say the same of gentiles. Americans like to be loved, and this is especially the case with American Jews, but one does not need to be loved by one's neighbour or even to be admired by him in order to get on with him. One does, however, need to trust him and a sufficient degree of trust has evolved between the Jew and his neighbours so that they can even quarrel without evoking the charge of anti-semitism.

Jewish organizations like to deny that there is such a thing as a Jewish lobby, which is, of course, nonsense, but it may fairly be said that the massive strength of the Zionist lobby is of comparatively recent origin. The Zionist Organization of America may be eighty years old, but Zionism as an effective force dates only from the holocaust. The rise of Hitler was not in itself sufficient to convince most American Jews of the need for a Jewish state, and they were in any case too preoccupied with their own problems. The depression was a trauma to all Americans, but especially to the Jews. They were familiar with poverty and hardship. They had known little else in Europe, but to experience it in America was quite another matter. They felt almost betrayed. The least one could expect of America was solvency, and if it could not even assure that, what was there to be said for it? The post-World War II years brought affluence, but it came with the taste of ashes. There could not have been many American Jewish families without a relative in the death camps. And with the grief came guilt, the feeling not merely that mankind had not done enough to save European Jewry from destruction, but that the Jews them-selves, and especially American Jewry, had not done enough. With the guilt, therefore, there came a determination that they should not be found wanting again. And finally, the apprehension. Could what happened in

Europe not happen in America? And if it did, where would the next haven be?

And yet with all the unreal fears, there has been a backlash and from a direction no one anticipated.

Ever since Jews have been a force in American life they have given their money, energies and influence to the black struggle for equality and thereby incurred something of the odium attached to the Black. They were among the most generous backers of the National Association for the Advancement of Coloured People and during the height of the civil rights campaign in the 'sixties, when whole armies of young people descended on the south, it is said that about half the marchers were Jews.

The revulsion against Nazi racialism which has made anti-semitism unrespectable has also placed a taboo on anything that could be even remotely construed as racism, so that the Black, as we suggested earlier, has, in a sense, become a direct beneficiary of the holocaust. Any criticism of Black leadership, policies or actions is made in the most muted terms imaginable, which is perhaps as it should be. Yet, at the same time, Blacks have assumed a freedom of utterance which is denied others and this has allowed a sort of licensed Black anti-semitism to emerge. That the Blacks, given their history, should dislike the white man is understandable, but that they should have particular antipathies towards the Jew is rather less so, and it is generally explained that in those areas where the Black is most emancipated and articulate, which is to say, New York, the white man he is most likely to encounter, whether as landlord, shopkeeper or boss, is the Jew. The Jew, therefore, has come to represent white exploitation. But isn't it more likely that the Jew represents a reproach? Here is someone who, in spite of every handicap of circumstances and history, has made it, has risen from the ghetto and is still rising, while he, the Black, remains where he is. His feeling of alienation in America has given him more than a passing sympathy for the Arabs, which has naturally brought him into conflict with the Jews, but what will almost certainly become the most serious source of conflict is the fact that the rules of the game which have characterized American life are being rigged in favour of the Black and, in effect, against the Jew. The *numerus clausus* is returning under the name of Affirmative Action; but then Americans have always had a genius for clothing unpalatable ideas in palatable terms. The Jew, as we have noted, has worked harder than most whites to bring equal rights to the Black. What he did not bargain for was that the Black should become more equal than others, and that advancement in the future, including access to universities and jobs, would depend less on merit than on numbers.

Now numbers have never been on the side of the Jews. They hate numbers. They go in dread of them and have done so ever since the first census taken by Moses ended in catastrophe. They have been nervous of census forms and have opposed questions on religion, in case it should be discovered that Jews are rather more numerous (or perhaps less) than they are generally thought to be. On occasion Jews have not hesitated to play the numbers game when it suited them, as, for example, in the complaint that they form only a half per cent of the executive staff of major American corporations, but on the whole they have never asked for more than an even break, and have usually been content with less. If they struggled against the *numerus clausus* in schools, universities and jobs, it was because they believed that entry should be based not on religion or racial origins, but on merit; a belief, which, they were led to think, was central to the American way of life.

A few years ago, when contemplating the Black problem (and one of the reasons why it preoccupied so many good Jewish minds was that it was possibly a relief from Jewish problems), Norman Podhoretz suggested miscegenation as a solution. Here was the melting pot again, though in a form not previously envisaged, certainly not by the Jew. But the idea never got off the ground because, apart from anything else, the Blacks didn't want it. While the liberal Jew, in the extremes of his liberality, was prepared to fade out of existence (one might call it genetic-disarmament), the emancipated Black wanted to remain exactly who he was, only more so, and began to rummage back into his past to rediscover himself. The Jew had not become Black, but in a sense the Black has become a Jew, or rather Jewish.

The process of rediscovery began rather earlier among Jews. One noticed it already in the late 'fifties and early 'sixties in the staging of Peretz and Sholem Aleichem off-Broadway and off-off-Broadway, and later on in the success of Rosten's *The Joys of Yiddish*. The whole movement possibly saw its apotheosis in the staging of *Fiddler on the Roof*, replete with mock Chagallia, so that, by 1970, if someone had cared to establish a dude *shtettle* in the Catskills with *shtieblach* and *kapotes* and *gartlech* and *shtreimels* and *samovars*, he would have prospered as richly as any dude ranch. The trend has accelerated in recent years, for reasons we have already examined, and there has been a revival of Jewishness, and even of Judaism.

Jews have a habit of harking back to past golden ages – perhaps golden ages are by their very nature things of the past. There was thus a golden age in Judea under Solomon, another in Israel under Ahab, a golden age in Babylon under the Parthians, a golden age in Spain under the Moors, a golden age in Poland under Casimir the Great, and perhaps our own times are more golden than any of them. Not all Jews are fortunately placed, and not a few are in the gravest difficulty, but given the size of the Jewish diaspora, and the number of lands among which they are scattered, it is impossible that they should all be prospering all of the time. If we take world Jewry as a whole, it can be said with fair honesty that they have never had it so good. They know it, which is the source of their apprehensions. Can it last? There is no reason why it should not, other than that it has not in the past, and it is Jewish history, rather than immediate threats, which is the source of apprehension. To which one must add that any apprehensions about the future of American Jewry are not half as deep or as widespread as apprehensions about the future of America itself. American Jews feel a little like a castaway who has struggled endlessly through troubled waters, and has finally been hauled aboard a great ship, only to find that the ship too is drawing water.

The art historian Bernard Berenson, a Lithuanian-born Jew, with a deep understanding of Jewish history, compared world Jewry to the peasants scratching a livelihood on the slopes of Etna:

The slopes of Etna afford landscapes enchanting to the eye as well as to every other sense. In their season the fragrance of orange and lemon blossoms is almost overpowering. The wheat grown there is of such excellence that it is held too good for local consumption and exported abroad, even out of Italy. In every respect this region is the garden of the Lord, a paradise . . . Once every fifty years or so this Eden, this paradise is visited by destruction. Etna vomits torrents of lava which overwhelm the countryside, and belches up clouds of cinders which cover it as with a sinister snowfall. Farms, villages, towns, cities are burnt and buried, thousands perish. Undiscouraged, the inhabitants of the region begin all over again, as we often do after so relatively mild an 'act of God' as a winter blizzard. Forgetting Etna's rages, or believing that they will not return in their day, they go to work and enjoy the exercise of their functions as if nothing could disturb or interrupt, let alone put an untimely end to them.

There is, however, this difference. The Sicilians can abandon their orange groves and settle, as some have done, in a more secure, if less exotic area of the globe. The Jew has no such alternative. They might, as Arthur Koestler has urged in a memorable essay, renounce their Jewishness if not for their own sake, then for that of their children. There are, however, people for whom Jewishness, or rather Judaism, is more important than life, and they are prepared to renounce much else that life may offer in order to transmit it to their children. They may be a minority, but they are a growing minority. But even those Jews who are indifferent to their culture and their faith find compensation in the mere fact of their Jewishness, the sense of belonging which it affords, the bonhomie, the feeling of mutual concern, the shared thoughts, the common responses, the shared identity and even, in the Jewish pagan, the feeling of antiquity. Sentiment lingers in the most hard-headed individuals and there is an understandable disinclination to renounce an identity which has been extant for some 4,000 years. The Jew, if he is nothing else, can tell himself that he is a Jew and draw comfort from the fact.

There are also Jews who, for reasons which it is not difficult to imagine, might be perfectly willing to renounce what they have left of their Jewishness, but are not entirely free to do so if only because such acts of renunciation can never be unilateral. He may defect from the Jews, but there is no assurance that he will be accepted by the gentiles. Disraeli, though baptized in childhood and a devout member of the Church of England, was always *der alte Jude* to Bismarck. Trotsky, though he renounced his Jewishness and denied he was a Jew, was never regarded by his enemies as anything but a Jew. And of course when Hitler arrived in Vienna from Linz, it was not so much the bearded Hassidim of the Leopoldstrasse who darkened his vision, but the de-tribalized, Germanized, cultivated Hebrews of the *Neue Freie Presse* and the Burgtheater.

Many Jews are now lost to Judaism, not through any conscious act of renunciation, but through unconscious drift. Yet the holocaust has forced an indissoluble element into the Jewish soul, so that no matter how far a Jew may be removed from his origins, his faith or his people, let there come but one knock at his door at an early hour, and he will become a Jew again *off tzalhuches*, if only for the hell of it.

Bibliography

Abrahams, I. *Jewish Life Under Emancipation*. London: St Clement Press, 1917.

Abrahams, I. *Jewish Life in the Middle Ages*. London: E. Goulston, 1932. New York: Atheneum, 1969.

Agar, H. *The Saving Remnant*. London: Hart-Davis, 1960. New York: Viking Press, 1960.

Ainsztein, R. *Jewish Resistance in Nazi Occupied Eastern Europe*. London: Elek, 1974. New York: Barnes and Noble, 1974.

Allon, Y. *Shield of David*. London: Weidenfeld and Nicolson, 1970.

Baron, S. W. *A Social and Religious History of the Jews*. New York: Columbia University Press, 1952.

Baruch, B. *My Own Story*. London: Odhams, 1958. New York: Holt, Rinehart & Winston, 1957.

Begin, M. *The Revolt*. London: W. H. Allen, 1951. Los Angeles: Nash Publishing Co., 1972.

Belloc, H. *The Jews*. London: Constable, 1922. Boston: Houghton Mifflin, 1922.

Ben-Gurion, D. *Rebirth and Destiny of Israel*. New York: Philosophical Library, 1954.

Ben-Gurion, D. *Recollections*. London: Macdonald, 1970. New York: Schocken Books, 1970, titled *Ben-Gurion Looks Back*.

Ben-Sasson, H. H. (Ed.). *A History of the Jewish People*. London: Weidenfeld and Nicolson, 1976. Cambridge, Mass.: Harvard University Press, 1976.

Berenson, B. *Rumour and Reflection*. London: Icon Books, 1952. New York: Simon and Schuster, 1961.

Berlin, I. *Karl Marx*. London: Oxford University Press, 1963. New York: Oxford University Press, 1963.

Bermant, C. *Israel*. London: Thames and Hudson, 1967. New York: Walker, 1967.

Bermant, C. *Troubled Eden*. London: Vallentine Mitchell, 1969.

Bermant, C. *Point of Arrival*. London: Eyre Methuen, 1975.

Bermant, C. *The Walled Garden*. London: Weidenfeld and Nicolson, 1975.

Birnbaum, N., & Lenzer, G. *Sociology of Religion*. London: Prentice-Hall, 1969. Englewood Cliffs, N.J.: Prentice-Hall, 1969.

Bolitho, H. *Alfred Mond*. London: M. Secker, 1933.

Buber, M. *Tales of the Hassidim*. New York: Schocken Books, 1947.

Carrington, N. (Ed.). *Mark Gertler: Selected Letters*. London: Hart-Davis, 1965.

Cohen, I. *Contemporary Jewry*. London: Methuen, 1950.

Cohn, N. *Warrant for Genocide*. London: Eyre and Spottiswoode, 1967. New York: Harper and Row, 1969.

Colt, M. L. *Mr Baruch*. London: Gollancz, 1958. Boston: Houghton Mifflin, 1957.

Darin-Drabkin, H. *The Other Society*. New York: Harcourt Brace Jovanovich, 1962.

Deutscher, I. *The Prophet Armed: Leon Trotsky 1879–1921*. London: Oxford University Press, 1954. New York: Oxford University Press, 1954.

Deutscher, I. *The Prophet Unarmed: Leon Trotsky 1921–29*. London: Oxford University Press, 1959. New York: Oxford University Press, 1959.

Deutscher, I. *The Prophet Outcast: Leon Trotsky 1929–40*. London: Oxford University Press, 1963. New York: Oxford University Press, 1963.

Deutscher, I. *The Non-Jewish Jew*. London: Oxford University Press, 1968. New York: Oxford University Press, 1968.

Dimont, M. I. *The Indestructible Jews*. London: W. H. Allen, 1973. New York: World Publishing Co., 1971.

Domb, I. *The Transformation*. London: privately.

Dubnov, S. *History of the Jews in Russia and Poland*. New York: Arno Press, 1920.

Elon, A. *The Israelis*. London: Weidenfeld and Nicolson, 1971.

Elon, A. *Herzl*. London: Weidenfeld and Nicolson, 1975. New York: Holt, Rinehart and Winston, 1975.

Epstein, I. *The Jewish Way of Life*. London: E. Goulston, 1946.

Epstein, I. *Judaism*. London: Penguin Books, 1959. New York: Penguin Books, 1959.

Field, F. *The Last Days of Mankind*. London: Macmillan, 1967.

Finkelstein, L. *The Jews, Their History, Culture and Religion*. London: Peter Owen, 1961. New York: Harper and Row, 1960.

Fleg, C. *The Jewish Anthology*. (Trans. M. Samuel). New York: Harcourt Brace Jovanovich, 1925.

French, Philip. *The Movie Moguls*. London: Weidenfeld and Nicolson, 1969.

Gershenfeld, L. *The Jew in Science*. Philadelphia: Jewish Publications Society of America, 1934.

Hilberg, R. *The Destruction of the European Jews*. London: W. H. Allen, 1961. New York: Franklin Watts, 1961.

Hitler, A. *Mein Kampf.* London: Hutchinson, 1969. Boston: Houghton Mifflin, 1939.

Horowitz, D. *The Economics of Israel.* Oxford: Pergamon Press, 1967. Elmsford, N.Y.: Pergamon Press, 1967.

Howe, I. *World of Our Fathers.* London: Routledge, 1976. New York: Harcourt Brace Jovanovich, 1976.

Jackson, S. *The Great Barnato.* London: Heinemann, 1970.

Jones, E. *The Life and Work of Sigmund Freud.* London: The Hogarth Press, 1962. New York: Basic Books, 1953–57.

Katz, J. *Tradition and Crisis.* New York: Free Press, 1961.

Katz, J. *Exclusiveness and Tolerance.* London: Oxford University Press, 1961. New York: Oxford University Press, 1961.

Kautsky, K. *Are the Jews a Race?* New York: International Publishers, 1926.

Kobler, F. *A Treasury of Jewish Letters.* London: East and West Library, 1952. Philadelphia: Jewish Publications Society of America, 1956.

Kraines, O. *Government and Politics in Israel.* London: Allen and Unwin, 1961. Boston: Houghton Mifflin, 1961.

Laqueur, W. *A History of Zionism.* London: Weidenfeld and Nicolson, 1972. New York: Holt, Rinehart and Winston, 1972.

Lee, S. J. *Moses of the New World.* London: Yoseloff, 1971. Cranbury, N.J.: A. S. Barnes, 1970.

Levitan, T. *The Laureates.* Boston: Twayne Publishers, 1960.

Levitt, M., & Rubenstein, B. (Eds.). *Youth and Social Change.* Detroit, Mich.: Wayne State University Press, 1971.

Lewinsohn, B. R. *Barney Barnato.* London: G. Routledge and Sons, 1937.

Lipman, V. D. *Three Centuries of Anglo-Jewish History.* London: Heffer, 1961. West Orange, N.J.: Albert Saifer, 1960.

Lowenthal, M. (Ed.). *The Diaries of Theodor Herzl.* New York: Dial Press, 1956.

Maimonides, M. *Guide for the Perplexed* (Trans. M. Friedlander). London: Routledge, 1928. New York: Dover, 1956.

Marcus, J. R. *The Jews in the Medieval World.* Cincinnati: The Sinai Press, 1938.

Marx, G. T. *Protest and Prejudice.* London: Harper and Row, 1968. New York: Harper and Row, 1967.

Marx, Karl. *Early Writings* (Ed. T. B. Bottomore). London: C. A. Watts, 1963. New York: McGraw-Hill, 1963.

Mendelsohn, E. *Class Struggle in the Pale.* London: Cambridge University Press, 1970. New York: Cambridge University Press, 1970.

Meyer, F. *Marc Chagall.* London: Thames and Hudson, 1964. New York: H. N. Abrams, 1957.

Montefiore, C. G., & Loewe, H. *A Rabbinic Anthology.* Philadelphia: Jewish Publications Society of America, 1960.

Moore, G. F. *Judaism in the First Centuries of the Christian Era.* Cambridge, Mass.: Harvard University Press, 1966.

Morse, A. D. *While Six Million Died.* London: Secker and Warburg, 1967. New York: Random House, 1968.

Myerson, A., & Goldberg, I. *The German Jews.* New York: Alfred A. Knopf, 1933.

Namier, L. B. *Avenues of History.* London: Hamish Hamilton, 1952.

Nedava, J. *Trotsky and the Jews.* Philadelphia: Jewish Publications Society of America, 1971.

Netti, J. *Rosa Luxemburg.* London: Oxford University Press, 1966. New York: Oxford University Press, 1966.

O'Connor, T. P. *Lord Beaconsfield: A Biography.* London: Fisher Unwin, 1879. Philadelphia: Richard West, 1973 (reprinted from 1905 ed.).

Parkes, J. *Anti-semitism.* London: Vallentine Mitchell, 1963. New York: Quadrangle, 1969.

Poliakov, L. *A History of Anti-semitism.* London, Routledge, 1974. New York: Vanguard, 1965.

Prittie, T. *Israel, Miracle in the Desert.* London: Pall Mall Press, 1967. New York: Praeger, 1968.

Pulzer, P. *The Rise of Political Anti-semitism in Germany.* London: John Wiley and Sons, 1964. New York: John Wiley and Sons, 1964.

Rabinowicz, H. M. *The Legacy of Polish Jewry.* London: Yoseloff, 1965. Cranbury, N.J.: A. S. Barnes, 1965.

Radin, M. *Jews Among the Greeks and Romans.* New York: Arno Press, 1915.

Ramsaye, T. *A Million and One Nights.* London: Frank Cass, 1964. New York: Simon and Schuster, 1964.

Reitlinger, G. *The Final Solution.* London: Vallentine Mitchell, 1968. Cranbury, N.J.: A. S. Barnes, 1961.

Robinson, J. *And the Crooked Shall be Made Straight.* New York: Macmillan, 1965.

Robinson, S. M., & Starr, J. (Eds.). *Jewish Population Studies.* New York: Conference on Jewish Social Studies, 1943.

Rose, H. H. *The Life and Thought of A. D. Gordon.* New York: Bloch Publishing Co., 1964.

Roth, C. *The Jewish Contribution to Civilization.* Cincinnati: The Union of American Hebrew Congregations, 1940.

Roth, C. *Gleanings.* New York: Bloch Publishing Co., 1967.

Roth, C. (Ed.). *Jewish Art.* London: Vallentine Mitchell, 1972. Greenwich, Conn.: New York Graphic Society, 1971.

Roth, L. *God and Man in the Old Testament.* New York: Macmillan, 1955.

Rubin, J. *Do It!* London: Cape, 1970. New York: Simon and Schuster, 1970.

Runes, D. D. (Ed.). *The Hebrew Impact on Western Civilization.* New York: Philosophical Library, 1951.

Ruppin, A. *The Jews in the Modern World.* New York: Arno Press, 1934.

Ruppin, A. *The Jewish Fate and Future.* Westport, Conn.: Greenwood Press, 1940.

Russoli, F. *Modigliani.* London: Thames and Hudson, 1959. New York: H. N. Abrams, 1959.

Samuel, M. *The World of Sholem Aleichem.* New York: Alfred A. Knopf, 1943.

Schechter, S. *Studies in Judaism.* Plainview, N.Y.: Books for Libraries, 1903.

Schoenberg, A. *Letters.* London: Faber and Faber, 1964 (Ed. Edwin Stein).

Scholem, G. *Messianic Idea in Judaism.* London: Allen and Unwin, 1971. New York: Schocken Books, 1971.

Schwartz, S. M. *The Jews in the Soviet Union.* New York: Arno Press, 1951.

Simon, L. *Ahad Ha-am.* Philadelphia: Jewish Publications Society of America, 1960.

Simon, L. *Studies in Jewish Nationalism.* Westport, Conn.: Hyperion Press, 1975.

Sombart, W. *Jews and Modern Capitalism* (Trans. M. Epstein). New York: Burt Franklin, 1913.

Spiro, M. E. *Kibbutz: Venture in Utopia.* New York: Shocken Books, 1963.

Syrkin, M. (Ed.). *Golda Meir Speaks Out.* London: Weidenfeld and Nicolson, 1973. New York: Putnam, 1973.

Talmon, J. L. *The Unique and the Universal.* London: Secker and Warburg, 1965. New York: George Braziller, 1965.

Talmon, J. L. *Israel Among the Nations.* London: Weidenfeld and Nicolson, 1970. New York: Macmillan, 1970.

Trachtenberg, J. *The Devil and the Jews.* New Haven: Yale University Press, 1943.

Vallentin, A. *Einstein.* London: Weidenfeld and Nicolson, 1954.

Villiers, D. (Ed.). *Next Year in Jerusalem.* London: Harrap, 1976. New York: Viking Press, 1976.

Weizmann, C. *Trial and Error.* London: Hamish Hamilton, 1949. New York: Schocken Books, 1966.

Weizmann, V. *The Impossible Takes Longer.* London: Hamish Hamilton, 1967.

Wiseman, T. *Cinema.* London: Cassell, 1961.

Wouk, H. *This Is My God.* London: Cape, 1959. Garden City, N.Y.: Doubleday, 1959.

Zeman, Z. A. B., & Scharlau, W. B. *The Merchant of Revolution: The Life of Alexander Israel Halphand.* London: Oxford University Press, 1965. New York: Oxford University Press, 1965.

Zucker, N. L. *The Coming Crisis in Israel.* Cambridge, Mass.: The MIT Press, 1973.

Index

INDEX